Loyalty Rules!

Loyalty Rules!

■

How Today's Leaders Build
Lasting Relationships

Frederick F. Reichheld

Harvard Business School Press
Boston, Massachusetts

Printed in the United States of America
05 04 03 02 01   5 4 3 2 1

Library of Congress Cataloging-in-Publication Data
Reichheld, Frederick F.
    Loyalty Rules! : how today's leaders build lasting relationships / Frederick R. Reichheld.
        p. cm.
    Includes bibliographical references and index.
    ISBN 1-57851-205-0 (alk. paper)
    1. Customer loyalty. 2. Customer relations. 3. Employee loyalty. 4. Leadership. I. Title.
    HF5415.525 .R45 2001
    658.8'12--dc21

                                                                        2001024195

The paper used in this publication meets the requirements of the American National Standard for
Permanence of Paper for Publications and Documents in Libraries and Archives Z39.48-1992.

In loving memory of my parents,
Jane and Charles Reichheld

Their lives embodied this simple formula:

LOVE X COURAGE X PERSEVERANCE = LOYALTY

Contents

■

Preface

■

This book is designed to be a practical handbook for building loyal business relationships. While some may consider it odd for a handbook to be organized according to a code of principles, too many handbooks are little more than mere catalogs of tools. In the case of loyalty, there is no shortage of tools; the constraining factor in most companies is a deeply flawed understanding of objectives. A hammer, for example, is a marvelous tool, but in the hands of someone with misguided objectives, it can become a destructive weapon. Similarly, tools such as data warehouses, customer-relationship management software, and rewards programs all have outstanding potential, but when a leadership team is confused about the principles that underpin true loyalty, the use of these tools is often counterproductive. Loyalty cannot begin with tools; it must begin with leaders who recognize the enormous value of building and maintaining mutually beneficial relationships.

General George Marshall described the importance of principles and objectives over tools this way: "If you get the objectives right, a lieutenant can write the strategy." Accordingly, this book spends at least as much time on the underlying objectives for building loyalty as it does on the how-to's. The principles and practices described herein are derived from my experience with Bain & Company's loyalty practice during the 1990s, as well as from a series of CEO Loyalty Roundtables and Master Class executive seminars that I organized. While the same principles (or rules) of loyalty apply to all business relationships—including suppliers, dealers, and investors—*Loyalty Rules!* focuses primarily on customers and employees because these are the most central relationships in most businesses. Nevertheless, examples from the full range of business relationships will illustrate the universal nature of these principles.

Loyalty Rules! is intended to build on the economic framework established in my previous book, *The Loyalty Effect* (Boston: Harvard Business

School Press, 1996). By delineating the microeconomic framework linking customer and employee retention to accounting profits, my earlier book argues that loyalty makes financial sense. By demonstrating how a 5 percent increase in retention can yield between 25 percent and almost 100 percent increases in profits across a variety of industries, I hoped to convince more companies to concentrate additional resources and energy on building loyalty. Indeed, the numbers startled many executives and set off a rush to create tools for boosting retention.

My primary goal in writing *Loyalty Rules!* is to ensure that the energy and resources invested in building loyalty are invested productively. There is still much confusion about what it means to be loyal in business and whether the rules have changed as we shift into the new economy. To some, the idea that loyalty is important to success has become a distinctly radical proposition. But the rules have not changed—loyalty is more vital than ever. All too often, it is a company's own strategies and internal systems that unwittingly undermine its efforts to build customer and employee loyalty.

During my more than twenty years of consulting at Bain & Company, my work has spanned a wide range of industries and clients. Not only have I observed that loyalty remains relevant to personal success, but I am convinced that without it, success in any meaningful sense is impossible. When executives come to appreciate the many dimensions and true value of lasting relationships, then loyalty helps bridge the gap between the philosophical world and the practical, between the world of ethics and the world of economics. My real hope is that more and more companies and leaders will come to see loyalty not only as a driver of growth and profits, but as a central measure of their success, to understand that loyalty provides the acid test of their leadership.

Acknowledgments

∎

I am most grateful to my partners for creating the Bain Fellow position and tailoring it to accommodate my desire to focus on writing and research while still maintaining important ties to the firm. None of this would have come to pass had it not been for the support and encouragement of Tom Tierney, Bain's worldwide managing director from 1992 through 1999. John Donahoe, Tom's successor, has reinforced that support along with Phyllis Yale, leader of our Boston office, who graciously accepted the responsibility for managing the evolution of my relationship with the firm. All three of these leaders represent wonderful illustrations of the kind of leadership described in this book—leadership founded on operating principles that are truly worthy of loyalty.

Many Bain partners have shaped my thinking about loyalty and leadership over the years—too many to thank here individually. But I especially want to recognize Phil Schefter, who made important contributions to this project, both through our collaboration on a *Harvard Business Review* article focusing on the relevance of loyalty to the new economy, and through his thoughtful criticism of the manuscript for this book. Chris Zook also found time in his busy schedule to read the entire manuscript and offer thorough and thoughtful suggestions for improvement.

The executives whom I have used as examples of loyalty leadership have been most generous with their time and support. The list of CEOs who participated in one or more of our loyalty roundtables is provided below. These sessions were enormously valuable in helping to articulate and pressure-test the rules of loyalty. Special thanks are due to the four CEOs (noted by an asterisk) who also courageously volunteered to teach with me in Master Class seminars on loyalty-based leadership.

Jack Brennan, CEO, The Vanguard Group
Roger Brown, CEO, Bright Horizons Family Solutions
Truett and Dan Cathy, CEO and EVP, Chick-fil-A
Scott Cook, Chairman, Intuit
Tom Donahoe, Vice Chairman, Price Waterhouse
*Jim Ericson, CEO, Northwestern Mutual
*Bob Herres, CEO, USAA
Tim Hoeksema, CEO, Midwest Express
Mike Phillips, CEO, Frank Russell Company
Ed Rust, Jr., CEO, State Farm Insurance
*Andy Taylor, CEO, Enterprise Rent-A-Car
*Rich Teerlink, CEO, Harley-Davidson
Tom Tierney, Worldwide Managing Director, Bain & Company
John Whitacre, CEO, Nordstrom

Another CEO, Steve Walker of Walker Information, has made a uniquely important contribution by helping me turn the Loyalty Acid Test Survey from an idea into a reality. Steve contributed the resources and time of his firm (particular thanks to Mark Drizin and Chris Woolard) to finalize the survey design and to implement the beta test of loyalty leaders. Walker Information's joint project with the Hudson Institute (National Employee Relationship Report) also provided the baseline of employee loyalty described in chapter 1.

Now to the writing process itself: Although my writing skills seem to be improving with continued practice, I could never have managed to complete this manuscript without the capable and enthusiastic assistance of Nancy McLaren, who served as my editor throughout the project. Throughout her years as an English teacher, I suspect that none of her students received even a small fraction of the red marks that my manuscripts have earned, nor did they appreciate them nearly as much as I have. Nancy's collaboration has been invaluable.

Linda Polmear, my assistant at Bain, successfully juggles a host of responsibilities, including speaking engagements, research projects, CEO Loyalty Roundtables, and Master Classes—all while maintaining an upbeat and cheerful outlook that infects everyone with whom she comes in contact. She has played an enormously important role along every dimension of my work at Bain.

Finally, and most importantly, I want to thank my wife, Karen. For over twenty years, she has exemplified what it means to be a partner worthy of

loyalty. The rules of loyalty, which it took me years to recognize and articulate in this book, to her are so patently obvious that she finds it incredi-
ble that they are not already well understood throughout the business
world. Karen's deep, intuitive wisdom on these subjects has provided the
litmus test for evaluating my ideas. When they make sense to her, I know
that I finally got them right.

Loyalty Rules!

1

Timeless Principles

■

Loyalty, the key to success in today's economy? Be serious! What relevance could such a quaint, old-fashioned notion hold for a world in which customers defect at the click of a mouse and impersonal shopping bots scour databases for ever better deals? What good is a small-town virtue amid the faceless anonymity of the Internet's global marketplace? Loyalty must be on a fast track toward extinction, right?[1]

Wrong. Chief executives at the cutting edge of e-commerce—from Cisco's John Chambers to eBay's Meg Whitman, from Dell Computer's Michael Dell to Intuit's Scott Cook—care as deeply about customer retention as does any top-notch bricks-and-mortar executive, and consider it vital to the success of their online operations. Whitman reports, "Loyalty is the primary ingredient in eBay's secret sauce." Web-savvy leaders know that loyalty is an economic necessity; acquiring customers on the Internet is enormously expensive, and unless those customers stick around and make lots of repeat purchases over the years, profits will remain elusive. And they know it's a competitive necessity; in every industry, some company will figure out how to harness the creative potential of the Web to create exceptional value for customers, and that company is going to lock in many profitable relationships at the expense of slow-footed rivals. Without the glue of loyalty, even the best-designed e-business model will collapse.

But that's *customer* loyalty. We all know that *employee* loyalty is another story. It takes a typical Silicon Valley firm only two years to lose half its employees. With the new economy's surge in job hopping and career surfing, how can any company hope to hold on to its workers? And how about supplier loyalty? The burgeoning Internet-based auctions, which blow apart traditional supply-chain relationships, seem to make loyalty all but irrelevant. Investor loyalty? Online trading has accelerated investor annual churn rates toward 100 percent. Employee, supplier, and investor loyalty—all must be anachronisms of the digital economy.

Wrong, wrong, and wrong again. Customer loyalty hinges, as it always has, on committed teams of high-caliber employees and suppliers, which in turn require a core of owners committed to building an enduringly successful enterprise. The challenge of building loyalty has indeed stiffened as the new economy has blossomed and presented enticing alternatives for customers, employees, and the whole range of business partners. But along with the enormous potential of the new economy have come increased risk and volatility. In this environment, it's become clear that loyalty is an even more vital asset for success in the age of the Internet. Building loyalty has in fact become the acid test of leadership.

It's a test that most leaders are flunking. Fewer than half of all employees of U.S. companies now consider their employer to be worthy of loyalty.[2] Bemoaning the decline in loyalty, leaders fault the Internet, rapid changes in technology, shifting government regulation, cutthroat competition, fickle customers, and greedy, short-term investors. Some have concluded that loyalty is no longer relevant in modern society, where self-interest sets the tone for employer-employee relations. But they are kidding themselves. People yearn now more than ever for leaders and institutions worthy of their trust and commitment—to help guide and enrich both life and work. When business leaders observe diminished loyalty in the people around them, it is not because a confusing new economy has robbed loyalty of all relevance, but rather because the core principles embodied in their leadership have proven unworthy of loyalty.

THE CASE FOR LOYALTY

Loyalty remains the hallmark of great leadership. It provides a far more exacting standard for leadership excellence than do the profits demanded today by impatient shareholders. The long-term rewards of loyalty ultimately outstrip even the most spectacular short-term profits. We are not, however, talking about a trade-off between loyalty and long-term profits. After all, what kind of customer, or supplier, or dealer, or employee would cast his or her lot with a leader who could not offer outstanding financial potential? Loyalty obviously demands superior profits, but it demands more. It requires that those profits be earned through the success of partners, not at their expense. Loyalty can be earned only when leaders put the welfare of their customers and their partners ahead of their own self-serving interests.

Herein lies the essential paradox of business loyalty. If loyalty is really about self-sacrifice—that is, about putting principles and relationships ahead of immediate personal financial gain—what relevance can it possibly hold for business, which is in large part driven by the pursuit of self-interest?

Too few managers can answer this question coherently. They have convinced themselves that maximizing shareholder value provides the sole principle for successful business practices, and that through faithful commitment to this principle, they have fulfilled their professional and ethical obligations to partners. In reality, though, these leaders are confusing profits with purpose. Whether they know it or not, they have abandoned what I'll call the "high road" of business practice. A single-minded focus on financial results will not create the conditions for loyalty or long-term success, and it may well lead an organization down a slippery slope to the "low road." On the low road, where money matters more than people, it becomes standard practice to take advantage of customers, employees, vendors, and a host of other business associates whenever they are vulnerable. Here, the goal of strategy is to create market power; the job of leaders, to utilize that power to strangle competitors, bully vendors, intimidate employees, and extract maximum value from customers—all in faithful duty to shareholders, whoever those shareholders happen to be this month. In this Darwinian struggle, only the toughest individuals survive, and trust is a weakness to be exploited.

Low-road strategies can generate impressive financials, for a time, and buoyant earnings and stock price provide the necessary bribes required to keep followers committed. Eventually, however, the low road leads to trouble. There will come a time when the firm gets blindsided by a competitor, or fails to anticipate a shift in market preferences, or discovers that a new technology has made its business model obsolete. And then, the true value of loyalty will become apparent. When profits inevitably get squeezed and stock price plummets, the company can no longer fund the bribes. Yet somehow, leaders must rally their partners to fight rather than switch; customers, employees, dealers, and suppliers must bind together and find a solution. Unless leaders have built relationships based on loyalty—loyalty to something more fundamental than today's earnings or stock price—then nothing will keep partners from jumping ship the instant a better opportunity comes along.

Many executives have confused employees, vendors, dealers—and even themselves—about the relationship between treating people right and financial success. The idea that the sole purpose of business is to generate profits, or that maximizing shareholder value matters more than treating people with dignity and respect, is absurd. Yet these common misperceptions are no more absurd than their mirror images. It is equally absurd to think that businesses can treat people right without achieving outstanding financial results, or that adhering to high standards of decency and consideration is somehow inconsistent with maximizing growth and profits.

There is indeed a high road in business, and it is the only road to lasting success. If you hope to lead others successfully or for very long, you must break through the widespread disillusionment and confusion by demonstrating that your leadership is founded on principles worthy of loyalty; principles that will inspire commitment among customers, employees, and investors; principles that cultivate partner growth and prosperity, not simply your own profits. You must show all your partners—including shareholders—how these principles create the most solid foundation for financial excellence and sustained success.

Wishful thinking? Read on, and you'll find plenty of examples of successful loyalty leaders who can serve as practical role models for your journey along the high road. What's their secret to building loyalty in this increasingly volatile environment of the new economy? Well, for starters, they understand the enormous value of loyalty, so they measure it.

MEASURING LOYALTY
THE LOYALTY ACID TEST

Climbing to the high road requires the right tools—in particular, tools to measure loyalty as carefully as profits. Satisfaction metrics are a good first step, but don't stop there. Satisfaction, a fleeting attitude that lacks durable staying power, is a poor substitute for loyalty and sets far too low a standard of excellence. Far better than satisfaction scores are measures such as customer and employee retention rates—real behaviors with real financial consequences. But even retention rates don't tell the whole story. Sometimes customers stick around simply because they aren't aware of alternatives or because they are hostage to long-term contracts. Some employees stay put only because they lack ambition or other options.

Loyalty is the gold standard for measuring the quality of a relationship. True loyalty endures through the best of times and the worst and melds mutual interests into shared goals. Are your relationships with your partners worthy of their loyalty? You have to ask them. This is precisely what many of our model loyalty leaders have done—they have taken the acid test, applying what I call the Loyalty Acid Test Survey (see appendix) to hundreds of their customers and employees.

The Loyalty Acid Test Survey is a relationship report card specifically designed to help leaders evaluate and strengthen key relationships. A handful of "loyalty leader firms" (firms that have achieved the highest level of loyalty in their segment) beta-tested this tool, with some striking results. They discovered, for example, that between 70 and 75 percent of their employees agreed with the statement "I believe this organization deserves my loyalty." Though the firms are not satisfied with this result and are taking steps to improve, they fully appreciate their relative advantage. Exhibit 1–1 compares the plight of the average U.S. company with the initial loyalty leader results. From a representative national sample of over 2,000 employees, only 45 percent agreed that "I believe my organization deserves my loyalty," and 32 percent were neutral. The worst news, however, is that 23 percent actively disagreed.[3]

Consider the predicament faced by leaders of firms on the lower end of the loyalty scale. They would like their customers to be loyal, but meanwhile, unbeknownst to the leaders, most of their own employees are not at all convinced that the company deserves loyalty. How the employees treat customers in their daily interactions will almost certainly convey their misgivings. Unless management teams measure and analyze organizational loyalty with a tool like the Loyalty Acid Test Survey, they are operating in the dark. Chances are, their energy is misdirected and resources are allocated to fix symptoms rather than root causes.

To build superior loyalty, you need an analytical framework and tools

Exhibit 1-1

THE LOYALTY ACID TEST: EMPLOYEES

"I believe this organization deserves my loyalty."

■ Agree   ■ Disagree

45%	
22%	

U.S. Average

72%	
9%	

Loyalty Leader Sample

?	
?	

Your Company

0%   20%   40%   60%   80%   100%

to analyze and strengthen key relationships. The Loyalty Acid Test Survey is designed to help you prioritize your challenges and create an effective game plan for maximizing the loyalty of your business partners. Adaptations for employees, customers, suppliers, dealers, and investors can be downloaded from the Web. You will also find instructions for comparing your results with the most up-to-date loyalty leader benchmarks cataloged on our Web site, www.loyaltyrules.com, the unique source for this data.

So what do these numbers and the years of research tell us? How do the best companies earn such an impressive loyalty advantage? The answer begins with a single insight. The center of gravity for business loyalty—whether it be the loyalty of customers, employees, investors, suppliers, or dealers—is the personal integrity of the senior leadership team and its ability to put its principles into practice. Consider the evidence displayed in exhibit 1–2. Of the 1,057 employees surveyed who agreed that "senior leaders of this organization are people of high personal integrity," 63 percent

Exhibit 1-2

IMPACT OF LEADERSHIP INTEGRITY: NATIONAL SAMPLE

"I believe this organization deserves my loyalty."

■ Agree   ■ Disagree

65%

9%

Employees agree that leaders have high integrity

18%

54%

Employees disagree that leaders have high integrity

| 0% | 20% | 40% | 60% | 80% | 100% |

agreed that "I believe this organization deserves my loyalty." Of the 444 who disagreed that their senior leaders had high integrity, only 19 percent considered their organization worthy of loyalty. As you will see in the pages ahead, the rules for building loyalty in the new economy are essentially the same rules that have always created loyalty. Timeless principles of integrity such as truth, fairness, and responsibility continue to create the gravitational core for organizational loyalty. Indeed, their validity and importance have only increased in the age of the Internet.

THE HIGH ROAD AND THE INTERNET

Although the Internet has accelerated churn in many sectors of the economy, leaders who understand the basis of true loyalty recognize it as a powerful tool for strengthening relationships. Indeed, the electronic market space is a most hospitable environment for high-road strategies. By directly linking companies with their suppliers and customers, the Web can dramatically deepen relationships and effect enormous efficiencies. But little of this potential can be realized unless these relationships enjoy a high level of trust. For customers on the Web, where business is conducted at a distance and risks and uncertainties are magnified, trust is more important than ever. Online customers can't look a sales clerk in the eye, can't size up the physical space of a store or an office, and can't see and touch products. They have to rely on images and promises, and if they don't trust the company presenting those images and promises, they'll shop elsewhere. In fact, when Web shoppers were asked to name the attributes of e-tailers that were most important in earning their business, the number one answer was "a Web site I know and trust."[4] All other attributes, including lowest cost and broadest selection, lagged far behind. Price does not rule the Web; trust does.

When customers do trust an online vendor, they are much more likely to share personal information. This information enables the company to form a more intimate relationship with customers and to offer products and services tailored to their individual preferences, which, in turn, further increases the level of trust and strengthens the bonds of loyalty. Such a virtuous circle can quickly translate into a durable advantage over competitors.

The story is much the same for integrated supply-chain relationships. Unless firms are comfortable engaging in highly transparent relationships and sharing internal information, including costs and profit budgets, with their partners, little benefit can be achieved through reduced inventory levels, coordinated scheduling, or joint planning. Open, transparent relationships work only when both sides are committed to mutual success.

In addition to rewarding trust generously, the Internet opens new opportunities to build trust. Everyone knows, for example, that communities flourish on the Web. Less understood is how the trust built up in such communities can be transferred to the companies that host them. Here, eBay provides a great example. In the past, fears about reliability and fraud prevented the exchange of used merchandise between strangers from developing into a big business. But eBay used the unique capabilities of the Web to establish and enforce the rules of engagement. Buyers and sellers rate each other after each transaction, and the ratings are posted on the site. Every member's reputation thus becomes public record. Although there are still kinks to be worked out—linking screen names to specific individuals, for example—progress to date has been astonishing. In a sense, eBay is using the Internet to bring small-town rules of trust to the most challenging of markets—a global network of strangers.

The Internet not only creates communities, but speeds the search for truth. In the past, convenient store locations, aggressive sales forces, and a general lack of information shielded companies from the penalties of providing anything less than the best product and service quality; customer inertia was mistaken for loyalty. Thanks to the Internet, however, those shields have been dismantled. Through chat rooms and online ratings services, customers can check companies' reputations and results and share referrals instantly by copying e-mails to dozens, or thousands, of associates. They can compare supplier price and quality in real time, all the time. Winners in the new economy will welcome—and benefit from—the unprecedented level of candor characterized by the high road.

SUSTAINABLE ECONOMIC ADVANTAGE

One of the greatest challenges confronting players in the new economy lies in building the kind of sustainable economic advantage necessary to deliver superior results. Not so long ago, this challenge manifested itself in the relatively straightforward goal of building structural cost advantages, which could be expected to yield a competitive edge for decades. Today, a company like IBM is displaced by Compaq, which is then leapfrogged by Dell Computer, all in the period of a few short years. Winning business models deteriorate quickly as core elements in the value chain shift and evolve. Shifting alliances and outsourcing arrangements reshuffle competitive positions. Since nearly limitless information is readily available through the Internet, competitive strategies are easier to decipher and to copy. Proprietary data and processes are more difficult to protect. Not only is information flowing more readily from company to company, so are employees. Witness the executive search business, which has mushroomed from a cottage industry to more than $10 billion in annual fees.

Quite likely the only possible source of sustainable competitive advantage in the new economy will be the bonds of loyalty you generate. If this strategy seems like an uphill battle in today's environment, remember that sustainable advantage means outperforming your competitors. Although defection rates across your industry may be climbing, you need to build relationships that are stronger and more enduring than your competitors'. However small the advantage, it will compound into substantial economic benefits as you grow.

In my previous book, *The Loyalty Effect*, I documented the outstanding financial results generated by leaders who can build a measurable advantage in loyalty.[5] By dissecting the microeconomic forces that link loyalty to profits, we explained the enormous growth and cost advantages of loyalty. We showed that in industry after industry, the high cost of acquiring customers renders many customer relationships unprofitable during their early years. Only in later years, when the cost of serving loyal customers falls and the volume of their purchases rises, do relationships generate big returns. The bottom line is this: An increase in customer retention rates of 5 percent increases profits by 25 percent to 95 percent. Those numbers startled many executives, and the book set off a rush to craft retention strategies, many of which continue to pay large dividends.

When my colleagues at Bain and I applied the same methodology to analyzing customer life-cycle economics in several e-commerce sectors—including books, apparel, groceries, and consumer electronics—we found classic loyalty economics at work. In fact, the general pattern of early losses followed by rising profits is exaggerated on the Internet (exhibit 1–3). At the beginning of a relationship, the outlays needed to acquire a customer are often considerably higher in e-commerce than in traditional retail channels. In apparel e-tailing, for example, new customers cost 20 percent to 40 percent more for pure-play Internet companies than for traditional retailers with both physical and online stores. That means that the losses in the early stages of relationships are larger.

In future years, though, profit growth accelerates at an even faster rate. In apparel e-tailing, repeat customers spend more than twice as much in months 24–30 of their relationships as they do in the first six months. And since it is relatively easy for Web stores to extend their range of products, they can sell more and more kinds of goods to loyal customers, broadening as well as deepening their relationships over time. The evidence indicates, in fact, that Web customers tend to consolidate their purchases with one primary supplier to the extent that making purchases from the supplier's site becomes part of their daily routine. This phenomenon is particularly apparent in the business-to-business sector. For example, W. W. Grainger, the largest industrial supply company in the United States, discovered that longtime customers whose volume of purchases through Grainger's traditional branches had stabilized increased their purchases

Exhibit 1-3

CUSTOMER LIFE-CYCLE ECONOMICS IN E-COMMERCE

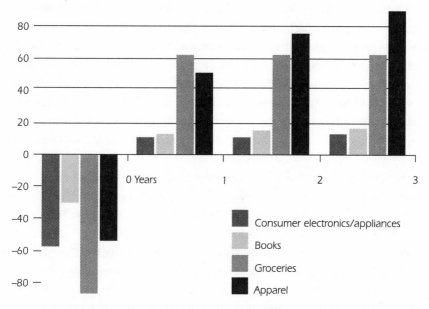

substantially when they began using Grainger's Web site. Sales to these customers increased at three times the rate of similar customers who used only the physical outlets.

In addition to increasing their own purchases, loyal customers also frequently refer new customers to a supplier, providing another rich source of profits. Referrals are lucrative in traditional commerce as well, but, again, the Internet amplifies the effect since word of mouse spreads even faster than word of mouth. Online customers can, for example, use e-mail to broadcast a recommendation for a favorite Web site to dozens of friends and family members. Many e-tailers are now automating the referral process, letting customers send recommendations to acquaintances while the customers are still in the e-tailers' sites. Because referred customers cost so little to acquire, they begin to generate profits much earlier in their life cycles.

One e-commerce leader reaping the economic benefits of referrals from loyal customers is eBay. More than half its customers arrive through referrals. "If you just do the math off our quarterly financial filings," CEO Meg Whitman has told the *Wall Street Journal*, "you see that we're spending less than $10 to acquire each new customer. The reason is that we are being driven by word of mouth."[6] eBay has even found that the costs of supporting referred customers are considerably lower than those for customers brought in through advertising or other marketing efforts. Referred customers tend to use the people who referred them for advice and guidance rather than calling eBay's technical support desk. In effect, loyal customers not only take over the function of advertising and sales, but even staff the company's help desk—for free!

The combination of all these economic factors means that the value of loyalty is often even greater on the Internet than in the physical world. For any company doing business on the Web, the implication is clear: You cannot generate superior long-term profits unless you achieve superior customer loyalty. Moreover, the increased speed of change, the need for flexibility in individual roles and team structures, and the cutthroat war for talent have further intensified the need for employee loyalty. By loyal employees we mean more than those who simply show up and obediently carry out your commands. True employee loyalty includes responsibility and accountability for building successful, mutually valuable relationships. Finally, the ever-increasing need for loyal and committed suppliers, dealers, and investors increases as the Internet creates the opportunity—indeed, the competitive imperative—to build a more integrated network of relationships.

This emerging model of competitive excellence and sustainable economic advantage can be achieved only through more transparent and trustworthy partnerships within communities of mutually beneficial relationships. There has never been a more propitious time for leaders committed to the principles of loyalty.

FINDING THE RIGHT ROLE MODELS

Where should you look for practical examples of loyalty leadership in the new economy? It might be tempting to turn to some of today's highfliers. Isn't their success proof of their leadership excellence? A word of caution is in order here. Many of the Internet's putative business superstars have not yet demonstrated that they can generate profits, let alone weather the tough times that test the loyalty of customers and partners. Many digital-era savants are now closer to bankruptcy than to the billionaire status that was fleetingly theirs. Even those who survived the dot-com meltdown of the late 1990s may never live up to the lofty expectations of media pundits or the stock market.

Look instead to organizations whose exemplary track records of customer and employee retention have endured throughout the good times and the bad. Look to organizations with long track records of integrating technological innovations, including the Internet, into their core business in order to build stronger relationships. Look to organizations whose leaders have consistently put the interests of customers, employees, and their other business partners ahead of their own. Look to organizations such as the following:

- Harley-Davidson, which recovered from near bankruptcy in the 1980s by building mutually beneficial relationships, based on simple core values, with all stakeholders. Returns to investors have ranked among the top-tier returns of all public companies, and despite Milwaukee's tight employment market, a long line of applicants awaits job openings at Harley.

- Enterprise Rent-A-Car, which raced past Hertz and Avis to become the largest car rental firm in North America. It continues to grow at more than 20 percent per year in an otherwise sluggish industry. With over 45,000 employees, the company manages to hire more college graduates than does any other firm in the United States by putting the interests of customers and employees ahead of those of the owners.

- The Vanguard Group, the mutual fund industry's growth leader. The organization built its $550 billion in assets under management by putting long-term investment returns to its customers first. With more than 40 percent of transactions now on the Web, Vanguard maintains the lowest costs and the highest customer retention rates in its industry.

- Southwest Airlines, the only consistently profitable major airline in the United States for every year since 1973. The airline has employee turnover rates of 4 to 5 percent, in an industry with rates typically double that. In the notoriously cyclical airline business, Southwest has never had a layoff. With the lowest ticket prices, the company still ranks at the top in customer service and safety.

- Dell Computer, which so effectively utilized the Internet to revolutionize the sales and production of personal computers that it has become the global market share leader. By focusing on building the most valuable customer experience, Dell has made itself the profit leader.

- Cisco Systems, whose employee turnover ran less than 10 percent during the 1990s although it is headquartered in Silicon Valley, where turnover averaged 25 to 30 percent. Not only does every employee carry an ID badge embossed with the company values, but all bonuses are dependent on meeting customer satisfaction goals.

- Northwestern Mutual, the company that has consistently focused on creating superior value for its policyholders. The "Quiet Company" has so successfully parlayed its superior customer retention into lower costs and faster growth that it can no longer be categorized as a high-end niche player; it is the industry leader in individual life insurance.

- MBNA, the only credit card company that considers customer retention so important that it reports the statistic in its annual report. The company retains 97 percent of its profitable customers.

- Chick-fil-A, whose store operator turnover runs 5 percent, compared with the competition's 35 to 40 percent. Founder Truett Cathy has so effectively marshaled loyalty effect economics that he can afford to let his operators earn compensation double or triple industry averages, while still generating sufficient cash to grow the chain while remaining a private company.

- SAS, the leading statistical analysis (e-intelligence) software firm, whose 5 percent turnover rate among software engineers compares with the industry's average of more than 20 percent. By hiring the right kind of people and providing them with a career and lifestyle that reinforce work-family balance (employees enjoy free health care and child care), SAS is building an institution in a notoriously fickle market space.

- USAA, the preeminent insurer of military personnel and veterans, whose customer turnover is so low that the primary root cause of defection is death. USAA's top management believes so strongly in the importance of customer retention that the managers base their own bonuses on this metric. USAA demonstrates how customer loyalty and employee loyalty go hand in hand; the firm's telephone staff turnover runs 9 percent, compared with more than 20 percent for the industry.

- The New York Times Company, where customer retention is tracked as carefully as profits, and where retention performance (above 90 percent) stands head and shoulders above the rest of the newspaper competition, which churns readers at rates of 25 to 50 percent.

- U.S. Marine Corps, the only branch of the U.S. military that has managed to meet its staffing targets—primarily because of superior recruiting and retention success. Rather than dropping standards to meet staffing demand, the Marines constantly raise them. The Corps' motto, *Semper Fideles*, helps convey to outsiders the central role that loyalty plays for the Marines.

- Intuit, the leader in personal financial software, whose employee turnover runs half the Silicon Valley average. Intuit has weathered several storms, including a blocked merger with Microsoft and a fundamental shift in its business model from shrink-wrapped software to the Internet by remaining loyal to its founder's values.

The list goes on, but the stories all have the same refrain. Loyalty is not dead. It rules the new economy—just as surely as it ruled the old. Leaders who grasp its true nature and economic potential understand that loyalty cannot be a one-way street. They earn people's loyalty when they treat them in a manner that inspires their trust and commitment. Model leaders understand both the short-term costs and the superior value of long-term investing in human capital, of attracting and retaining a select business team. They know that when you treat people with dignity and respect, communicate honestly, help people discover their full potential by guiding them into roles that play to their special strengths, and strive to create and nurture mutually beneficial partnerships, then you will become a leader worthy of trust and commitment and your business will thrive.

Partnerships must adhere to the rules of loyalty, or they will become nothing more than unstable, self-serving alliances. True partnerships must be driven by mutual caring, respect, responsibility, accountability, and growth. In a true partnership, each individual must willingly put the success of the relationship ahead of short-term, personal gain. And, of course, for each partner to prosper in the long term, the entire system of relationships with employees, dealers, vendors, and investors must successfully create value for the ultimate customer. Each individual must be willing not only to put the partner's interests ahead of his or her own, but also to make the interests of the final consumer the highest priority.

An impossible challenge? How can one inspire such self-sacrifice in an organization composed of ordinary mortals conditioned to follow the compass of their own self-interest? As you will see, this kind of selfless generosity is both sensible and practical, but only when leaders fulfill their responsibility. It makes sense when leaders select the right partners and guide them into roles in which they can contribute and receive real value. Leaders must also ensure that individuals are fairly rewarded for the collective success they help to create. When people trust that in the long run the success of their partners will drive their own personal success, then they can logically and wholeheartedly commit themselves to the service of others.

To earn this trust, leaders must demonstrate far more than good intentions. They must demonstrate the wisdom, discipline, courage, and commitment to ensure mutual accountability and responsibility from every partner. Only with strong leadership can relationships be restructured according to a set of principles that regularly rewards those who consistently treat others right. Leadership is indeed the key to transforming business relationships into something far greater and more powerful than the mutual pursuit of greed and self-interest. Only outstanding leadership can transform common business relationships into real partnerships truly worthy of loyalty.

The leaders profiled in this book prosper because they have built and nurtured just such a network of loyal partnerships—and they have helped those around them do the same. Because their personal integrity sets the standard, and because their own loyalty to core principles never wavers, these leaders inspire the mutual pride, trust, and commitment that bind people together even in times of turbulence and adversity. Think about it. Wouldn't you feel proud to be part of an exclusive team renowned for taking the high road? Wouldn't you remain loyal to a leader who dedicated both time and money to helping you achieve your fullest potential, and who cared more about building and maintaining loyal relationships than about his or her own bank account? Why would leaders be so generous? Out of charity?

Loyalty leaders do not act out of charity. In fact, their records show that they have prospered magnificently. Most of those profiled in this book will retire with a personal net worth in the tens or hundreds of millions; a handful have already become billionaires by devoting themselves to their partners' success and by inspiring others to follow suit. They know that their efforts to make their employees and customers worthy partners, and to align interests and share rewards, will ultimately lead to their own success and prosperity. These leaders have earned stellar loyalty credentials because they have discovered how to create a network of mutually beneficial relationships that both build, and are sustained by, loyalty—to one another, to the firm, and, even more importantly, by commitment to a shared set of values and principles we call the *principles of loyalty*.

THE SIX PRINCIPLES OF LOYALTY

The six principles of loyalty encompass standards of excellence, simplicity, honesty, fairness, respect, and responsibility. But they are not idealized abstractions far removed from the routine operations of the workaday world. On the contrary, they are embodied in simple, straightforward actions that drive measurement systems, compensation, organization, and strategy:

1. **Play to win/win**
   Profiting at the expense of partners is a shortcut to a dead end.

2. **Be picky**
   Membership is a privilege.

3. **Keep it simple**
   Complexity is the enemy of speed and responsiveness.

4. **Reward the right results**
   Worthy partners deserve worthy goals.

5. **Listen hard, talk straight**
   Long-term relationships require honest, two-way communication and learning.

6. **Preach what you practice**
   Actions often speak louder than words, but together they are unbeatable.

After extensive research and analysis, my colleagues at Bain and I are convinced of the universal nature of these six core principles of loyalty. The model leaders in this book have put them to work in a wide variety of industries and situations that range from Silicon Valley start-ups to century-old institutions, from the highest to the lowest of technologies, from manufacturing to services, from small firms to large, and from public to private—and even to mutual—ownership. The leaders' backgrounds, personalities, and management styles range just as widely, from ferociously competitive former jocks to bookish introverts, from soft-spoken, grandfatherly counselors to fire-breathing table thumpers. But underneath such differences, these leaders demonstrate a consistent pattern for shaping their business into a network of mutually supportive partnerships.

The principles of loyalty at first glance may seem so obvious as to be self-evident truths, but don't be fooled. Although these principles are timeless, they are also revolutionary. They reflect basic inner truths as well as fundamental economic realities that all too many leaders ignore at their peril. Those who truly understand and practice them are receiving Loyalty Acid Test Survey scores that put them on the honor role. They are building track records comparable to the masters of loyalty-based leadership discussed throughout this book. Reading their stories will help you to understand more fully how these principles work in the real world, and to diagnose and strengthen your own relationships, with potentially revolutionary results.

The executives selected to be my exemplars remain steadfastly loyal to these principles. They know that their organizations cannot exist solely to maximize shareholder value, or solely to put customer interests first, or solely to be the best place for employees to work. Because loyalty leaders recognize that all these people must be well served if their loyalty is to be earned, they are committed to providing superior value across the board, and they pare away any impediments to this goal.

You will see the six principles of loyalty in action in the case studies that follow. First, however, we must highlight the single most important lesson that the executives we will study have to teach, a lesson derived from their concept of leadership and its intrinsic responsibilities. These executives all agree that the fundamental job of a leader is to be a role model, an exemplary partner whose primary goal is to help people grow to their fullest human potential. To build loyalty, they say, you must first be loyal to others by helping them build relationships on the right principles. Then, your leadership actions must not only reinforce these principles, but embody them.

When your associates see that you are faithful to the timeless principles of loyalty, then they will be loyal in return. And when they follow your example, when they begin to restructure their own network of relationships according to your model, when they begin to place the interests of their partners and customers ahead of their own, watch out! You will have initiated a chain reaction with breathtaking consequences. You will have unleashed the loyalty effect, the spiraling economic advantages that reward those who follow the high road.

2

Loyalty Leadership

∎

Putting Principles into Practice

Who are the leaders worthy of becoming your role models as you trek the high road? Who has consistently and courageously put the principles of loyalty into practice in today's challenging environment? This chapter profiles several leaders who have built loyalty through their personal integrity, superior business strategies, and masterful implementation of the six principles of loyalty.

THE ENTERPRISE RENT-A-CAR STORY

When Andy Taylor returned home to St. Louis in 1973 to rejoin Enterprise Rent-A-Car, the small company his father had founded sixteen years earlier, he had no inkling that he was on a road that would lead to the top of the car rental industry. Leaving the West Coast company he had joined out of college meant taking a pay cut, but he had washed and shuttled cars for Enterprise as a teenager, and his fond recollection of the company's philosophy lured him back. Today, as CEO, he preaches the same simple philosophy his father, Jack Taylor, taught him: "Put customers first and employees second, and profit will take care of itself."

Through this formula of service to others, Taylor has built the most loyal group of employees and customers in the industry—and turned the car rental industry on its ear. Before the competition could say "maximize shareholder value," they found themselves staring at Enterprise's taillights in the distance. Click your way onto enterprise.com, the firm's Web site, and you will discover that Enterprise has become the largest car rental company in North America, bigger than Avis or Hertz, with a fleet exceeding half a million vehicles. While the rest of the industry languished through the 1990s with sluggish growth and sputtering profitability, Taylor steered Enterprise into the passing lane with growth rates exceeding 20 percent per year.

Even industry insiders find Taylor's track record extraordinary. Enterprise kept on growing at phenomenal rates without the bread-and-butter airport business and without the large advertising budgets of its major competitors. The firm defies the norm in other ways as well: Its prices are as much as 20 percent below typical airport rates; customers routinely get door-to-door service; and branch managers generally earn substantially more than they would at Hertz or Avis. Although this mix of lower pricing, superior customer service, and richer compensation is true to the Taylor credo, according to the standard bottom-line philosophy it would seem like a recipe for bankruptcy.

Nothing could be further from the truth. Somehow profit takes care of itself, as Jack promised it would. Experts estimate that Enterprise is the most profitable firm in its industry, so profitable that its rapid growth is funded through internally generated cash flow and privately placed debt. Despite the investment surge required to launch it to the top of the industry, Enterprise's profitability has enabled it to remain a privately held company.

What is going on here? Taylor admits that even he is a little overwhelmed by the sheer magnitude of Enterprise's numbers: over $5.6 billion in revenues, a fleet exceeding 500,000 cars, 46,000 employees, and more than 4,400 branch offices. The company continues to open branches at the rate of one a day and is the largest recruiter of college graduates, hiring over 5,000 per year, even though, to some, careers in car rental lack cachet. What's more, Enterprise is one of the largest single purchasers of new cars annually—4 percent of U.S. cars built—and the largest seller of used cars in the United States. What is the magic formula? Taylor describes it in terms of loyal relationships:

> At Enterprise, loyalty is everything. If we don't satisfy customers so that they come back, we can't build the business. If we don't have happy, well-informed employees who feel bonded with the company's success, we won't deliver the kind of excellent service that satisfies customers. Loyalty has been the key to Enterprise's success.[1]

Enterprising Strategy

Enterprise's loyalty-based strategy is so successful precisely because it is unique. Taylor explains, "A major difference between Enterprise and our competitors is that their business is cars and ours is people. They focus on building their fleet of cars; we focus on building our employees' careers."[2] But there are other important differences as well. Taylor's father, Jack Taylor, recognized early on that his small business could offer special value only if he focused on building leadership in a specific niche. The airport car rental business was then dominated by the big three—Hertz, Avis, and National—with combined market share in excess of 90 percent. In contrast, in the 1960s the home-market rental business, which consists primarily of replacement cars for customers whose cars are being repaired, was fragmented among dozens of local firms. The Taylors opted to serve this customer segment by focusing on customers' special home-market replacement car needs. By offering competitive rates and convenient service to insurance adjusters who needed replacement cars for clients when their cars were stolen or damaged, the Taylors grew their business and accumulated loyal partners.

Essential to the firm's growth has been the steadfast commitment of its leadership to the simple network of local branches that best serves the home market. In the words of Andy Taylor, "One key to our growth has been our ability to say no to revenue opportunities which don't fit our system."[3] In this way, Enterprise provides service that offers truly special value to its target customers and that earns their loyalty.

Decentralized Organization

Today 90 percent of the U.S. population lives within fifteen miles of an Enterprise Rent-A-Car branch. Andy Taylor learned long ago the value of organizing his business into small, stable teams with maximum responsibility, flexibility, and accountability. Enterprise can deliver superior service at a profit because employees at each branch have free rein to make the decisions that affect their own customers and the profitability of their unique branch. Although headquarters has initiated important systemwide technology upgrades, Taylor relies primarily on local initiatives for service and cost improvements.

Each branch, though company-owned, is a separate profit center, structured to operate as an independent, entrepreneurial business. This structure, which Taylor calls a confederation of partnerships, simplifies the management of growth, and he acknowledges it as the most critical feature of his ongoing strategy. It does more than enable rapid growth and the flexibility to make rapid changes. It also provides better career development opportunity for employees, who get to run their own businesses much earlier in their careers than in most other companies. Branch managers are responsible for several million dollars' worth of assets. The high level of financial responsibility creates more rewarding jobs for them and keeps them focused on maximizing fleet utilization. Taylor believes that individual accountability is the basis for a good partnership, and his small, independent branch structure makes it impossible for managers to miss either subpar or outstanding performance.

This simple structure also accelerates the learning process. Enterprise openly shares the financial results and customer satisfaction scores of every branch office and every region. As a result, everybody can compare results and see which branches have developed winning practices, such as a van driver's practice of offering free soft drinks to customers during summer months and an assistant manager's allowing customers to return rental cars after hours. Because the compensation of branch and assistant branch managers is based on their branch's profits, the managers are eager to learn from their peers. Friendly rivalries are encouraged, and it is not unusual to see competing branches wager a dinner on monthly profit reports. Every employee is motivated to find innovative ways to increase customer retention and referrals in order to build enduring relationships with the right kind of customers.

High Tech and High Touch

You might not expect a company focused on maintaining relationships, a company that distinguishes itself by personal touches like picking customers up at their homes, to excel at technology as well. But Enterprise knows it must do both. The firm is an acknowledged leader in electronic commerce, noted particularly for its development of advanced technology that allows insurance companies to authorize reservations and billings electronically. In 1999, Enterprise was included (along with eBay, Amazon.com, and Dell Computer) in *CIO* magazine's list of the 100 companies most likely to win in the new economy. Taylor considers information technology to be such a strategic advantage for delivering exceptional customer service that he has Enterprise's technology division report directly to him.

The enterprise.com Web site is a worthy model for its simple, straightforward, and speedy interactions with customers and prospective employees. Furthermore, Enterprise is one of only a handful of companies that manage their own satellite networks, an enormous advantage when it comes to keeping track of its hundreds of thousands of vehicles, linking thousands of locations, and connecting electronically with its business partners.

Enterprising Employees

At Enterprise, leaders look to hire people who can grow into general managers, people who within just a few years will essentially be running their own business at a branch office. This career track is appropriately compared to a real-world M.B.A. Everyone starts at the bottom, but no one is treated as a mere underling. All branch employees are accorded dignity and respect; they are expected to dress professionally, and they are paid as professionals. Starting pay is far above industry norms, from $25,000 to $35,000 depending on the location, but the expectations are also far above average. Like professionals, trainees are expected to grow and to produce results for their team. If they do, they can anticipate exciting futures because Enterprise is growing and promotes from within.

Everybody learns through personal experience exactly what it takes to succeed: serving customers well, being good team members, and contributing to the branch's bottom line. Within eighteen months management trainees can be promoted to assistant branch managers, sharing in branch profits. Continued success will give employees the opportunity to run their own branches, which can quickly bring their annual compensation to more than $50,000. In fact, compensation for highly successful employees will grow more than 20 percent per year and can top $200,000 within ten years of their college graduation.

Taylor never limits the number of executives who earn these substantial paychecks. On the contrary, he revels in their success and regularly monitors a report that shows how many achieve the top tier of compensation. Since he gauges his own accomplishment by the success of his partners, Taylor is gratified that his count is higher than at firms with revenues several times those of Enterprise. Leaders of those other firms quite likely feel compelled to minimize the number of highly paid executives; they consider such overcompensation unnecessary, even wasteful or unfair, for a nonheadquarters job. Taylor, on the other hand, wants his talent to stay out in the field, where it can create the most value for customers and frontline employees.

Another reason Taylor and his leadership team want to see their employees earn outstanding paychecks is that Enterprise's system of partnership-based compensation aligns their interests financially. Every officer in the company, from the newest assistant branch manager to Andy Taylor himself, receives a base salary of no more than $35,000 and a share of profits from all the branches in his or her "lane," or region. So everyone wins when a manager figures out how to expand local branch profits. Even though this policy has led to some extraordinary levels of compensation, Taylor strongly believes that he should never change the deal and constrain the upside of his most successful people. It wouldn't be smart, because he would lose the commitment of his star performers and compromise his ability to attract exceptional talent into the firm. Moreover, it wouldn't be fair. The executives at Enterprise are committed to fairness and to being faithful to their customers, to their employees, and, above all, to the principles on which the company was founded as they continue their remarkable journey up the high road.

THE VANGUARD STORY

At this point you may be convinced that loyalty principles can transform an industry such as car rental, which can easily be broken into small, entrepreneurial units. But can these same principles and practices have impact in a big, centralized bureaucracy?

Consider The Vanguard Group, the mutual fund operation with 8,000 of its 11,000 employees located at its headquarters outside Philadelphia. Vanguard is organized as a mutual, perhaps the least entrepreneurial form of ownership conceivable, with no stock option incentives for executives, no equity currency for acquisitions, and no investor/owners to hold management's feet to the fire. Yet, by focusing on building mutually beneficial, loyal relationships, Vanguard is doing to its industry precisely what Enterprise has done to car rentals. With over $550 billion in assets and annual growth of nearly 30 percent, Vanguard has sailed past some stiff competition, including Merrill Lynch. Founded in 1975, fifty years after the first mutual funds were created, the firm has proceeded to lap the field. In the process, Vanguard consistently delivers superior service to customers, awards above-market compensation to crew members, and operates at costs about 75 percent lower than competitor levels.

What strange wind has filled Vanguard's sails, and by what mysterious star does its captain navigate? Founder John Bogle maintains that the answer is simple: Vanguard has consistently put the interests of customers first, kept costs low, and stayed the course.

Discovering That Special Course

From the outset John Bogle has been advising Vanguard customers to "stay the course," and he is a man who practices what he preaches. But even he floundered a while before discovering the course worth staying. Several guiding principles, such as the commitment to putting customer interests ahead of his own, were already clear when Bogle first spun Vanguard out of the backroom operations of Wellington Management. The company, however, was barely staying afloat as customers bailed out by redeeming more shares than they were buying for eighty straight months. But Bogle remained undaunted.

He hoped Vanguard's turnaround would begin in 1976, when he introduced the company's new flagship product, its 500 Index Fund. The superiority of index-fund investing was one of Bogle's core beliefs that dated back to his college thesis at Princeton. He believed that the lower management fees of index funds would lead to higher returns over the long run, because they encourage managers simply to hold representative stocks in order to match market performance rather than trading more actively—and expensively—in an attempt to beat the average. Although Bogle's wisdom was corroborated in later years, this first index offering flopped, garnering just $12 million from its $150 million underwriting target, and for two years underperforming the market.

Results were so underwhelming that Bogle veered off on a radical tack. He deep-sixed his sales force and shifted to a strictly no-load format. Then, instead of launching an aggressive advertising campaign to replace his sales force, he throttled advertising to a bare minimum and implemented a series of strategies that also seemed inimical to growth. He refused to allow telephone transfers for index funds, and for some funds he added redemption fees—unpopular policies, especially with active traders. He even rejected the standard practice of subsidizing new account sales at the expense of existing customers, concluding that such a practice was disloyal.

Miraculously, his counterintuitive strategies began to power the firm's growth. Today, Vanguard's advertising budget represents only a fraction of the industry norm, yet the firm continues to outgrow the competition. What kept Bogle committed to his unorthodox plan throughout the discouraging early years? How could he hope for success with paltry advertising, no sales force, and marketing policies that discourage active traders, the industry's most profitable customer segment? Bogle explains it this way: "Faith. I believed then as I do now that our philosophy of providing superior value to our customers—by providing index funds with costs as low as humanly possible—is the right course."[4]

Low Costs through Employee Loyalty

Bogle kept the faith, and the results have been astonishing. With the fervor of an Old Testament prophet, he preached the gospel of minimizing costs and maximizing customer value, and the firm responded by squeezing expenses to a level that others in the industry considered impossible. Today, Vanguard's costs run less than 30 basis points (0.3 percent of assets), in contrast to a mutual fund average of 120 basis points!

You might expect Vanguard to be paying paltry wages to maintain such a dramatic cost advantage. In fact, employees did agitate for better compensation. They were proud to be part of the most ethical organization in the industry. They were proud that their hard work had more than doubled productivity between 1985 and 1995, when Vanguard managed to reduce the number of employees per $1 billion in assets from fifty-five to twenty-two. But they felt they deserved greater reward for their commitment.

Bogle listened—even when the truth was hard to hear—and he learned. Part of his deep appreciation for the value of employee loyalty is the understanding that loyalty must be a two-way street. In 1993, he turned to his assistant, Jack Brennan, for a fair solution. Brennan responded with the Partnership Plan, a compensation program that aligns the interests of employees with those of customers, who, of course, want maximum returns from their mutual fund investments. Brennan's plan measures Vanguard fund returns against competitor returns. When Vanguard delivers superior results to its customers, the employees share in the surplus. Brennan describes the plan:

> Of course, the way the Partnership Plan works, employees don't start
> on their first day at above-market compensation. Partnership must be

earned through performance and loyalty. Participation grows for new employees as their salary and tenure grow. After seven years, increases are based solely on salary, which in turn is based on performance and promotions. For most employees, the bonus is capped at 30 percent. Since we have been outperforming competitors by such a wide margin, the plan payout has increased every year since its inception.[5]

Despite the success of the Partnership Plan, employees know that generous paychecks are only one reason to work at Vanguard. Gus Sauter, a thirteen-year Vanguard veteran and managing director in charge of index funds, had five different employers before joining Vanguard. He appreciates the differences:

> For me, the nonmonetary compensation at Vanguard is enormously important. We really do put customer interests first, and we try to do the right thing for our people. I love the small-company feel of Vanguard, and I have friends at all levels of the company. Also, I've been given an enormous amount of responsibility. Maybe our paychecks are not what we could earn on Wall Street—but here, you can believe in what you are doing. Vanguard wants us to do the right thing, even if it means turning away millions in revenues from the wrong kind of investor. John Bogle wants us to take the high road, and he has set a wonderful example. He told me not to accept any investments that are not in our customers' best interests—even from his brother![6]

The Changing of the Guard

When Bogle required heart transplant surgery in 1997, he selected Jack Brennan to succeed him as CEO. Asked how the company would change with Brennan at the helm, Bogle responded: "Oh, I don't think it will change at all. We've left a tremendously strong value system."[7] This value system is virtually synonymous with the six principles of loyalty detailed in this book.

Although the loyalty principles at Vanguard have not changed in more than twenty-five years, its stable foundation has enabled change of seismic proportion in just about everything else. For example, in 1975, Vanguard funds were distributed by brokers who charged load; by 2000, all funds were no-load and purchased directly. In 1975, no money was managed in-house; by 2000, hundreds of billions were managed internally. In 1979, Vanguard had only one outside manager; some twenty years later, there were dozens of outside investment managers. In 1980, Vanguard was essentially a retail firm; by 2000, one-third of its assets were institutional. In 1996, the company did no business overseas; by 2000, its markets included the Pacific Rim, Europe, and the Internet. As recently as 1995, Vanguard offered no advice or guidance to customers; within five years, there was a thriving financial planning and advisory service available on an award-winning Web site.

Because of the chaotic pace of change, Brennan felt compelled to reassert the firm's immutable values in a handbook for Vanguard's leadership: "In the future, nothing about Vanguard's values will change, but everything about the way we do business must change."[8] CEO fixation on customer loyalty has *not* changed with the transition from Bogle to Brennan, however. Brennan has continued Bogle's tradition of scrutinizing customer defections to gauge the success of Vanguard's mission. He believes that Vanguard's low redemption rate of 10 percent, about half the industry average, has been a vital force behind his firm's superior growth and its remarkable cost efficiency.

Worthy of Trust

Why has Vanguard customer loyalty continued to build despite the shifts toward online trading and mutual fund marketplaces, trends that are roiling the industry? Of course it hasn't hurt that Bogle's faith in the superiority of index investing has been borne out by experience: Vanguard's 500 Index Fund outperformed the vast majority of actively managed funds throughout the 1990s. But there is more. Click on to Vanguard's Web site, and you will begin to understand. Despite pouring more than $100 million into the site's development, Vanguard does not greet your online visit with sales hype for its products. Rather, the site is designed to inform and educate customers, even if that means leading them away from a purchase. For example, you will see messages advising caution before investing in any fund that is approaching its dividend distribution date, so that investors won't be hit with an unanticipated tax liability. Or you may see certain funds flagged because their recent performance has been particularly strong. The descriptions of such highfliers usually bear a note of caution from CEO Jack Brennan, warning that recent returns may not be sustainable in the future. That's quite a contrast to most fund companies, which lure investors by aggressively promoting the returns of hot funds.

Vanguard understands that building trust leads to more enduring relationships—and more profits—whereas a quick sale may simply leave a customer feeling cheated. Brennan explains the underlying rationale:

> Trust is our number one asset at Vanguard. We recognize you can't buy trust with advertising or salesmanship; you have to earn it—by always acting in the best interests of customers. We didn't design our Web site to sell more products and services. We designed it to educate our customers and provide better and more timely information and advice so that they can make better decisions. As customers learn to trust us, they generate a surprising amount of growth.[9]

In other words, Brennan is continuing in the tradition established by John Bogle when he created Vanguard in 1974. Bogle founded the company on a set of principles that would make it special, different from every other mutual fund. He called Vanguard his "noble experiment," an experiment to test the principle of focusing on the best interests of the customer rather than those of the company or its executives. In other words, as *Forbes* concludes in a 1999 cover story on the firm, "Vanguard is in the business of selling virtue."[10]

THE HARLEY-DAVIDSON STORY

Virtue is probably not the first thought that comes to mind when you picture a squadron of tattooed, leather-clad bikers cruising on their Harleys—but to the leaders of the Harley-Davidson Motor Company, these bikers embody principles of the highest order. The firm's annual report trumpets that it has "the world's most loyal customers."[11] And who can argue? How many firms inspire customers to tattoo their bodies with the company logo? Were it not for the company's faithful customers, Harley-Davidson, the time-honored U.S. firm, would never have survived the onslaught of Japanese competition in the 1980s, when it was almost buried in the same scrap heap as the other 140 U.S. companies involved in the manufacture of motorcycles.

Instead, Harley's performance has made it one of the hottest growth stocks on the New York Stock Exchange. *Fortune* examined the performance of the top 1,000 public companies between 1987 and 1996 and discovered that only 17 had multiplied total shareholder return by 35 percent or more per year.[12] Harley ranked ninth on that list, bracketed by companies such as Intel, Microsoft, Micron Technologies, and Home Depot. What is the secret formula for such remarkable returns to shareholders? *Forbes* offers one insight: "It's that loyalty, that intangible asset, that has convinced investors that Harley is a real growth stock."[13]

Out of the Dust

In 1981, the company was certainly not considered a growth stock, and loyalty was becoming a scarce commodity. Customer defections, coupled with the aggressive sales strategies of foreign competitors during the years from 1969 to 1981, when Harley was owned by entertainment conglomerate AMF, made Harley's leading market share in U.S. motorcycles plummet. When AMF finally put the firm up for sale, it looked like the end of the road for Harley until it was rescued by its management team in a last-minute leveraged buyout. Rich Teerlink joined the firm two months after the buyout as the chief financial officer. His primary role during the first four years on the job was to help stave off bankruptcy, which, in December 1985, loomed only a few hours away.

In those days, any pool of oil on the road would prompt the quip that someone must have parked a Harley there. In fact, the company's reputation for poor quality and poor reliability, combined with an economic recession and the onslaught of Japanese competition, gave management few degrees of freedom as it struggled to resuscitate the once-proud company. Teerlink, whose down-to-earth style belies his financial sophistication and University of Chicago M.B.A., eventually rose to become CEO from 1989 to 1997. Although he stepped down as chairman in 1998, he remains on the board. He describes the situation during the turnaround:

> If it were not for a core of unbelievably loyal customers who stuck with us through the tough times, Harley-Davidson would not exist today as an independent company. Somehow, they kept the faith and gave us the chance to repair and rebuild our relationships with the rest of our stakeholders, including our unions, salaried employees, suppliers, dealers, and investors.[14]

Learning from the HOGs

Teerlink prized loyal customers and wanted to be sure his organization would never take them for granted. Searching for ways to keep leaders hardwired into customer concerns, Harley-Davidson's leadership team came up with a program called the Harley Owners Groups, or HOGs. Harley headquarters helped its dealers organize associations of riders as well as rallies, tours, and parties that continually fueled their shared passion for riding. Teerlink and the rest of the leadership team regularly attended HOG meetings and listened to complaints as well as to praise. While they were frying bacon for the bikers and polishing fenders, they watched HOGs customize their bikes and found inspiration for new models. Harley management's steady dedication to the development of the HOG program has paid off. Teerlink firmly believes that HOG stands out as one of Harley's most successful loyalty-building efforts. This pathbreaking program has continued to be as active after his retirement as before.

Teerlink talked to customers about the firm's philosophy and the importance of mutually beneficial relationships among all the firm's stakeholders. This message is obviously attractive to customers and dealers—even suppliers and unions—but it is precisely the kind of talk most loathed by investors. The typical investor would prefer to hear a CEO chant, "The reason our firm exists is to maximize shareholder value."

And yet, few investors are complaining about Harley. Teerlink and the management team utilized their partnership philosophy to fuel one of the most storied turnarounds in corporate history. After surviving the bankruptcy scare in 1985, the firm returned to public ownership in 1986. The rest of the Cinderella story is public record: Market share rebounded to over 55 percent of the large bike market. Despite an initial 40 percent layoff in 1982, Harley's leadership team won the loyalty of workers and broke new ground in effective union relations. Additionally, the firm's success in transforming its unreliable, oil-leaking clunkers into a state-of-the-art product line made it a poster child for the U.S. quality movement. Of course this transformation was mutually beneficial for investors, since an initial investment of $100 in Harley stock in 1986 would have grown to more than $16,000 by the year 2000, representing an annual return of over 40 percent.

The formula that Teerlink and his colleagues followed to produce this remarkable turnaround builds superior, loyal relationships, and it is the same formula the firm uses today. They recognize that the firm's competitive advantage is based on these special relationships:

> Building and maintaining the relationships that make the Harley-Davidson experience unique and our business successful is a big part of what we are all about. Pure and simple, these relationships are a competitive advantage for Harley-Davidson. . . . No matter where you look, we have developed long-lasting relationships that produce positive results for everyone touched by Harley-Davidson.[15]

The principles underpinning these relationships have not changed since they were first articulated in the early 1980s. Veteran employees throughout the organization can recite them by memory, and they are handed out to newcomers on laminated plastic cards. The credo is short and direct:

- Tell the truth.
- Be fair.
- Keep your promises.
- Respect the individual.
- Encourage intellectual curiosity.

Picture the irony here. Many employees, including most of the executive team, own and ride Harley motorcycles; if you walk through a factory, you'll see a crew that could double as extras for Brando's classic *The Wild One*. As the staff editor at *Training* magazine observed, "Here's a bunch of hard-core bikers producing the most infamous icon of go-to-hell individualism in America, and it turns out they're all worked up about relationships?"[16] As you will see in later chapters, Harley's success is fundamentally a story about the power of leaders who inspire almost fanatical loyalty by helping people build successful relationships.

THE DELL COMPUTER STORY

Can the loyalty principles that apply in traditional businesses like motorcycles and mutual funds also work in the warp-speed world of computers?

Michael Dell's success in transforming the personal computer business proves that they can.

Rising from a college dorm room operation in 1983 to the second largest manufacturer and marketer of computers in the world in 2000, Dell Computer Corporation is one of the most noteworthy success stories of the 1990s. With current growth at more than five times the industry average, Dell is already the number one e-commerce company in the world. Its Web site sold more than $30 million per day in 1999 (compared with $3.5 million at Amazon.com) and expects to earn more than half of its revenues over the Internet in the early 2000s.

Most people know that Dell pioneered direct distribution in the PC business and offered superior prices by cutting out the middleman. By rapidly adapting to a Web environment, the company reduced its sales, general, and administrative costs from 15 percent of revenues in 1994 to 9 percent in 1999. But few people recognize that Dell is about much more than low costs. Michael Dell knew that building a business solely on low costs does not create a sustainable advantage. As he explains in *Direct from Dell*, "What was really important was sustaining the loyalty among our customers and employees."[17] Many strategists claim that a business should focus on being either low cost or high service, but leaders such as Michael Dell, Andy Taylor, and John Bogle have demonstrated that by taking the high road—by focusing on partnership and loyalty—they can deliver both superior service and remarkably low costs.

Choosing Customers Dell-iberately

Early in Dell's formative years, there was very little loyalty in the PC industry. Average customer repurchase rates were only about 20 percent. With 80 percent of customers freely switching brands, PC margins rapidly approached the kind of returns typical of undifferentiated commodities— with many companies being acquired or exiting the business. Michael Dell broke away from the pack by recognizing that the best opportunity to transform this commodity business into one based on principled relationships and loyalty was in sales to corporations. He focused his company's resources and efforts accordingly. Dell designed a product line and services ideally suited to corporate clients. And Dell, indeed, has become the provider of choice in this segment.

Several other major decisions have contributed to Dell Computer's unique status in the industry. The company decided to serve some individual consumers, but only experienced users whose product and service needs are most similar to those of Dell's core corporate customer. The enormous market for beginners—who have a voracious appetite for product support and education—was left to companies such as Compaq, Gateway, and Packard-Bell. Also, rather than risk compromising the value offered to its target customers, Dell focused even more intently on its core strengths by exiting the retail channel entirely. Conventional logic held that if a company were going to build sufficient market power to become a long-term winner in PCs, it would have to gobble up the prodigious market share controlled by the retail superstores. News stories at the time hammered Dell for the decision to jettison its retail business, claiming that it would severely limit the company's growth.

But rather than slowing growth, the firm's decision to simplify its focus actually accelerated growth. Michael Dell explains:

> The real value was that it forced all of our people to focus 100 percent
> on the direct model. That single-mindedness was a powerful unifying
> force.... We had to identify those opportunities that made the most of
> our strengths and go after only the best ones ... [so that we could] hold
> ourselves accountable to our customers, employees and shareholders.[18]

A further unifying force is the firm's clear, simple, and unwavering commitment to work in the customer's best interest, even at the expense of short-term revenue opportunities. For example, Dell never sells its mailing lists or customer information, viewing this as a violation of the customer's privacy.

Another key element of Dell's loyalty model is intensive two-way communication with customers, says Michael Dell: "The best way we've found to stay in tune with our customers and keep them happy is to engage in a cooperative, mutually beneficial dialogue."[19] This discussion includes face-to-face meetings, online surveys, and online focus groups. Dell himself continues to spend substantial time on the Web interacting with customers, sometimes as an anonymous Dell employee so that he can get the unvarnished truth about how customers feel about his company and the service it provides.

Communication also plays an important role in the successful relationships Dell Computer has forged with its vendors. Early on, the company made an important strategic decision to avoid manufacturing at Dell anything that could be made better and cheaper by another company. This policy not only reinforces the firm's ability to focus on what it does best, but also removes the cost of holding inventory. Considering the rapid price decline and obsolescence of many computer components, a large inventory places an enormous drag on most competitors' earnings. Dell describes his preference for outsourcing: "Choose what you want to excel at and find great partners for the rest. . . . Today our rule is keep it simple and have as few partners as possible."[20] Dell Computer now has fewer than forty suppliers, which provide more than 90 percent of its materials needs. Dell adds, "The lesson is simple: complexity kills. Bring suppliers into your business and provide them with all the information they need to make an informed decision."[21] Dell could never have grown as fast as it has without its superior network of vendor partnerships.

Building a Company of Owners

Of course, in a hypergrowth industry like computers during the 1990s, the most prized commodity is talented employees. Their loyalty is an absolute necessity. Michael Dell devoted an entire chapter of *Direct from Dell* to the subject of building employee loyalty. The chapter's title, "Build a Company of Owners," encapsulates his employee strategy:

> You need to engender a sense of personal investment in all your employees—which comes down to three things: responsibility, accountability, and shared success. . . . Mobilize your people around a common goal. Help them to feel part of something genuine, special and important, and you'll inspire real passion and loyalty.[22]

Dell practices what he preaches. He has organized the company into small teams, each with clear P&L (profit and loss) responsibility for one customer, product, or geographical segment. As an organizational unit grows too large, he can subdivide it appropriately since a core part of his organizational philosophy is to "stay allergic to hierarchy." Every team is held accountable for its financial and customer service results, and every employee is rewarded with stock options in the firm. This organizational simplicity and consistency has helped build one of the greatest business successes in the United States. There are so many millionaires among Dell employees that they have their own name, Dellionaires. But it is much more than financial success that keeps outstanding people at Dell. The loyalty of employees to one another and to the company has enabled this once tiny, undercapitalized start-up to grow at an astonishing rate, eclipsing enormous rivals along the way. And it is why Michael Dell remains so confident about his firm's ability to continue its skyrocketing trajectory far into the future: "It's about people who are thoroughly invested in each other's growth. It is, in the truest sense of the word, a loyal partnership."[23]

THE INTUIT STORY

You've seen the principles of loyalty triumph in computer hardware, so what about software? Consider Intuit, the widely admired market leader in personal finance software. Scott Cook founded the company in 1983 with a simple precept as his foundation: Do right by the customer. But he found the climb up the high road was not an easy one. Despite his impressive pedigree—Harvard M.B.A., Procter & Gamble brand manager, and Bain & Company manager—and despite a business plan that promised to revolutionize how people could organize their finances, Cook was turned down by more than twenty venture capitalists who didn't see a bright future for his ideas. So he raised $500,000 from his own savings and from friends, family, and assorted credit cards in order to fund his own start-up. His goal was to make customers' lives better by creating a product so simple and intuitive that it was easier to use than a pen and checkbook for organizing their personal finances. The results of his dogged pursuit of this goal have been remarkable.

It's not hard to understand why people are so impressed with Intuit's success. Its flagship product, Quicken, has not only become the most popular financial software in the world but the best-selling retail software application of any kind. Intuit's Quickbooks and TurboTax lead their categories of accounting software for small businesses and personal tax filing software, with over 70 percent market share. Intuit remains one of the few companies that has gone head to head against Microsoft in a major product category and emerged victorious. In fact, Microsoft became so frustrated with its inability to outdistance Quicken with its own offering, Microsoft Money, that it offered to buy Intuit for $2 billion, which at the time would have been the biggest software deal in history. When the U.S. Department of Justice opposed the deal, however, the two firms decided simply to remain enemies.

This was only one trial that Cook and his leadership team have overcome—with the help of loyalty. For example, during its start-up phase, Intuit burned through all its money, and all the employees who remained had to work for months with no salary. Now, that's superior loyalty!

More recently, in the late 1990s, the firm was blindsided by the rapid shift to Web technology and had to scramble to reengineer the firm for an Internet world. This reengineering required a completely new business model since Intuit had been geared solely for retail distribution of software. On the Internet, the only sources of revenue would be from advertisers and business partners such as banks and insurers who wanted Intuit to peddle their products. Stock analysts wrote off the company as a has-been. They saw what Amazon.com had done to book retailers and foresaw an even bleaker future for retailers of software products. In August 1997, a *Fortune* magazine article entitled "Is Intuit Headed for a Meltdown?" quoted an industry analyst: "'*Quicken* is over! It's done. It's almost a nonfactor.'"[24] This pessimism sent Intuit's stock into a tailspin; it dropped to less than half its peak value, severely testing the loyalty of employees who had stock options ready to be cashed in.

But within a year, Intuit had reinvented itself and roared back to transform its Internet entry, Quicken.com, into the Web's personal finance powerhouse with over 76 million page views in April 1998. To what does Cook attribute his firm's resiliency? He credits the firm's operating values:

> *Do Right by All Our Customers.* Doing right means acting with the best interests of the other party in mind. We commit ourselves not only to meeting expectations, but exceeding them. An important word in this phrase is *all*—it includes every relationship at Intuit. We treat each other, our business partners, and our shareholders with the same care and respect with which we treat our customers. . . . We know we've succeeded in doing right when all our customers feel that they have benefited from their association with us.[25]

These immutable values on which Cook and his leadership team operate the company have allowed Intuit to bounce back from crisis and to change on a dime. These values almost went without saying when all employees worked together in the same room, but as the firm grew, it became neces-sary to codify them in writing. To ensure that everyone was involved in the process, Cook closed the company for a day, took over the San Jose con-vention center, and split the group of 500 employees into twenty-five teams to draft a statement of the firm's vision and operating values.

Cook credits the process of institutionalizing these values as a vital step that has allowed Intuit to continue along the high road. Intuit's annual reports show that the operating values have consistently played a central role in guiding the company. The following lines from Cook's introduc-tion to the 1998 report demonstrate that Intuit stands for much more than simply creating value for the shareholder:

> With our business partners, Intuit takes a team approach, helping each partner succeed and thereby helping the partnership succeed, a win-win-win approach. We actively seek solutions where Intuit wins, our partners win, and our customers win. When all three work, powerful results can happen.[26]

Cook believes that achieving superior financial results does not require making trade-offs with values. The key is having the right values, and then living by them. Intuit's track record of treating people right and its result-ing reputation for integrity are unparalleled in its industry. Employee turnover rates run at 13 percent, one-half the Silicon Valley average. The firm's dominant leadership position in its sector of the software market is also unparalleled. Has integrity taken a heavy financial toll on Cook? Hardly. His Intuit shares (including those he and his wife have contributed to a charitable trust) will push him into the loyalty billionaire club, and his enormous credibility in the new economy is evidenced by his recruit-ment to the boards of both Amazon and eBay. *Fast Company* comments, "Intuit isn't just one of the most compelling success stories in software his-tory. It's one of the classiest software companies in history."[27]

THE CISCO STORY

Among the classy success stories of building loyalty in the roller-coaster world of Silicon Valley, we can hardly ignore the saga of John Chambers. When he became CEO at San Jose–based Cisco Systems in January 1995, the company had just over $1 billion in sales and a market capitalization of $9 billion. Five years later, sales had accelerated past $20 billion, making Cisco the fastest growth company of its scale in the history of business. The company's stock priced surged to more than $80 per share, pushing Cisco's stock market capitalization to more than $500 billion.

Then orders from the technology sector, Cisco's core customer base, screeched to a halt. Quarterly sales plunged 30 percent, compared with a 66 percent annual growth rate just six months earlier. Cisco's stock price plummeted by more than 80 percent, and Chambers had no alternative but to announce plans for the first layoffs in the firm's seventeen-year history. The same business press that had anointed John Chambers CEO of the year now lambasted him for his atrocious forecasting and speculated that Cisco could never bounce back to its former greatness. In fact, many observers wondered if Chambers's loyalty-based principles made sense in the warp-speed world of the Internet, where technologies cycle from invention to obsolescence in mere months.

There are no guarantees when it comes to business success, and only time will tell how well Cisco will rebound. But Chambers has given the firm a big edge for a resilient recovery. He has led the firm according to a set of principles including trust, customer focus, frugality, and open, honest communication. He has made Cisco a role model for utilizing the Internet to reduce costs and simplify business processes. He has not only preached these principles, but he has practiced them with integrity.

Of course, Cisco will suffer defections as it endures the difficulties ahead, but they should be few relative to those of the competition, which has also been walloped by the decline in technology purchases. Obviously, there is no magic shield to insulate companies from the effects of such large declines. However, it is precisely in the most difficult times that loyalty will yield its greatest value. Because Chambers built the company as a network of partnerships based on principles worthy of loyalty, Cisco should enjoy the advantages of customers, employees, and partners who remain committed to getting things back on track.

A Web of Partners

Current economic conditions aside, it's important to examine just how Cisco reached its predominant position in the industry. Without Cisco, the Web as we know it would not exist, since at least 75 percent of Internet communications now travel over Cisco equipment such as its routers and switches. Cisco has been called the quintessential Internet company with good reason. Fully 90 percent of its internal communications now take place online, and its customers place more than 85 percent of their orders over the Web. The firm has so thoroughly Web-integrated its operations with those of suppliers that Cisco does not even stock finished products. By creating an electronic supply chain with thirty-two manufacturing plants worldwide (thirty of which are owned by suppliers), the company can begin manufacturing build-to-order products within fifteen minutes of receipt of an order. But building effective relationships with suppliers is only part of the story. Cisco sells more than half of its products through dealers or resellers who are also thoroughly integrated into the company's online communications system. Cisco's Internet-based business model demonstrates how heavily such a strategy relies on building effective partnerships throughout its network of customers, suppliers, and dealers. And it illustrates how well the Web can work to enable such a community to function.

Cisco has also put enormous priority on building a network of long-term relationships with its employees. Headquartered in the middle of Silicon Valley, where employee turnover ran 25 to 30 percent per year throughout the 1990s, Cisco maintained voluntary turnover rates consistently lower than 10 percent. An important part of its strategy has been growth via dozens of acquisitions, and voluntary turnover in those acquired companies was only 6 percent per year, versus the norm of 20 to 40 percent in the first two years after acquisition. Asked how he measures the success of corporate acquisitions, Chambers replies, "Real simple. Retention of people and [customer] revenue that you generate two or three years later."[28]

Chambers not only demands monthly attrition reports for his own employees but for those of acquired companies as well. In most deals, Cisco insists that there will be no layoffs without the assent of both Chambers and the CEO of the acquired company. And it's hard to argue with the logic of his intense concern for loyalty. Chambers calculates that the price per acquired employee ranges from $500,000 to $3 million. No wonder he treats his people as precious assets and appreciates the value of loyalty. And no wonder he is so deeply disappointed that the firm was forced to resort to layoffs to cope with collapsing product demand. There is little doubt in anyone's mind that Cisco had no alternative, and will do its best to treat people fairly.

Communicating Culture

That brings us to the role that Chambers considers most central to his leadership responsibilities as CEO. He sees his primary job as building the right culture—one that enables partners to build mutually beneficial relationships by focusing on delivering customer value. Admittedly, the company's rapid expansion into fast-evolving markets prevents Chambers and his senior executive team from participating in most of the daily decisions. But what they can do is create a culture by preaching the values and principles that must guide decisions across the firm and throughout its network of partners. In fact, Chambers found a simple but creative way of reinforcing Cisco's values: embossing them on plastic cards attached to every employee's ID badge. All nine values on the cards—Quality Team, No Technology Religion, Stretch Goals, Teamwork, Open Communication, Trust, Frugality, Empowerment, and Drive Change—support the overarching objective of putting customer interests first.

During the summer of the year 2000, Chambers invited his twenty-plus top executives to his home in Carmel, California, and asked them how well the company was living up to these values and what changes should be considered for the new century. The result? Not only were the values reaffirmed, but the customer satisfaction target, which drives everyone's bonus, was raised from 4.23 to 4.30 (on a 5.0-point scale). For Chambers, the key to building and sustaining relationships has always been to clarify the values that serve as their foundation, and then to keep raising the standards of excellence. He knows that arrogance and complacency, the two most serious threats to any successful company, start at the top; the only defense is for leaders to raise the performance bar, not just for profits and revenues, but for fidelity to the firm's values. By placing principles and relationships above gigabytes and megahertz, Chambers has created the foundation for Cisco's long-term success in the most challenging of industry sectors.

THE MORAL OF THESE STORIES

So what is the moral of all these stories? What can you extrapolate from the stresses and successes of these loyalty leaders to help you along your own pathway? Clearly the high road often traverses difficult terrain, but these leaders did more than survive. They thrived by steadfastly doing the right thing. Indeed, only in the most difficult times are principles truly tested and proven for others to witness and to understand.

Early in its turnaround, Harley came face-to-face with bankruptcy and was forced to lay off 40 percent of its workforce. Vanguard struggled through years of customer outflows at the start. Enterprise ran up against the auto industry Goliaths that acquired the other rental companies and ran them for inventory management instead of for profits. In 1992 and 1993, Dell stumbled badly, saw earnings deteriorate, and had to survive a cash crisis before finally managing to get back on track. Intuit was written off as dead two or three times over its seventeen-year history. Cisco has made perhaps the costliest stumble of all time, losing $400 million in market value. But John Chambers's previous experiences during disastrous reversals at IBM and Wang taught him the importance of never slipping off the high road. Even in the most trying times, these loyalty leaders have neither grasped at industry fads or management fashions nor looked for quick fixes to boost their earnings. Instead, they have had the courage to ask themselves how they could do a better job in living up to their principles, how they could become more worthy partners. As a result, by building relationships worthy of trust and commitment, they have fundamentally transformed the economics of their industries—and the lives of the people their businesses have touched.

The moral of these stories is that loyalty leaders don't ask for loyalty *from* their partners; they don't even make it an objective. Their objective is to be loyal *to* partners by remaining true to core principles and always working in their partners' best interests. By being loyal, leaders will earn the loyalty of those around them. And earning partner loyalty becomes the measure of their leadership.

To follow in the footsteps of these loyalty leaders, you, too, must use partner loyalty as the measure of your success. You must have the courage to take the Loyalty Acid Test—regularly—to learn how many of your partners believe you deserve their trust and loyalty. As you read through the following chapters, you will gain a more detailed understanding of the principles of loyalty that have guided our model leaders. Then, as you listen carefully to partner feedback, you will discover the inconsistencies between your practices and the principles. By constantly striving to close the gap between principles and practices, you will find yourself on the high road. This is the only path to becoming a loyalty leader.

3

Play to Win/Win

■

*Profiting at Your Partners' Expense
Is a Shortcut to a Dead End*

On the high road, it is not enough that your competitors lose; your partners must win. So focus exclusively on business opportunities where you can be the best, and align partners around the overarching objective of upgrading the customer experience. Only an unrelenting focus on customer value can sustain the economic and the ethical superiority of high-road strategies and create the conditions for trust, commitment, and mutual success.

Fire up your Web search engine, input the keyword *loyalty*, and you will discover that the notion of loyalty has been hijacked and tortured by opportunistic marketeers. Your search will reveal more than 100,000 loyalty-related pages overwhelmingly dominated by loyalty cards, loyalty marketing, loyalty programs, and my personal favorite, loyalty schemes. It seems that loyalty has been reduced to a potpourri of marketing gimmicks designed to manipulate customer behavior with cheap bribes. Some airlines, for example, apparently think that frequent-flier miles can win customer loyalty in spite of canceled flights, overcrowded planes, lost baggage, and surly flight attendants. Credit card and telephone companies, grocery chains, publishers, and Internet service providers are experimenting with similar shortcuts to loyalty. If they think a frequent-flier mile can engender real commitment—commitment that will outlast the inevitable barrage of enticements from competitors—they have a lot to learn about the basics of loyalty.

That is not to say that a well-structured rewards program for valued customers lacks great potential, especially in the e-commerce world, where tracking consumer purchase patterns and rewarding optimal behavior is extremely efficient and effective. Web-based marketing techniques can provide excellent tools for tracking and learning from customer behavior patterns. But even the most effective loyalty marketing incentive cannot compensate for mediocre service or value, nor can it redress a relationship based on flawed principles. Even the best marketing scheme provides no better basis for customer loyalty than do golden handcuffs or long-term contracts for the genuine loyalty of employees or suppliers. Unless a company gets the fundamentals right, founding its relationships on a set of principles and practices worthy of trust and commitment, these so-called loyalty programs simply confuse customers and partners and trivialize the true nature and importance of loyalty and the loyalty effect.

Loyalty is not about bribery and hostage taking. It's not about jackpot schemes or frequent-flier miles. It is about earning people's enthusiastic commitment to a relationship that will improve their lives over the long term. When partners trust that you have the capability and commitment to help build their success, they will commit to doing the same for you, and profits will soar. But they must see more than good intentions; they must see a rational strategy for creating superior economics. For instance, the customers and employees of Enterprise Rent-A-Car remain committed based on real value. As kindhearted as he is, Andy Taylor could not be trusted to pay his partners so generously without the significant cost advantage afforded by Enterprise's focused and disciplined strategy. Similarly, being a customer, an employee, or a supplier of Michael Dell has become increasingly rewarding because his firm has attained a structural cost advantage of 5 to 10 percent over his competitors. And despite Jack Brennan's high-minded aspirations, Vanguard needs its ninety-basis-point cost advantage over the average mutual fund to remain such a paragon of loyalty.

In fact, every loyalty leader described in this book has built structural economic advantages through focused competitive strategies grounded in a thorough understanding of industry economics and customer segmentation and competitor capabilities. These leaders have extended their advantage by ensuring that all partners understand the strategy and their role in making it succeed. When partners are convinced that the strategy can create superior value for the ultimate customer, and they trust that leaders will follow high-road principles and will work hard to ensure that each partner succeeds and is rewarded fairly, then they can concentrate their full energies on the most essential goal—delivering customer value.

HIGH-ROAD STRATEGIES
MORE THAN PROFITS, NEVER LESS

The unrelenting focus on customer value provides both the economic and the ethical superiority of high-road strategies. If partners are enthusiastic about working hard to grow profits for themselves, then they are all the more inspired when those profits are earned through meaningful service and value to customers. Some managers, forgetting this key component of job satisfaction and self-fulfillment, presume that structuring mutually beneficial relationships among partners is sufficient. But being mutually beneficial doesn't necessarily make a business relationship worthy of loyalty. Lots of business relationships are characterized by a "you scratch my back and I'll scratch yours" philosophy, as are pork-barrel politics, bribery, price-fixing, and kickback schemes. These relationships may fatten wallets or yield temporary strategic advantages, but they cannot meaningfully enrich the lives of those involved, and they rarely inspire the zealous commitment to shared success common among the constituents of loyalty leaders. On the contrary, by violating common standards of decency and ethical behavior, they demean everyone involved.

The high road is about more than profits for you and your partners. It is about building a win/win strategy in which the entire chain of relationships with employees, dealers, vendors, and investors creates superior value for the ultimate consumer. Only the continuous creation of customer value superior to that of any competitive alternative can sufficiently fund the aspirations of a worthy organization and its network of partners.

Never Stop Climbing

Few companies have logged as many miles on the high road as has State Farm Insurance. North America's leader in personal property and casualty insurance has been committed to building trustworthy, enduring relationships with its customers and agents since 1922. With consistently outstanding customer and agent retention statistics, market share nearly twice that of the next largest competitor, and retained surplus in excess of $45 billion, the company's credentials are superb. Despite these credentials, it is not always easy to maintain the high road, laments Ed Rust, Jr., State Farm's CEO: "We do always try to take the high road, but sometimes it gets pretty cloudy up there and it's hard to know which path really is the right one."[1] As Rust and his management team well know, sustaining mutually beneficial relationships through win/win strategies is never easy. Each shift in marketplace needs, competitor capabilities, or technology brings tough trade-offs and difficult choices.

One case in point is State Farm's 1996 decision to revise its contract with its agents, the first such change in more than thirty years. Faced with the inevitability of competition from new Web-based direct marketers of insurance, State Farm's leadership knew that the company needed both to reduce costs and to improve service quality by strengthening its agents' customer relationships and by augmenting its local agent offices with twenty-four-hour phone centers and Internet capabilities. Because of inflating insurance prices—driven largely by escalating repair costs, legal expenses, and technology investments—the existing commission structure was rewarding agents too richly for providing merely adequate service. So the company's leaders structured a new contract to ensure that only those agents who delivered outstanding levels of quality and service to their customers could continue to prosper. No company more highly values the partnership it has built with its agency force than State Farm. Nevertheless, the leadership felt compelled to introduce the new contract because the only way to remain on the high road, and the only way to maintain outstanding opportunities for all partners, was to ensure that value to customers constantly improves.

Some agents did indeed feel betrayed by this change. They felt entitled to their generous compensation, arguing that since the company's profits appeared healthy, there was no need to change. But State Farm's leadership team knew that company profits were not excessive. Moreover, the team understood that no partner is entitled to prosper unless he or she contributes to ever better levels of value for customers. A leader must never let partners forget this basic fact, because no partner—agent, supplier, employee, or investor—is entitled to win individually if the entire network cannot deliver superior results for the customer.

Too often, programs aimed to increase employee loyalty focus almost exclusively on improved benefit plans or work-family balance. Although these programs can represent wise investments, they must be funded by the creation of value for customers. The single most important thing a leader can do to build loyalty is to help employees create the kind of customer value that will inspire pride in their work, and create the basis for sustained economic success.

It would have been very easy for State Farm's leadership team to duck its responsibility and leave the contract revision for the next generation of leaders. State Farm was already widely admired as the best in its business. As a mutual organization, it had no shareholders to demand higher profits. Rust and his colleagues could have coasted along with apparently satisfactory performance for many years because of the strength of their brand and their capital surplus. Why then did these leaders choose to confront the agent contract problem and face the aggravation of countless road trips and late-night sessions to explain the need for change to groups of resistant agents? Why did they decide to take on the inevitable battles, risks, and headaches?

The reason is that they had the courage to face reality and to act decisively in accord with their convictions. They knew that the Internet would change the economics of the business and the levels of service demanded by customers. What's more, it was their responsibility to help all their partners aspire to the highest standards of performance, levels that would maintain superior customer value and keep the company at the top of its industry. So the firm's leaders understood that they had to keep raising the targets for all their partners—including resistant agents—to help them avoid complacency and strive to be the best.

If you're like many other managers, you may think that you are setting sufficiently high targets to reach your stated goal of delivering "superior customer value," and you may believe that you are delivering it. But a wise manager would track actual customer retention. Typical firms lose half their customers in less than five years—and customers don't defect when they are truly receiving superior value. With the advent of the Internet, customers' shopping bots will compare real value with increasingly sophisticated algorithms, and price and service comparisons posted in real time on the Web will unmask value frauds. Word of mouse will spread the truth at lightning speed. The result will be skyrocketing defection rates for all firms but those offering truly superior value.

How can you be sure that the Internet will be your ally and not your downfall? Only by setting performance standards for your organization and its partners at sufficiently high levels can you guard against the impending customer exodus. Watch loyalty leaders as they inspire their partners to reach for the stars. They preach a simple message: Delivering anything less than the absolute best value would surely be disloyal to customers and unworthy of their reciprocal loyalty. Delivering second-best value to customers doesn't deserve a silver medal; on the contrary, it is an act of betrayal and cannot attract the highest caliber of employees, suppliers, agents, dealers, and investors, whose commitment is needed to build and sustain success.

Refuse to Be Satisfied

Jack Brennan seizes every opportunity to remind his crew members of Vanguard's fundamental operating principle, that success comes from the creation of superior value for customers: "We have a number of critical success factors—each of which is vitally important—but one of them overrides everything else. We must always be focused on providing the highest possible value to our clients at all times."[2] This message underpins his annual partnership speech, his graduation addresses, his speeches for Vanguard's orientation classes, and his one-on-one conversations. Brennan admits that his crew accuses him of being in a state of perpetual dissatisfaction about the level of value being delivered to customers, of being unrelenting in his search for ways to become even better. He believes that his job is to help institutionalize dissatisfaction. This is why he not only tracks customer retention but regularly surveys his customers about their satisfaction *and* their loyalty.

Only by helping partners reach for the stars—by targeting customer value that is even "better than the best"—can a leader ensure that the organization will stay on the high road to success. Too many leaders shrink from the demands of this goal and fail to insist that their organizations target the very best value. It is much easier, and seems less risky, to shoot for fair or reasonable value. For example, there are lots of index funds in the market today besides Vanguard's offering. But most have significantly higher expense ratios and turnover rates, which levy higher tax burdens, so these funds offer inferior value to customers. Investment professionals—many of whom maintain personal accounts at Vanguard because of its superior value—abandon the high road ethically when they fail to steer their customers to Vanguard. The problem is that Vanguard refuses to pay commissions. As a result, brokers and advisers not content with their advisory fee (the pricing that is visible to customers) steer their clients toward lower-value funds that funnel an extra 10 to 15 basis points back to the adviser. In other words, instead of acting in their customer's best interests, the advisers retreat to the practical position of acting in their own best interests and push the inferior product—which at least provides them with a living. This attitude, though, is shortsighted and intellectually dishonest.

When business is merely about making a living, it no longer inspires a network of partners to play a meaningful role in serving others. Instead, it steals their energy, convinces them that business is about profiting at the expense of others, and confirms their suspicion that loyalty is a foolish notion indeed. Only with the courage and wisdom to demand the absolute best value for customers, and to establish sufficiently high standards for employees, dealers, agents, and suppliers, can leaders climb to the high road and enrich the lives of everyone touched by their business.

Not Just the Best Motorcycles, but the Best Ownership Experience

As an aspiring loyalty leader, you must work hard on the continuous improvement of cost and quality in your organization. But even the achievement of six-sigma standards of excellence does not allow you to ease up on the throttle. To ensure that your organization continues to set the standards of excellence, you must focus on the basics of cost, quality, and timeliness *and* on discovering new levels of excellence for your customers' lifetime experience.

Harley-Davidson is decidedly a leader of the pack in creating new ways to make its customers' lives better. Admittedly, during its turnaround, Harley's leadership team simply kept the organization focused on developing better-quality bikes. But once quality had been revved up, the team expanded its search for other kinds of improvements. By observing how riders were customizing their bikes and noting which modifications were attracting the biggest crowds at rallies and in parking lots, the firm developed ways to offer these same enhancements at a lower cost than the bikers could manage on their own. Jeff Bleustein, Harley's current CEO, explains: "Our customers love to customize their bikes—it's like a grassroots folk art movement. We just try to make it easier for them."[3] Of course, Harley's goal is to earn a fair margin of profit on this work, but the result is a happier set of customers who recognize that the company is working hard for their benefit.

Along the same lines, Harley decided to rebuild engines in its Milwaukee plant rather than make customers search out local shops that couldn't offer the same efficiencies, quality, or reliability. Because the Harley factory already possesses the specialized tools and dies used to manufacture the engines, and because Harley's financial strength and technological knowledge enable the company to guarantee the rebuilt engines, its customers are better served.

Bleustein and his management team continually try to deepen and improve the experience of owning one of their products, often by making it more fun. They have created a line of clothing and accessories with the distinctive Harley styling, and they have developed Harley-Davidson cafés in New York City and Las Vegas featuring motorcycle memorabilia and distinctive Harley design features. "We want Harley riders to feel ownership in the restaurants," says Bleustein. "Of course another important benefit has been to demonstrate to the broader public that Harley riders are actually pretty nice people who are fun to be around. We expect these restaurants will provide us with some new motorcycle customers as well."[4]

Customers can now buy Harley-Davidson insurance and get financing through the company. Harley has also created a series of adventure tours—to places like the Grand Canyon, South Africa, and the Rhine Valley—that give riders a chance to extend their riding experience in memorable, exciting, and even educational ways. And in 2000, the company announced that a museum in Milwaukee would be devoted to celebrating the heritage of the Harley experience—a new Mecca for the Harley faithful.

Since Harley's core expertise is limited to building and marketing motorcycles, for most of these new activities Harley has chosen a partner that is the leader in its field. Some of these activities are real profit enhancers for the business, but the fundamental objective of the activities is not to provide revenue growth; that's only one part of the picture. These initiatives are all linked into an integrated strategy to enrich the lives of Harley customers. Bleustein summarizes the real mission of this strategy: "We want to fulfill the dreams of our customers through their motorcycle experience."[5]

Own the Customer Experience

Michael Dell is more concerned with fast computers than with fast motorcycles, but he gets just as excited as Bleustein when he talks about the importance of constantly upgrading his customers' lifetime experience. Banners reading "The Customer Experience: Own It" are posted on most bulletin boards at Dell's Round Rock, Texas, headquarters. Thousands of employees wear laminated ID cards inscribed with the Dell mission: "To be the most successful computer company in the world at delivering the best customer experience in the markets we serve."

The Internet offers most businesses a rich set of possibilities for improving the customer lifetime experience, but few firms have matched Dell's initiative. For example, Dell created Premier Pages, customized Web sites for thousands of the company's best customers and even some of its best prospects. These pages provide quick access to customer-specific information about Dell's products and services.

Twenty-four hours a day, customers can configure, price, and buy systems at the agreed-upon price. They can also check on order status, arrange delivery dates, and perform troubleshooting through Dell's virtual help desk. Many of Dell's customers use their Premier Page to keep track of their systemwide computer purchases for improved asset management. Customer help desks have direct access to Dell's pages, which speeds diagnostics and generates uniform solutions across geographically diverse locations. This complete integration into the customer's operation has enabled Dell to help customers purchase their computer needs more efficiently and has elevated Dell into the role of a valued partner whose primary goal is to help customers achieve superior results, not just a vendor pushing for more computer sales.

At Dell, employees diligently search for ways to add more value to products and to make the lives of core customers easier and more profitable. They know that even little details can make a big difference. For example, Dell will load all of a customer's required software—including proprietary applications—at the factory and configure the machine optimally so that it will run correctly right out of the box. The factory will even attach asset-control tags. This service saves time and money for the end user, who had been accustomed to waiting in line for expensive on-site technical staff support. Dell charges only a minimal fee for the service and clearly cares less about the extra revenue than about earning customer loyalty.

Michael Dell spotted this opportunity because of his mind-set not only to improve Dell's existing products and services, but also to search out new activities that could help customers put his computers to work more effectively. On customer visits, he observed the handling of his products and services all the way from the initial order to receipt by the end user. He frequently noticed piles of Dell boxes outside the customer's technical support area as expensive technicians unloaded, configured, and reloaded appropriate software. It was clear to him that Dell could provide these services far more easily and efficiently—just as it was clear to Harley executives that they could customize bikes and rebuild engines better than anyone else.

Another example of how Dell has utilized the Internet to create quantum improvements in customer experience comes at the other end of the purchase cycle. Despite the company's efforts to smooth the delivery of ready-to-use computers directly to its customers' desks, boxes of computers still accumulated outside the customers' technical assistance offices. This time the boxes weren't full of new equipment awaiting installation. They held perfectly functional, used equipment that had been replaced by the latest in state-of-the-art technology. Obviously, customers were having problems getting rid of their older generation of computers. Thus the DellAuction Web site was born. Now customers can go directly online to advertise and sell their surplus equipment to buyers who are happy to find the recycled bargains. Dell is providing truly superior customer service, its first priority, while also banking a percentage of every DellAuction sale and removing a barrier to the purchase of more computers. Dell's leadership won't stop here in the search for opportunities to utilize the Internet to improve customer experiences, and Michael Dell warns that other firms must follow suit: "The Internet is like a weapon sitting on the table ready to be picked up by either you or your competitors."[6]

Leaders at Dell have moved to institutionalize their fixation on improving the customer experience by creating an eight-person Customer Experience Council, which reports to one of the firm's vice chairmen. This group scrutinizes every detail of customer interactions with the company and its products. Dell's team includes each of the various divisions and functions that must work together to create the kind of enhanced customer service that distinguishes Dell Computer from its competition and that continually strengthens customer loyalty. The importance that Michael Dell places on this process is clear: "Make no mistake—we recognize that the fuel of our growth is a superior customer experience."[7]

INSIST ON WIN/WIN SOLUTIONS

In your quest to upgrade customer service and performance standards, remember that you won't succeed unless you have your partners' full support. Because change entails risk and uncertainty, partners will resist unless they trust you and are convinced of your commitment to their success. They must know that you will never profit at their expense and that you will work hard to find win/win options. The challenge is not only to serve the needs of the ultimate customer, but also to help each of your company's partners succeed.

Make Partners, Not Enemies

With their company's legendary commitment to maintaining mutually beneficial relationships, Harley-Davidson's leaders have been masterful in finding win/win solutions. For example, the firm has integrated the Web into its operations in a manner that has actually strengthened its relationships with dealers, in stark contrast to many other organizations that are alienating their historical channel relationships in the rush to exploit Web profit opportunities. Many consumers were interested in shopping online, and the company also knew that few local dealers could afford to stock the entire range of Harley merchandise. But the first proposal for a solution— a centralized Web site that would offer Harley's full line—was vetoed by CEO Jeff Bleustein because it would undercut the local dealers, who would inevitably lose business. Bleustein insisted that the team go back to the drawing board and collaborate with Harley's dealer council to come up with a solution that would muster mutual enthusiasm.

That solution was worth the wait. Now when customers search for Harley apparel or merchandise on the Web, they are routed to the firm's central Web page and asked to choose from a list of Harley's participating e-commerce dealers or to enter their zip code to find the nearest one. A click on the dealer name routes them to the local dealer's own Web page. Each dealer that sells online may opt to provide its own Web order and fulfillment system, but most have chosen to participate in the e-commerce program from Harley, which has contracted with several leading third-party suppliers of Web marketing and fulfillment services.

This result is a model win/win solution. Customers win because they now have Web access to a wide range of Harley's merchandise. The dealers win because they earn the retailing profits from all Web sales and establish a connection with new local customers, who may come in to buy motorcycles and services. The company wins because it has set the standard of excellence for Web site design, expanded marketing and sales via the Internet, and strengthened dealer relations. Bleustein underscores his company's commitment to mutual success:

> Every time a new technology comes along, it provides new opportunities that test our relationships. At Harley-Davidson, we are committed to building mutually beneficial relationships based on trust and respect. While it's too early to declare victory on our Internet approach, the process we used to arrive at this solution is a victory in itself. It helped us build even stronger relationships with our dealers and reinforced their confidence in our commitment to mutual success.[8]

Perhaps even more striking proof of Harley's commitment to finding win/win solutions is the company's decision to locate its new plant in Kansas City, Missouri. Although most manufacturers use the addition of new capacity as an opportunity to ditch their unions and to open plants in right-to-work states, Harley's leaders took the radical step of inviting the leaders from the firm's two major unions, the International Association of Machinists and the United Paper Workers International, to join the planning discussions. When Harley had been on the brink of bankruptcy, the unions had cooperated and accepted 40 percent layoffs. That crisis was long past, however, and Harley was now making lots of money. Although Harley's union-management relationships remained better than most, they were still adversarial, and management was not satisfied with the situation. Nonetheless, Rich Teerlink and Bleustein felt that it would not be fair to run away from the unions—and being fair is one of Harley's core values. Also, if Harley abandoned the unions, they would have undercut any opportunity to continue building better relationships in the existing plants. Almost certainly, union relationships would have deteriorated.

So Teerlink and Bleustein seized this opportunity to win/win. They formed a joint task force with the two union presidents and negotiated a process for building a partnership advantageous to each of them as well as to Harley's customers. Several Harley board members were quite skeptical, as were many of the union rank and file. The group nevertheless persevered, eventually selecting Kansas City for the new plant, and in the process agreed on a wide range of groundbreaking improvements in their relationship. For example, a new work-group structure placed the responsibility for quality and cost improvements on the factory floor. Job security was guaranteed for workers as long as the firm remained profitable. And a whole new level of cooperation was established; the plant manager and two union presidents even share an office in the new facility.

One story highlights the spirit and the practical advantages of this remarkable arrangement. The Harley plant manager and his backup team were out of town when a union employee noticed a problem with quality and took it upon himself to shut down the line. The union president, aware that the plant management team was away, assumed responsibility. Instead of sending employees home as he would have at the old plant, he took over and discovered that one of the machines needed adjustment. He called in the mechanics and had the line up and running in less than an hour. Not only were the workers, who received full paychecks, well served by this cooperative effort, but so were the dealers, customers, and shareholders, who were counting on a steady flow of bikes from the plant.

Many fundamental improvements from the Kansas City experiment have migrated back to the older plants, and Harley's leadership is delighted with the results of its loyalty strategy. Bleustein describes the results particularly in terms of employee attitudes:

> Not only has Kansas City met or exceeded all of our productivity targets, we have seen a real improvement in attitudes and cooperation at all of our plant locations. The best way to measure employee loyalty is to watch their level of openness to new ideas and their willingness to raise ideas and suggestions for improvement. By this measure, I see enormous progress across all of our plants.[9]

Enlist Your Partners' Input in the Hard Decisions

State Farm showed equal commitment to finding win/win solutions as it developed the new agent contract and worked to improve the performance of the agent distribution system. In the 1990s, many insurance companies were concluding that their agent distribution systems were becoming high-cost dinosaurs, and therefore were scrambling to set up alternative channels, including the Internet, to compete with their agents. State Farm, meanwhile, remained committed to discovering a win/win solution. Its leaders recognized that new technologies created enormous opportunities for reduced costs and superior service. But instead of undercutting their agents, the leaders invested in their growth and prosperity by integrating new technologies into the existing system. For example, customers now receive twenty-four-hour service: After-hours calls to agents' offices are automatically routed to a regional call center. Processing functions once performed by agents are increasingly centralized and automated. Plans for the Web are fully integrated with the agent's system to help agents forge even stronger relationships with their customers.

Rather than simply cooking up these new programs at headquarters, State Farm involved many agents and advisory councils in crafting the right kind of program. Openly sharing concerns about the existing contract, the threat from emerging competitors, and the need for new technologies, the managers spent thousands of hours with agents developing the best system to meet customer needs. Although the new contract was designed primarily to increase customer value, it was also designed to ensure that agents who delivered outstanding quality and value could continue to grow their incomes. Finally, instead of forcing the new contract down agents' throats, State Farm made adoption voluntary. Aware that unilateral demands don't strengthen relationships, the leaders worked hard to show the agents how the new contract could help customers, agents, and the company to win. Over half the company has already shifted to the new system. The process required enormous time and effort, but State Farm continues to enjoy the strongest and most loyal agency system in the industry.

It's no surprise that win/win strategies are also par for the course at Enterprise Rent-A-Car. Andy Taylor has fiercely resisted going into competition with the local car dealers, who are now highly valuable sources of customers. Though his firm might be well positioned, he has always rejected proposals to expand into new car sales. As the largest private purchaser of autos in the United States, Enterprise might easily beat the economics of the local dealer and significantly grow its own profits. But the company is not likely to follow this path. First, the organizational focus on its core competence, renting cars, might diminish. What is perhaps even more important, Enterprise has to balance its choices and is loath to embark on strategies that betray the interests of long-term partners. So the firm remains loyal, continues to get cars through the local dealers, and avoids strategies that would betray their dealers' interests. As a result of this loyalty, suppliers to Enterprise often willingly open their books and share their own profit goals and budgets because they trust Enterprise's leaders to work toward win/win solutions.

The loyalty benefits from win/win leadership are as compelling in the new economy as in the old. Cisco Systems is famous for aggressively out-sourcing noncore activities—a strategy dependent upon the company's reputation for building win/win relationships with vendors and resellers. Cisco strives never to undercut a reseller by serving a company direct. The company will even pay its salespeople a bigger commission when they keep a reseller in the loop. Of course, when a customer strongly prefers direct service, Cisco defers because they know there can be no win/win unless the customer is happy.

Loyalty Requires Discipline

Loyalty leadership demands that you find an avenue of joint success with all your partners. Trust among partners is built up over time, yet all it takes is a single instance of betrayal to destroy years of work building a relation-ship. If Harley dealers believed the firm had undercut them and was steal-ing their sales through a corporate Web site, the partnership would quickly have begun to unravel—just as it would have at State Farm if the firm were disloyal to its agents and started selling through other channels. Leaders who want to build loyalty and generate the loyalty effect must exercise extreme discipline to protect their partners' interests. They know that the key to winning is not to make sure their competitors lose, but to make sure their partners win.

PLAY ONLY WHERE YOU CAN WIN

Committing to win/win strategies cranks up the pressure to create truly superior economic opportunity for your organization and your partners. You cannot afford to waste time and energy with businesses and customers with which you don't have a legitimate opportunity to be the very best. If you want to win/win, you must have the discipline and focus to play only where you can win. CEOs of top loyalty companies know precisely when they have the wherewithal to win and when they don't. They don't compete for every new business that seems profitable for the moment; they invest only where they see the potential for building sustainable assets and relationships. There is no room for me-too products and services; loyalty leadership is based on the kind of structural economic advantage that results only from focusing on positions of strategic superiority, positions that enable a firm to be the best and to drive toward market leadership. Perhaps Jack Brennan of The Vanguard Group said it best in his 1999 partnership speech to employees:

> We manage our business with a disciplined strategy, believing that any company can only be great at a few things. And if we do those few things better than anyone else, and focus our success criteria on our clients only, with no other distractions, we will retain our lead in this business and even expand it over time.[10]

Resist the "Bargains"

It is far too early to know whether eBay will join the list of loyalty leaders, but the company is certainly showing many of the right signs. It passed a crucial test during the collapse in e-commerce-related stocks that followed the so-called irrational exuberance of the late 1990s. Because its stock price declined far less steeply than that of most other firms, CEO Meg Whitman could have purchased any of dozens of interesting companies at bargain-basement prices. Instead she demonstrated the discipline to remain focused on the firm's core auction-related business. When Whitman talks about the key to eBay's continued success, she first speaks of loyalty and follows quickly with the importance of focus.

Focus, Focus, Focus

When John Chambers first presented his vision of the future to the board of directors at Cisco Systems, he listed all the technology sectors in which Cisco needed to establish leadership if the firm were to create a sustainable position at the hub of the Internet. This strategy has been the guiding light for the firm. Today, Cisco's Web site lists the twenty business segments in which it competes and goes on to specify which sixteen have already achieved the number one slot and which four are poised at number two. The firm's growth strategy focuses investment only in those business arenas in which the firm can achieve leadership. Chambers appreciates the economic advantages of leadership, but he also knows that customers are generally leery of purchasing from a company new to a sector or to a technology. Many customers have been burned in the past when such suppliers backed away from a new initiative, leaving them high and dry. Chambers wants customers to know that when Cisco embarks on a new initiative, not only does the company intend to stay, it will invest for leadership.

Find Your Economic Sweet Spot

Andy Taylor also understands the risks and challenges of diversification: "One of the biggest factors in our success has been our ability to say no to opportunities that would pull us off track."[11] For decades Enterprise Rent-A-Car resisted the temptation to diversify and remained strategically focused on the home rental market. Especially when the firm was small, Enterprise didn't have the resources to fight a multifront war with Hertz and Avis. It thus focused intensively on a small sector in which leaders saw the potential to offer the best customer value—outstanding service at remarkably low prices. This pattern is consistent for high-loyalty companies. In defiance of some strategy textbooks that instruct executives to adopt either a low-cost or a high-service strategy, loyalty leaders aspire to accomplish both simultaneously in their area of specialization. Enterprise offers door-to-door service from highly motivated professional employees, while charging prices up to 20 percent below typical airport rates.

Enterprise can accomplish this remarkable feat of higher service at lower costs because its entire economic system has been streamlined to focus on the firm's target customers. By passing up airport locations and locating branch offices more conveniently for local customers, Enterprise has avoided expensive real estate charges and concession fees. Enterprise has also developed a unique reservation system that streamlines service to customers.

Fleet costs, which represent 50 percent of industry operating costs, have been lowered in a variety of ways as well. Because Enterprise is not beholden to any one auto manufacturer to move new-car volume, it can select optimal models for its customers and keep these cars on the road the appropriate length of time to maximize value to renters. Also, average rental periods in the home market are two to three times longer than airport rentals, so administrative costs are lower. Moreover, the home market offers a steadier demand compared with the airport's weekly cycle, which peaks on Wednesdays. Decentralized purchasing enables the firm to customize its fleet to local market needs; sport utility vehicles are likely to be available in rural suburbs and BMWs in upscale communities. This customized service coupled with local branch profit incentives has resulted in a fleet utilization advantage of more than 15 percent over competitors.

Such a clearly focused business strategy—a plan limited to a well-defined area of expertise and leadership—gives Enterprise an enormous economic edge to share with partners and customers. It is this real economic edge, not just some advertising hype or some short-term incentive or merely trying harder, that underpins the company's outstanding success. None of this success could have been achieved without the leadership discipline to focus only on the target activities and target customers that define the firm's economic sweet spot.

More recently, at the end of the 1990s, Enterprise began opening more locations at airports to serve its core home market customers when they travel out of town. By assiduously avoiding the short-term, bulk-commodity segment of the airport customer flow, Enterprise's airport branches have prospered. This strategic move will not only provide additional growth opportunities for Enterprise employees, it will also benefit a group of renters that has typically been underserved—the infrequent traveler. Most airport competitors gear their operations to the needs of the frequent business traveler, who prefers a high-tech, low-touch system. Hertz #1 Club customers, for example, simply look for the space number next to their name on the electronic sign at the bus stop, get in their car, where the keys are already waiting in the ignition, and drive away. Enterprise's target airport customers are looking for a different experience. They appreciate personal service, for instance, some advice on the best local restaurants or theaters. Because the average rental period is four days for the Enterprise customer, compared with one or two days for the frequent traveler, Enterprise can afford to offer superior pricing, along with its personalized service.

Tune Up Your Strategy

Look under the hood of any other high-loyalty company, and you will find a similarly well-tuned strategic engine that operates on the rational economic advantages offered by superior focus. Southwest Airlines, for example, has become the lowest-cost player in the airline business, with cost per available seat-mile of less than seven cents—more than 25 percent below the other large carriers. How? By concentrating only on discount travel and flying only one kind of aircraft. With more than 300 identically configured Boeing 737 airplanes, the firm enjoys simpler pilot training and scheduling, lower maintenance costs, smaller parts inventory, and superior purchasing economics. By avoiding advance seat assignments, Southwest has avoided computer system upgrades and can fill more seats per flight. The simpler fare structure also speeds transaction times and has enabled Southwest to shift more of its bookings onto the Internet—more than 30 percent of its revenues are attributable to online sales, more than twice the industry average. In the discount travel market, it's win/win all the way for Southwest Airlines. Customers are flying high with lower fares and fewer restrictions, and the company's profits continue to soar.

Northwestern Mutual created some of the lowest costs in its core individual life insurance business by focusing on certain customer segments, including executives and professionals; this focus results in the attractive economics yielded by higher average policy sizes. No longer dismissed as only a niche player, the firm has utilized its economic edge to become the largest issuer of individual life policies in its industry. Its strategy of narrower product line and customer targeting has not only financed its growth, but also generated sufficient cash that Northwestern Mutual, unlike so many of its cash-starved competitors, feels no pressure to convert to stock ownership.

Dell-ite Existing Customers

Dell's rise toward number one in personal computers has already been described in some detail, but the economic advantages of its strategic focus and leadership position need to be underscored. Its narrowed focus on the direct sales model has allowed the firm to streamline many business processes, including inventory management; Dell currently holds six days of supplies in inventory, a small fraction of competitor levels. This strategy not only saves cash but, of more importance in the world of rapid technological change, saves the markdown costs of obsolete inventory. Dell's special build-to-order capability can now custom-build a computer within a few days of receiving the order and ship it out the following day.

Dell's pioneering use of Internet connection with all its suppliers has enabled these partners to manage their own inventory costs more effectively, another benefit to the entire system. Dell and its suppliers don't have to guess in advance which products are going to be hot sellers; they simply respond to the flow of actual orders. Furthermore, Dell's innovative use of the Web keeps all its suppliers in direct touch and provides them with an online comparison of their performance.

Michael Dell turned a commodity PC business into a high-road loyalty firm not only by insisting that Dell Computer deliver low prices but also by insisting that the firm provide the highest standard of service in the business. Although many people think of Dell as a low-cost phone, mail, and Internet operation, in reality large corporate customers have a significant need for on-site relationship management and problem solving. To meet this need, Dell has deployed an army of sales consultants to provide this service. Its intense strategic focus has unquestionably been successful. Industry experts estimate that Dell has achieved a 5 to 10 percent sustainable cost advantage over its less-focused rivals. This edge explains how the firm can afford to offer outstanding service and still earn attractive profit margins.

Superior Value Needs Less Advertising

One more factor that should not be overlooked in Dell's superior economics is its relatively small advertising budget. The logic is obvious. Advertising, in general, is geared primarily to attracting new customers and new business, but loyalty firms are geared primarily to providing such outstanding value to existing customers that enthusiastic references and word of mouth create free advertising. When firms offer truly outstanding value, they get plenty of growth opportunity without big advertising expenses.

At most high-loyalty firms, savings in advertising alone can equal some competitors' entire profit margins. Enterprise's superior customer experience is generating industry-leading growth despite the company's smaller-than-industry-average advertising budget. The Vanguard Group has focused strategically on direct distribution of mutual funds to customers who appreciate the importance of low-cost, long-term investing in index funds. The superior service and lower costs resulting from Vanguard's focus have powered annual growth rates of nearly 30 percent, despite a Lilliputian advertising budget; for example, Vanguard's media spending is only 10 to 15 percent that of its large competitors' budgets. Demand from the large bike cruiser market grows faster than Harley-Davidson can build manufacturing capacity, although the company holds advertising below industry averages.

In every case, the leaders of these high-loyalty companies—as well as those discussed in later chapters—exercise superior discipline by strategically focusing only on business opportunities for which they can offer the very best value in the world so that both they and their partners can win. They know that real value, not superior salesmanship or brilliant advertising, is what generates winning growth and prosperity.

FOCUS ON THE RULES OF THE HIGH ROAD

One of the goals of this book is to provide you with practical advice for building loyalty in your company. Sharpening focus is a key step, especially as the Internet opens up so many new opportunities for growth. Since it is difficult to gauge whether your company is sufficiently focused, the Loyalty Acid Test Survey carefully probes this issue. Partners are asked how much they agree that the company focuses all of its resources and energy in areas where it can be the best. Successful loyalty leaders, however diverse their businesses, offer remarkably uniform advice to help you stay on course.

Get Rid of Distractions

The first step in improving focus is to rid yourself of distractions. An enormous portion of most leaders' time is spent struggling to improve business lines that cannot realistically be expected to deliver the best customer value and that have little strategic importance to the core of the company. These underperformers can nevertheless be seductive and lure you off target. There always seem to be opportunities to improve their financials, and since the stronger business lines rarely scream out for help, you may let laggards' problems monopolize your valuable calendar. As a result, you neglect the core of your business, which deserves intense focus in order to grow and continuously improve. In the face of rapid technological changes, the threat of new competitors, and changing customer needs and preferences, delivering absolutely the best value with consistency represents an awesome challenge, a challenge more than worthy of the complete attention of any leadership team.

Michael Dell, for example, emphasizes that it's at least as important for a firm to "figure out what you're not going to do as it is to know what you are going to do."[12] In 1994, Dell Computer was successfully growing sales in the retail market, primarily in stores such as Circuit City and CompUSA. These chains were expanding revenues at more than 20 percent per year, but after four years of effort, Dell's management team still could not figure out how to earn significant profits from this business. Even though retail was not a major part of the company's sales, it was a major distraction for the team—as is the case with most problem children in the corporate family of businesses. Every big decision became more complicated as the team wrestled with trying to predict how the superstore chains would react.

Finally, Dell's top managers put the retail division on notice. It would have to find a way to earn sufficient profit or exit the business. The division scurried to add potentially lucrative new accounts like Wal-Mart and Best Buy, but the bottom line didn't improve. More important, no one could devise a solid plan to differentiate Dell products and service from the competition. It had also become clear from market research that customers who purchased Dell products through retailers were less satisfied with their experience than those who purchased direct. Thus, the retail channel was diminishing the value of the brand and the firm's reputation as a truly special company. And perhaps most important, leadership recognized that to continue participating in a business in which Dell provided merely adequate value would be to leave unchecked a cancer that could eat away at employees' pride, energy, and clarity of purpose. By the end of the year, Dell decided to exit the mass market, a move that Michael Dell believes was vital to achieving the strategic focus he sought for his organization. He explains:

> We had product people working to support both the indirect and the direct channels, and doing half a job on each. We had manufacturing people wondering whether to build a plant that supplied the retail

channel, which demanded different specifications, or a plant for the direct model. We had sales representatives dealing with service and support conflicts from the customers that we had created ourselves by trying to be both direct and indirect at the same time.[13]

Beware of the Rotting Core

In your attempt to pare away distractions, remember that they don't always come from a new business line that hasn't lived up to expectations. For example, Enterprise Rent-A-Car discovered that the core business on which the company was founded forty years earlier had itself become a distraction and was no longer yielding reasonable profits. When originally founded by Jack Taylor as Executive Leasing, the company's core business was leasing automobiles to individuals. Leasing continued to represent the bulk of the company's revenues until the end of the 1970s, when daily rentals took over the lead. It wasn't until 1991, however, that the leadership team recognized that a structural change had taken place in the leasing market and that Enterprise needed to refocus.

The auto manufacturers had decided to get into the leasing business themselves during the 1980s, and Enterprise steadily lost leasing share to them. Because manufacturers chose to subsidize the cost of cars leased through their own dealers, it was difficult for Enterprise to compete; the company could no longer deliver its distinctive level of superior service while earning a decent profit. But after studying the leasing market carefully, looking for niches where it could offer special customer service and value, Enterprise discovered just such an opportunity in small, commercial fleets that ranged from 10 to 100 cars.

These small businesses have maintenance, insurance, and service needs too complex for local car dealers, yet their businesses are too small to earn the attention of large, national leasing companies. Enterprise's network of local entrepreneurs is perfectly situated to deliver the best value to this segment, so the firm's leasing business continues to prosper in this focused, niche market. On the other hand, the commodity leasing segment is no longer a distraction. Enterprise's leadership recognized that it had no viable strategy for delivering the best value in the leasing business, and it has been wise enough to change its approach.

Be Wary of Wall Street Wisdom

Some of the most lethal distractions that suck leadership time and energy away from core priorities are provided by the constant flow of advice from Wall Street. If Michael Dell had listened to the investment community, he would still be in retail, just like Compaq, IBM (until 1999), Hewlett-Packard, and Packard-Bell—and probably with equally unimpressive financials. IBM's personal computer division purportedly lost more than $1 billion in 1998, and Compaq's CEO was fired for the firm's disappointing financial results in 1999.

Harley-Davidson's leaders once allowed themselves to become distracted by the investment community and were induced in 1986 to acquire Holiday Rambler, the recreational vehicle manufacturer. With an eye to increasing its stock price, management listened to the wisdom dispensed from Wall Street, which held that Harley-Davidson was too focused as a single-product company. Wall Street stood in awe of Japanese competition at that time and noted that several Japanese competitors, including Honda, Suzuki, and Kawasaki, had targeted the U.S. motorcycle market. What this overseas threat signaled to Harley's leadership was the need to focus even more intently on the core business and to make it even stronger. The stock market experts, however, sang the siren song of diversification and seduced the firm into a line of business that was independent of the motorcycle "fad" and that had little risk of Japanese competition.

Harley acquired Holiday Rambler in 1986 for $155 million. Wall Street, certain that this leading manufacturer of top-quality recreational vehicles provided an outstanding opportunity to diversify and to capitalize on the burgeoning population of retirees, applauded the move. The problem was that Holiday Rambler had little in common with Harley's areas of expertise and little to offer its loyal customer base. Despite nine years of vigilant management attention, it became increasingly clear that Harley could not add value to the franchise and that all stakeholders would be much better off if management resumed an intensified focus on its core motorcycle business. Holiday Rambler was sold in 1996 at a price well below Harley's initial investment.

How could a leadership team as savvy as Harley-Davidson's make such a costly mistake? Diversification of earnings was a fashionable concept among Wall Street savants at the time, and many companies were eager to show their responsiveness to these vocal proponents of shareholder profits. In retrospect it seems absurd that diversification would create greater and more lasting value for investors who, on their own and with the push of a computer key, could easily diversify their investment risk into dozens, hundreds, or even thousands of stocks. But this preposterous proposition persuaded many companies to complicate their business portfolios.

During this period, MBNA, the loyalty leader in the credit card industry, was a subsidiary of a regional bank that security analysts regularly criticized for its overdependence on MBNA's earnings. The bank's management diverted resources from MBNA to feed the growth of other divisions with much weaker prospects. Instead of encouraging the parent company to funnel all its available resources into the business with the highest loyalty in its industry and with the potential to become a market leader, the gnomes of Wall Street demanded diversification, thus slowing MBNA's rise to market leadership.

The lesson here is clear. Investors have a legitimate demand for outstanding financial results, but leaders who bow to investor advice on how to achieve them and who allow themselves to become distracted from their own tried-and-true strategy do so at their own peril. Holiday Rambler soaked up countless hours of management time as the company leaders courted the acquisition, negotiated the deal, integrated management, and on and on. In the end, the investment proved to be nothing but a decade's worth of distraction. Harley's leadership team had failed to develop a strategy for delivering distinctively superior value to any segment of the recreational vehicle market. There was little overlap with the core strengths Harley had built in its motorcycle business. Teerlink and his management team showed the good judgment to admit defeat and recommit themselves to their original strategy. Since then, there have been only two acquisitions of any note by the firm—both focused on strengthening the core motorcycle business. The firm's outstanding financial results since its misguided excursion with Holiday Rambler are testimony to its excellent strategic discipline and focus.

Grow from Positions of Strength

Your company must maintain a winning level of growth to attract and retain outstanding partners. The source of growth preferred by loyalty leaders is from deepening relationships with existing customers and from developing concentrated positions of strength rather than from spreading resources more thinly. For a thorough examination of the topic of how to grow from positions of strength, I highly recommend *Profit from the Core: Growth Strategy in an Era of Turbulence*, by Chris Zook with James Allen, Harvard Business School Press, 2000. Northwestern Mutual, for example, sells more than 55 percent of its new life insurance to existing customers. Similarly, Enterprise's expansion to airports is focused on serving a broader set of needs for its existing loyal customer base.

The second best way to grow is by acquiring additional customers that belong to the same segment as the firm's existing book of business. Dell's global expansion followed this disciplined growth strategy successfully, but most firms eventually discover that their traditional core segment can no longer provide sufficient opportunity and they must branch out. USAA, for instance, realized it would eventually run out of opportunity in its core military officer market, despite expanding from auto insurance to life insurance, credit cards, mutual funds, and a dozen other lines. The shrinking military just didn't allow room to expand the business further. In their search for the best growth opportunities, CEO Bob Herres and his team had already initiated a renewed push to the extended families of officers, but research had shown that the needs and economics of serving these associate members did not quite represent the same outstanding match with USAA's strengths. After careful study, Herres and his team decided to extend their target market to include all members of the military, not just officers. They based their choice on the finding that USAA could create products and service of distinctive value for this segment—and that the needs of this segment closely matched those of USAA's historic strength, its core officer segment.

For a final example of how to grow from a position of strength to create a win/win strategy, turn to the New York Times Company. During the 1990s, the circulation of the *New York Times* reached a plateau at about 10 percent of the New York metropolitan newspaper market, and management commissioned a research team to determine what it would take to gain more share. The answer was confounding. Reportedly, those who didn't read the *Times* found its stories too long, its vocabulary too challenging, and its ideas too complex. They wanted to see more sports coverage, a horoscope would be nice, and cartoons were a must. Dumbing down the newspaper would be disloyal to core customers and held little interest for the editors and journalists, yet the business leadership knew it must find some option to generate growth.

What the company eventually discovered was that each major city offered a group of readers with like-minded values and attitudes, very similar to the paper's core New York readership. To win their business, however, the company had to provide these readers with better availability and earlier paper deliveries than it could currently offer. So management decided to invest millions of dollars to address these shortcomings. Satellite feeds now link the seven additional printing facilities that were brought online between 1997 and 2000. The paper upgraded distribution capabilities and, for the New England and Washington editions, customized local weather and TV listings. The editors win because they can maintain and improve the journalistic integrity of the paper. Target customers across the United States win because they now get a *New York Times*, customized to meet local needs, with early and reliable delivery. And the business leaders at the New York Times Company win because their strategy has produced a resurgence in the growth of subscribers and an attendant expansion of advertising revenues. The result has been a classic win/win thanks to a strategy that maintained superior focus on the right kinds of customer and offered partners the opportunity to grow and prosper.

PUTTING PRINCIPLES INTO PRACTICE

To help you put the principles of loyalty into practice, each chapter will provide a checklist of actions that you should consider implementing. Each checklist presumes that you will have already given the Loyalty Acid Test to a sample of customers and partners (more detail on the Loyalty Acid Test is provided in the appendix and on the Web site www.loyaltyrules.com). The Web site will show you how to calibrate your results in detail in comparison with loyalty leaders. You can, however, follow this rule of thumb: Any item that receives less than 50 percent agree or strongly agree should be considered a problem area. Combined agree/strongly agree scores between 50 percent and 75 percent represent areas with no crisis, but with plenty of room for improvement. Any score above 75 percent agree/strongly agree signals an area of strength.

With the Loyalty Acid Test Survey results in hand, you will be ready to work through the following list of suggestions intended to help you ensure that the principle of "play to win/win" is incorporated throughout all your relationships.

ACTION CHECKLIST

- **Clarify your strategy**
  Ensure that your strategy for creating superior customer value is so clear, focused, and rigorous that you can write it in one or two paragraphs. Distribute it to all your employees and other partners, and post it on your Web site. It must identify your target customer groups and explain the economic rationale for why your organization can offer demonstrably superior value to these customers.

- **Test your partners**
  Quiz your employees, suppliers, dealers, and investors to see if they clearly understand who your core customers are, why you can offer superior value, and what their own role is in creating that value. Recruit a trusted third party to interview all the members of your leadership team to test for consistency in their understanding of your strategic rationale and most vital challenges. Carefully consider the percentage of partners who are neutral or who disagree on the following Loyalty Acid Test Survey items: *The company has a winning strategy,* and *I understand our strategy and the role I must play for our success.*

- **Create a customer experience council**
  Assign a very senior cross-functional group to search out and prioritize opportunities to improve your core customers' lifetime experience. Provide this group with sufficient resources, and make them accountable for results. They should start by building a framework for tracking and analyzing key dimensions of the customer experience.

  - ❑ **Create customer value metrics**
    Give the customer experience council the task of establishing performance standards for grading the customer experience. At a minimum, track cost, quality, and timeliness for key touch points (moments of truth at which the organization or its partners touch the customer). Benchmark your performance against the best competitors; set goals to be "better than the best." Using relative retention rates and Loyalty Acid Test scores, verify the accuracy of your standards. (Note: The top benchmark scores must correspond to superior retention rates and Loyalty Acid Test scores, or you are measuring the wrong things.)

  - ❑ **Grow from your strengths**
    Utilize the council's combined industry knowledge and interview customers to chart the predictable evolution of their needs. Study loyalty

leader innovations so you can create such a valuable customer experience that core customers want to give you 100 percent of their business. Make the customer experience council responsible for discovering and prioritizing the best opportunities to upgrade the customer experience for existing core customers.

❑ **Scrutinize customer needs and opportunities**
Get senior executives out in the field to observe customers as they utilize your product or service. Invite suppliers and dealers to join in this process where appropriate. Prioritize the best opportunities to build additional customer value.

❑ **Become an Internet champion**
Enlist the customer experience council to search for the most powerful and creative ways to use the Internet to improve the quality and value of your customers' lifetime experience. Establish priority lists, and set aggressive deadlines for implementation.

■ **Sharpen your focus**
Study the Loyalty Acid Test results for this statement: *The company focuses all of its energy and resources in businesses where it can be the best.*

❑ **Stop wasting time**
Challenge the organization to identify where time is being spent on businesses with no clear plan for providing the market's best value. Track leadership time to ensure that leaders invest most of their time in deepening relationships both with the best customers and with partners in businesses in which you have leadership, or clear potential for leadership.

❑ **Stop wasting capital**
Insist that business line managers achieve leadership (as demonstrated by superior profits and customer loyalty), or set deadlines for exiting the business. Rank-order all capital investment proposals according to how much they will increase customer value in business lines in which you are or can become the best.

■ **Teach the win/win philosophy**
Develop stories and case studies that explain the advantage of win/win solutions and the role they must play in your success. Utilize these stories in training at all levels of the organization. For all key decisions and proposals, insist that managers explain why their recommendations are in the best interests of core customers and how they will provide win/win opportunities for all key partners. Study your Loyalty Acid Test Scores for this statement: *The company is committed to win/win solutions.*

4

Be Picky

■

Membership Is a Privilege

Loyalty requires choices. Cultivate business relationships only when both sides can provide special value, or you will soon dissipate your resources and be special to no one. Be selective not out of arrogance, but out of the humility that recognizes the impossibility of being special to everyone. Choose prospective partners with care so that you can afford to invest in their success and stick with them for the long term—but not forever unless they earn the privilege. Loyalty must be a two-way street.

By ascribing to the first principle of loyalty and offering the best possible value to your target customers, you automatically start the cycle of superior economics that can be shared with all your partners. But take heed. You can quickly nosedive into mediocrity unless you utilize your strategic advantage to be discerningly selective about those partners. Nothing speaks more clearly about your values and principles than your choice of associates and whom you promote to positions of prominence and authority.

You may be thinking that this notion of being picky does not square with high-road behavior: It smacks of discrimination and favoritism, and flies in the face of the democratic ideal that everyone be treated equally. Perhaps this is why so many businesses are not sufficiently discriminating. Their marketing and sales incentives reward revenue generation and new customer acquisition as if all customers were equal, and their customer and employee satisfaction surveys are structured as if everyone's satisfaction were equally important. Even those companies wise enough to measure customer defection often forget that some defections are far more costly than others.

When it comes to running a business worthy of loyalty, not all employees, customers, suppliers, and vendors are equally worthy of membership on your team. Loyalty leaders will be the first to admit that they discriminate—not on the basis of race, religion, or gender but on the basis of character, capability, and performance. They know that it would be absurd and unfair to treat an unprofitable customer the same as a highly profitable and loyal one. It would be equally absurd and unfair to invest the same resources in an unproductive employee as in a highly productive one. And it would be absurd to bend over backward for suppliers or vendors who were uncommitted and incapable of helping you become the industry's best. Loyalty leaders understand that they can and should treat everyone honestly and fairly, with dignity and respect, but they also understand that they can afford to be *loyal* only to those who can help build mutually beneficial relationships that reflect the principles of loyalty.

High-road leadership demands constant, vigilant, and unrelenting discrimination. Loyalty leaders discriminate out of a profound humility that recognizes their limitations and admits to the impossibility of offering honestly superior value to everyone. C. William "Bill" Pollard, the widely admired chairman of ServiceMaster, offers this simple caveat in *The Soul of the Firm*: "I hope you believe that not everyone can work for your company."[1] It is plain common sense that business leaders who try to create special value for everyone will end up being special to no one. But there is more than economics behind this logic. Following the high road requires your people to put the interests of customers and partners ahead of their own—even when no one is watching.

This recognition makes loyalty leaders especially concerned about who is invited to join their team. With so many hours devoted to the workplace today, success and happiness can result only when these hours are shared by people with the capability to create financial results and with the character to treat each other right in the process. No wonder Southwest Airlines, screening carefully for the right personality and character traits, hires only 4 percent of its 90,000 applicants each year.

PICKING YOUR EMPLOYEES

Rich Teerlink, former Harley CEO, has always maintained that "people are our strongest source of competitive advantage."[2] His views are typical of loyalty leaders, who all list employee recruiting and selection among their most vital functions. They know that their employees are ambassadors to the outside world. Employee behaviors and attitudes—even more than leadership principles and ideals—communicate most directly to customers, suppliers, and others just what the company stands for.

A high degree of initial selectivity also affords leaders the luxury of being able to invest aggressively in the success of each person. They can stick with their superior employees much longer than less selective organizations can, so that everyone is motivated to dig in and fix problems rather than to opt for superficial solutions or to look the other way. The relationship becomes a two-way street. It is no coincidence that during the tight labor market of the late 1990s, when many manufacturers were struggling to find workers, Harley-Davidson plants had a waiting line of prospective employees. Harley offered an outstanding career opportunity, and applicants lucky enough to be selected knew that they could build a long-term career with the organization. Harley invested heavily to find the right kind of employees and worked hard to ensure they would want to stay for the long haul. The employee turnover rate at Harley has been only 4 percent.

U.S. Marine Corps recruits learn right up front that the Marines care deeply about commitment and loyalty. Their well-known motto, *Semper Fideles*, means "always faithful," or "always loyal." Interviewed in 1999, on the day of his retirement as commandant of the Marines, General Chuck Krulak commented, "Here I am on the last day of active service, and what better topic to talk about than loyalty!"[3] He has no doubt about the crucial link between loyalty and standards of excellence:

> The reason we have been the only branch of the service that has been able to meet its recruiting objectives is not because we've lowered our standards; we've raised them. Department of Defense recruiting guidelines require one test for drugs; we do it three times. They insist on 90 percent high school graduates; we demand 95 percent. You don't see us advertising that we'll pay for your college education or that we'll teach you a valuable skill. Every one of our ads carries one simple message: The Marines will offer you the opportunity to be challenged—physically, mentally, and morally. We target men and women of character.[4]

Krulak sees at work in the business world the same principles that he has experienced in the military. Upon his retirement from the military, after thirty-nine years with the Marines, he accepted a position as senior vice chairman of MBNA, the loyalty leader in the credit card business. "Only the best" is a prerequisite to recruiting success—in the military or in private business.

Truett Cathy, Chick-fil-A's founder, has always been picky about his business partners because he expects to build long-term loyalty: "We don't select or even seriously consider an operator unless we want the individual to be with us until one of us dies or retires." Not only are manager turnover rates at Chick-fil-A the lowest in the fast-food industry (less than 5 percent for store operators, versus more than 35 percent for the industry), but the turnover rate for counter crews is less than half that at competing chains (125 percent compared with more than 300 percent). Although Chick-fil-A management is hardly happy about 125 percent turnover, the competitive advantage is striking.

Michael Dell may not be quite as long-range in his planning as Cathy, but his ambitions are similar:

> Today we hire people with the long term in mind. We're not bringing them in to do a job; we're inviting them to join the company. . . . If you hire people with the potential to grow far beyond their current position, you build depth and additional capacity in your organization.[5]

Loyalty leaders are uniform in setting high standards for new employees, and they are remarkably uniform in the practices they have learned to attract and retain the right employees. They all create a uniquely attractive opportunity, they all are keenly involved in the recruiting process, and they all take pains to ensure that employees' first experiences on the job reflect their value to the company as well as the values of the company.

Special Employees Deserve Special Opportunity

Chapter 3 discusses the importance of focusing on a target group of customers if you intend to create special value for them. The same is true if you are going to attract the right employees. It is easier and more productive to create a uniquely attractive opportunity when you narrow your focus to a particular employee niche. You can know a narrower segment in much greater depth and customize both recruiting and ideal career paths.

Andy Taylor has bucked industry norms with his targeted recruiting efforts. Walk into any branch of Enterprise Rent-A-Car, and chances are you will be greeted by bright, friendly, and helpful crew members whose vitality is palpable. Virtually all Enterprise employees are college graduates, energetic men and women to whom Enterprise can offer a truly special career opportunity. The company looks for clean-cut and polite, yet fun-loving new recruits who are willing to work hard and compete for the outstanding experiences and financial compensation the company offers. Despite their college degrees, they must be willing to start at the bottom just like almost every senior executive at Enterprise—including Taylor himself.

In general, the labor-intensive car rental industry tries to keep wages as low as possible. Not surprisingly, second-rate compensation rarely attracts first-rate talent. But Taylor and his leadership team have followed a very different path. New hires at Enterprise start at pay levels 25 to 50 percent higher than those of the competition, levels that can grow at 20 percent annually for strong performers.

Superior compensation is just one of the ingredients that enable Enterprise to be more picky about who is hired. Just as important, Enterprise employees find it highly gratifying to be part of a company that regularly startles customers by its superior level of service and value. Many customers are astonished when their cars are delivered to their home by a professionally dressed college graduate, or when a branch employee drives them to the registry after discovering their driver's license has expired. And mechanics at local garages and body shops—mechanics who frequently make referrals for car rentals—enjoy Enterprise's Wednesday tradition of sharing pizza or donuts.

Since personal skills are so crucial in building good relationships, Enterprise values EQ—emotional intelligence—at least as highly as IQ in recruiting employees. In fact, the firm has its own fun EQ questionnaire, designed to highlight applicants with exceptional EQ, as well as a cadre of recruiter specialists who team up with local branches to pick the top candidates from thousands of applicants.

Another example of the benefits of careful employee selection is the success of Chick-fil-A, the loyalty leader in quick-service restaurants. Much of Chick-fil-A's success results from the company's ability to be pickier than the competition, especially for the store operator position, which attracts graduates of West Point and Annapolis as well as management alumni from talent troves such as Accenture—credentials unheard of elsewhere in the fast-food industry. Chick-fil-A can both attract and retain such outstanding talent because it offers a uniquely attractive entrepreneurial opportunity to earn as much as $200,000 to $300,000 with no more equity investment than an up-front $5,000 franchise fee.

Its superior operator pool then allows the company to attract a higher-quality part-time workforce. Like its competitors, Chick-fil-A targets high school students to work the counter, but it goes after the upper end of the class, typically higher achievers and more dedicated workers who have long-term intentions of attending college. These students appreciate the superior training that they receive from top-caliber operators, and Chick-fil-A further entices them by offering part-timers $1,000 to $2,000 in scholarship money. Even bigger scholarships of up to $18,000 for Berry College in Rome, Georgia, are awarded to dozens of top employees each year. The firm has also created a pipeline of talent for its full-time recruiting needs; more than half of the new restaurant operators have worked previously in Chick-fil-A stores as part-timers.

You may be thinking that deep pockets can always provide quick and easy access to first rate-employees, but it's not that simple, and money alone is no guarantee. Loyalty cannot be bought. You do not necessarily need the highest compensation to build an employee loyalty advantage. For example, SAS, the market leader in statistical analysis software for e-intelligence, has developed a strong hiring program even though its compensation for new software engineers doesn't match salary packages at Oracle or Microsoft. But with turnover rates of 5 percent in an industry where 20 percent is the norm, SAS stands out as a recruiting success story.

The success of SAS is the result of creating a differentiated career that appeals to a distinctive type of employee. In addition to occasionally going head-to-head for new hires with Microsoft and Oracle at schools like MIT, Cal Tech, and Princeton, SAS focuses its recruiting on colleges such as the University of North Carolina and the University of Kansas. These schools are generally less competitive and attract students with different priorities from those on the fastest, most intensive academic and career tracks. By creating challenging and stimulating jobs in a workplace that is also compatible with a more balanced lifestyle, by developing a beautifully manicured corporate campus in Carey, North Carolina—an ideal town for raising a family—and by pampering employees with benefits like on-site day-care centers, free health care, piano lessons from the pianist who plays at the cafeteria during lunch, and flexible schedules, SAS has become the employer of choice for its niche.

Don't Delegate Employee Selection

Senior executives of high-loyalty organizations know that the destinies of their firms will be determined by the people they recruit, so top leaders—including CEOs themselves—spend as much of their time as possible on this vital function. You would do well to follow Michael Dell's example.

> I'm always looking for good people, and I expect others on our team to do the same. At Dell, we look for people who possess the questioning nature of a student and are always ready to learn something new. . . . And whenever humanly possible, I look for them myself.[6]

The need for such senior involvement stems partially from the fundamental fact that successful firms must win the war for talent by recruiting and retaining the most capable employees. But competence is not the dimension that interests these senior leaders the most, because competence can be easily judged and can be developed through training and education, especially if candidates have the right aspirations and attitudes. The more subtle dimensions that merit CEO attention have to do with the attitudes, character, and cultural fit of prospective employees—personal qualities that tend to be well established early in life. Jimmy Collins, the president of Chick-fil-A, interviewed all prospective store operators to ensure that they would be positive ambassadors of the company and would represent its values to their communities.

> Our customers in Lubbock, Texas, don't know what our mission statement is—and they probably don't much care. On the other hand, they do know Nell [Nell Russell, who retired in 1999 after 27 years with the company] and what kind of person she is. To them, Nell is what Chick-fil-A stands for, and the way Nell treats her staff and her customers is the clearest reflections of our values.[7]

As Collins prepared for his own retirement in 2001, he began to delegate the job interviews to the next generation of leaders at Chick-fil-A, but he carefully trained those leaders to look for the right qualities in candidates.

At Home Depot, the company that has used principles of loyalty to transform home improvement retailing, the volume of hires has reached 75,000 per year. Not surprisingly, leaders have had to delegate hiring responsibility—but they have worked hard to ensure that prospective employees are carefully screened for values and cultural compatibility. Now, every store has a computer kiosk at which candidates can key in personal information and learn more about employment opportunities. An important portion of this process involves a screening test that evaluates each individual's core values. The candidates are apparently willing to be quite candid with the computer, which probes to learn whether this is the kind of person who cares about serving others.

Southwest Airlines has developed some of its own techniques for identifying candidates with outstanding personality and character traits. The company conducts group interviews and simply asks the job applicants to talk about themselves. Recruiters watch candidates when it is not their turn to speak. Those who listen carefully to others and display empathy and encouragement are ranked highest. Those who ignore others and concentrate instead on writing notes for their own speech are bypassed, no matter how impressive their presentation or credentials.

State Farm's agents are the firm's primary representatives to the outside world, so the company is extraordinarily picky in selecting candidates for this position. In the 1990s, the firm structured a system that both enables agents to earn compensation far above the industry average and allows the company to be extremely selective. Most new agent candidates must now work in a local or regional office, where they learn the company's internal processes and get to know its partners and its culture. At the same time, State Farm's leadership can evaluate their performance and cultural fit with the firm firsthand and steadily improve the average quality of its agent force.

Be Picky about Employees' Initial Experience

The first forty hours of on-the-job experience make an indelible cultural imprint on employees. It frames their understanding of the company and its business. For this reason, loyalty leaders devote enormous attention to the design of employees' first forty hours, including details that other leaders might consider trivial. Most senior executives in high-loyalty firms find the time to get involved personally, not only in the selection of newcomers but also in their orientation and training. When you pick employees carefully, you can afford to invest more in training and in creating the ideal initial career experience.

For example, Home Depot refuses to throw undertrained employees in front of customers because that would make both the customers and the employees unhappy. So the company gives new cashiers a full week of training before sending them out to the floor. By the time these new hires face customers, they're equipped with the confidence and skills they need to provide outstanding service and to make them proud of their work. Store managers further increase the odds for a successful start-up by avoiding predictably frenetic Saturday and Monday mornings for a trainee's first solo run. Meanwhile, competitors scratch their heads trying to figure out how Home Depot can afford to invest a week of training in the inherently high-turnover cashier position. But it is precisely this policy that keeps turnover at Home Depot lower than at the competition and that helps generate the economic advantages of a loyal workforce.

You've already seen that Enterprise Rent-A-Car carefully manages its employees' initial career experiences, insisting that everyone begin at the bottom rung of a branch. Efficiency experts might raise their eyebrows at seeing well-educated professionals, who are overqualified and expensive, performing such basic functions as delivering cars or working the front counter, but Enterprise knows that this strategy will ultimately produce managers who can build a business from the bottom up, with customer needs at the forefront.

MBNA, the loyalty leader in bank credit cards, is famous for its scrutiny of prospective employees, who face six rounds of interviews, including at least two with officers of the company. CEO Charlie Cawley imprints the following statement on the back cover of every annual report: "Attention to detail drives everything we do." Then he strives to live up to these words.

For example, Cawley insists that new college hires start out in the collections department. Listening to stories about tragic financial reversals, divorces, and lost jobs may not be the most fun-filled way to begin a career, but it's the best way to learn about the costs to the company and its customers when credit line extensions lead to disappointing outcomes. Defaults on MBNA accounts run far below the industry average because every executive is practiced in dealing with these system failures and in minimizing their likelihood. No matter where these employees land during their careers at MBNA, they will appreciate the lessons learned from their frontline training. They will understand the importance of choosing the right kinds of customers and offering them the right level of credit, and they will know the right way to treat those who get into financial trouble. Of course, heavy systemic investment in career development would make no sense at all unless a high percentage of MBNA's recruits stayed on for years. And they do. The firm's turnover rate is just 12 percent, far below the industry average. In this light, it is not surprising that MBNA recruited General Charles Krulak, former Commandant of the Marine Corps, as vice chairman to oversee its human resources and to ensure constantly higher standards of excellence in recruiting and basic training.

One of Krulak's first initiatives was to upgrade the already outstanding recruiting process by ensuring that only top-performing MBNA employees, only the best of the best, were tapped to meet with prospective employees in their early interviews. The initial interview is, of course, the all-important beginning of the employee experience. Krulak wanted to make sure that MBNA employees considered recruiting an honor, not a burden to off-load onto a staff assistant. The irony in most firms is that the best people are also the busiest, so they are the least likely to be available for recruiting trips. Unless senior executives get involved and make it a top priority, these stars rarely get allocated to the vitally important process of attracting and selecting the future generations of employees. Now, MBNA accepts only the best as its recruiters, and they are trained by Krulak himself.

Be Picky about Who Stays and Who Gets Promoted

When you hire carefully and then invest heavily in your recruits' development and initial career experiences, you can reasonably demand superior performance. Jack Brennan at Vanguard has found that the best way to ensure that only high-performance employees stay on board is to set "stretch goals." If teams are really stretching to accomplish their objectives, then they will be selective about who earns the right to stay on the team. Vanguard's turnover rate among phone personnel runs at 14 percent—well below the industry average—and Brennan is committed to paring it further. He knows, however, that the danger of further reduction is the likely retention of weaker performers unless, at the same time, he continues to raise the organization's goals and performance standards.

Many loyalty leaders have not only raised performance standards, but also created up-or-out career paths that make it very difficult for executives—even those not in top management's line of sight—to coast or become complacent. High-performance cultures cannot tolerate mediocrity or selfish behavior. Although Andy Taylor does not have a formal up-or-out policy, he notes that it is unusual for people in the management training program to stay at Enterprise unless they are promoted. The company works hard to help people succeed, but it is very careful to promote only those who can serve as role models and who will attract, educate, and retain the right kind of employees with the right kind of values.

The system at Chick-fil-A works much the same way. Jimmy Collins reports that "the vast majority of our operator turnover is among operators whose performance is below average."[8] Although it is unusual for Chick-fil-A's leaders to have to terminate their relationships with an operator, they do pay special attention to those stores whose performance falls into the bottom 15 to 20 percent. These stores, called "targeted units," are tracked as a separate group and receive extra time allocations from Chick-fil-A's field consultants. Customer survey frequency is doubled, and improvement plans are developed with each operator. This special attention is not meant to turn up the pressure on underperforming units; it is meant to help them get back on track. As Collins says, "We err on the side of mercy."[9]

Chick-fil-A's leaders know, however, that if operators don't improve performance, they will probably leave. The compensation system is geared to reward performance, not effort, so some will leave because they are not satisfied with their income. Moreover, the entire corporate culture is built around achievement of superior financial results. As Collins says, "We have so many outstanding performers in our system, low performance operators feel they just don't fit in."[10] Every Chick-fil-A store operator knows where he or she stands in comparison to the other 600 or so operators. All that the operators have to do is hit a button on their in-store computers, and they will see where they rank in terms of sales, sales growth, profits—and, in essence, compensation.

Forced ranking systems are not unusual in high-loyalty organizations. The Marine Corps, the loyalty leader among the branches of the U.S. military, has a very structured up-or-out system based on forced rankings of officer performance. Enterprise Rent-A-Car branches all know how their profitability stacks up in comparison with the other branches across the

United States. John Chambers force-ranks all Cisco executives based on the results of customer evaluations.

Though this strategy may seem unnecessarily brutal, to be a loyalty leader you must retain and reward only the partners who perform. Of course you want every one of your people to succeed and to stay on board. On the other hand, you also must understand that it would be disloyal to the organization to retain employees who cannot hold up their end of the bargain, which is to deliver performance mutually beneficial to your entire network of partners.

Even more than by the employees it retains, a company's true values are revealed by its leadership's selection of candidates for promotion into positions of power and authority. Leaders promoted into prominent positions make the most powerful magnets when it comes to attracting the right kinds of employees. Smart recruits with long-term goals will be considering whether these are the role models they want to emulate.

Knowing that promotion decisions communicate so loudly and publicly what a firm really cares about, Andy Taylor put a great deal of thought and effort into his firm's promotion system. As a result, despite its entrepreneurial culture, Enterprise does not simply promote the candidate with the highest profits or operating margin per car. In addition to these important inputs, a successful candidate must also score strongly in customer satisfaction rankings and in the development of high-potential candidates below him or her. In other words, Taylor is emphasizing that only those leaders who can build loyal customer and employee assets earn promotion to positions of greater power and influence in his organization.

SELECT YOUR CUSTOMERS WITH CARE

Even when selective hiring is more theory than practice, most leaders acknowledge its importance. However, being picky about *customers* may be a foreign concept. Isn't it true that growth is good, and bigger is better, especially when Wall Street analysts are breathing down your neck? In fact, loyalty leaders are extremely picky about targeting only the right customers—those for whom their firms have been engineered to deliver truly special value. While a few high-profile businesses are better off soliciting as many customers as possible—Microsoft's Window's operating system, for example—these are the exceptions, not the rule.

Most companies that want to maximize sustainable growth and profits are wise to focus only on the right customers. Every customer acquisition involves an up-front investment that will be paid back only if the customer's loyalty can be earned. Bringing in the right kinds of customer can result in long-term cash flow annuities, continued growth from referrals, and enhanced satisfaction from employees, whose daily jobs are improved when they can deal with appreciative customers. Attracting the wrong customers will result in costly churn, a diminished company reputation, and disillusioned employees. In many e-commerce businesses, steep up-front customer acquisition costs make the stakes even higher.

Pick Customers Carefully for Faster Growth

Ironically, by focusing on selectivity and discrimination rather than on unbridled customer acquisition, high-loyalty firms are growing into market leaders. For example, Northwestern Mutual has grown to become the largest U.S. issuer of ordinary life insurance by insistently focusing on providing traditional life insurance to its target niche of small business owners, professionals, and executives. Dell Computer, by being more selective about its customers than any of its competitors, is growing at least twice as fast in all its market segments. Enterprise Rent-A-Car has risen to number one in the car rental industry by carefully avoiding the corporate frequent travelers who dominate the airport rental segment. Loyalty leaders have discovered the secret to accelerating and sustaining growth: Pick the right customers.

Perhaps the paragon of customer pickiness is The Vanguard Group, which is growing faster than any major competitor and is on a trajectory to become the largest mutual fund group in the world. John Bogle, Vanguard's founder, was always opposed to growth for the sake of growth: "We've never wanted to be the biggest, just the best."[11] Bogle's objective was always to serve customer interests better than anyone else, a standard that has continued since his retirement. So how did he gauge the firm's success? "Redemption rates," he explained, " I watched them like a hawk."[12] In the mutual fund industry, redemptions can signal customer defections, and Bogle analyzed them more carefully than new sales statistics to ensure that Vanguard's customer strategy was on course. Low redemption rates meant the firm was attracting the right kind of loyal, long-term investor. The inherent stability of this loyal customer has been key to Vanguard's cost advantage. Providing special value to this target customer is a core principle of building a successful partnership.

Bogle's pickiness became legendary. He scrutinized individual redemptions, especially large ones, with a fine-tooth comb to see who let the wrong kind of customer on board. When an institutional customer redeemed $25 million from an index fund purchased only nine months earlier, Bogle saw a failure in the system. Vanguard employees knew to expect his probing inquiry and warning not to let it happen again.

Bogle acknowledges that he was probably the only business leader in the world who "spent more time looking at big redemptions than at big sales." Bogle warned his team: "We don't want short-term investors. They muck up the game at the expense of the long-term investor."[13] At the end of his chairman's letter to the 1995 Vanguard Index Trust, Bogle reiterated: "We urge them [short-term investors] to look elsewhere for their investment opportunities."[14]

Jack Brennan, Bogle's successor as Vanguard's CEO, feels just as strongly about the importance of choosing the right kind of customer. He continues the tradition of carefully tracking redemption rates and using them as a fundamental gauge of the health of his company. He regularly makes speeches about the importance of customer retention and credits this advantage—which of course is dependent upon superior customer selection—for Vanguard's superior growth. He explains:

> Between 1983 and 1998, the industry's redemption rate increased by about 25 percent, while Vanguard's decreased by 25 percent. In the direct marketing segment of the mutual fund business, Vanguard's new sales represent 25 percent of total new sales, which is about our share of assets. But our cash flow, that is, our new sales net redemptions, represents about 55 percent of the industry total. It's our advantage in customer loyalty that is pushing our assets up faster than the rest of the industry.[15]

Pick the Right Customers to Reduce Costs

Vanguard's customer selectivity contributes to its retention advantage, which in turn accelerates growth. Brennan and his associates also appreciate that picking the right customers helps them reduce costs. Since taking the baton from Bogle, Brennan has improved Vanguard's astonishingly low costs even further. When he took the helm as CEO in 1996, Vanguard's flagship S&P 500

Index Fund costs ran 0.20 percent of assets. By 1999, this had declined to 0.18 percent—a 10 percent improvement.

One notable example of Vanguard's customer selectivity has been widely publicized in the business press. An institutional investor who tried to invest $40 million in one of Vanguard's funds was turned away because Vanguard suspected that the customer would churn the investment within the next few weeks, creating extra costs for all the existing customers. The shocked customer complained to Brennan, who not only supported the decision but used it as an opportunity to remind his team members why they needed to be selective about the revenue they accepted.

This notion that customers drag with them an inherent level of cost efficiency is rarely considered. Conventional wisdom considers operations and service departments to be the drivers of cost efficiency. Few businesses realize, however, that the types of customers selected by a particular sales or marketing focus also greatly affect cost efficiency. But loyalty leaders such as Michael Dell are intensely aware of this reality. Dell's decision to avoid the most broad-based consumer segment for most of the 1990s resulted from a careful cost analysis that showed how new computer users soak up inordinate levels of service support that can quickly drain personnel and fiscal resources.

For most of its history Dell has focused on corporate sales. In 1999, Dell did announce plans to expand its share of the home market, but this sales initiative has targeted exclusively the most expert individual consumers.

Dell narrowed its customer segment by focusing on the Internet as its primary consumer channel. Since only consumers who already had a computer could get online, these were almost certainly experienced users, who would be less expensive to serve. While Dell's competitors may not yet fully appreciate its picky customer focus, they do marvel at its resulting low costs. They are very unlikely to achieve similar efficiencies until they understand how their mix of customers constrains the potential for cost efficiency.

The reason that Enterprise Rent-A-Car assiduously avoids the large-corporate-account, frequent-traveler segment is that these rentals hurt fleet utilization because of cyclical demand and short-duration rentals; they also inflate administrative costs with their specialized, national-account billing system requirements. Even when Enterprise opens a branch near an airport, it has an explicit strategy for avoiding bulk, commodity business in favor of the infrequent travelers.

One final example of a business that generates important cost advantage by selectively picking customers is Northwestern Mutual. Northwestern focuses its agents on upper-income professionals, business owners, and executives. Its financial representatives are taught never to oversell, so that policyholders can afford to continue premium payments even in economic downturns. This strategy, in turn, improves the firm's customer retention, which reduces administrative costs. Additional evidence of Northwestern's pickiness is found in its market penetration statistics. Its penetration in the segment of executives and professionals with incomes over $100,000 is two to three times that of its overall market share. Because the company is so selective, most of its business is conducted with just those customers its system is tuned to serve most efficiently.

Furthermore, though insurance customers typically have multiple policies, Northwestern covers a higher percentage of its customers' needs than does any other company in the business. Increasing business with existing customers is far more efficient than courting newcomers; underwriting an existing customer is much simpler—to say nothing of computer records and processing. About 55 percent of the firm's new life insurance is on existing policyholders. No wonder its costs are the lowest in the industry— and no wonder it can offer better value to attract and retain its target customers. Imagine how your costs would drop if you did most of your business with inherently lower-cost customers and if most of your growth came from that same group of loyal customers.

Don't Lure Butterflies, Collect Barnacles

Unless you're managing customer acquisition carefully, you're probably letting the wrong ones in the door. Marketing and sales departments too often invest in lures to attract butterflies when they should be searching for barnacles. Consider the menagerie of prospective customers in your industry. Then consider who is the ideal match for the superior, long-term value your firm can deliver. These are the customers who are likely to stick around for a lifetime if they are treated right. These are the barnacles. Butterflies, in contrast, tend to flit around to today's sweetest deal, or to the company that happens to have the most dazzling new fad or the latest technology.

Since barnacles are hard to pry away from their current affiliations, the marketing job is much easier if the focus is on netting butterflies. If incentives for marketing and sales executives are based on volume of new customers, as is common, there will inevitably be a high yield of butterflies in the count. Price breaks to attract new customers and advertising campaigns that stress the latest fad or fashion are sure to yield an inflow of just those customers whose loyalty is hardest to earn and whose lifetime value to the company is the lowest—often actually negative when lifetime accounting is calculated correctly.[16]

Many loyalty leaders have discovered how to identify potential customer barnacles and have designed their marketing investments accordingly. They have also learned how to shoo away butterflies. MBNA, for example, has found that broad mailings to solicit new credit card customers yield a high percentage of butterflies who are attracted by their need for extra credit—and who often can't pay their bills. So MBNA has focused on affinity marketing, which attracts members of clubs and organizations, college alumni, and even fans of sports teams. The primary appeal to the customer is the affiliation, not the immediate need for credit. And MBNA carefully measures retention statistics for each group of customers and for each type of solicitation to learn how to avoid butterflies and how to lure a thriving colony of barnacles. Despite its rapid rate of growth in the relatively mature market of MasterCard and Visa bankcards, MBNA has kept its loan losses well below the industry average.

The New York Times Company provides another excellent example of loyalty-based leadership and the powerful consequences of being picky in marketing and sales investments. Chapter 3 described how the company's decision to refine its customer focus accelerated growth because the paper could concentrate on adding subscribers who would remain loyal for many years. Executives knew that typical subscriber acquisition campaigns, broad-based media advertising coupled with price discounts, would lure swarms of butterflies. They were acutely aware of their paper's industry-leading retention rate—above 90 percent for subscribers who had been getting the paper for two or more years, versus the competition's annual 40 percent defections—and were loath to diminish this advantage.

With this in mind, the company analyzed marketing programs and subscription campaigns to identify which brought in the richest mix of tenacious barnacles, and company executives reallocated investment dollars accordingly. Direct marketing campaigns based on cost-effective acquisition of target customers are now reevaluated weekly. Ever since the company interviewed long-term *New York Times* customers to find out which shows they watched, television advertising has been focused on CNN, the History Channel, and MSNBC. Acting on this type of careful analysis, the *Times* has managed to further increase its retention rates. Long-term readers now defect at only 8 percent per year.

Advertising, in general, is a risky way to acquire new customers since barnacles are most heavily influenced by referrals from existing customers and by real performance criteria rather than by seductive media campaigns. Loyalty leaders such as Enterprise and Vanguard are choosy about the placement and message of the relatively little advertising they do.

Vanguard, for instance, eschews ads that tout the company's superior performance, opting instead for a "steady as she goes," long-term-value orientation. Though many of Vanguard's competitors advertise hot performance, a volatile and transitory criterion, none come close to matching Vanguard's track record. (Based on five-year performance records, 68 percent of Vanguard's stock and bond funds ranked in the top quarter of their Morningstar categories.[17]) By emphasizing the performance of one particularly hot fund, the competitors are attracting butterflies who, ironically, end up costing much more than the initial ads that lured them.

Price discounts are just as bad as ads for hot but unsustainable performance. These are nectar to the butterflies. For this reason, Enterprise, despite its enormous cost and price advantage, does not tout price in its advertising campaigns. Rather, it emphasizes the unique level of service provided by sharply dressed professional employees—"We will pick you up"—because this approach attracts Enterprise barnacles, who value Enterprise's superior level of service above all else.

The following suggestions reflect the practices that loyalty leaders employ to avoid a butterfly infestation:

- Analyze the list of your long-term, loyal customers to determine what product or promotional campaign attracted them in the first place. Make these the priority marketing investments.

- Since barnacles are best attracted by referrals and not advertising, invest in referral programs and communication networks.

- Butterflies often cherry-pick individual products, so develop bundled product lines that appeal most to customers who intend to consolidate their purchases with one supplier.

- Target customers who are interested in procuring service and parts from the same source as their original purchase.

- Be cautious targeting young customers; their frequent moves and changes in life situation make them unlikely barnacles.

- Avoid price discounts to attract new customers; but if you must encourage trial, distribute free samples to the best target segments.

- Avoid business customers with high employee turnover and any consumers who move frequently.

- Avoid marketing to customers with historic patterns of frequent switching from supplier to supplier.

Don't Reward Volume Alone, Only Quality Volume

Take note of how loyalty leaders structure their employee evaluations and incentives. This subject—the best practices in measuring performance and structuring rewards—will be discussed in greater depth in chapter 6, but because of its importance, we will touch on it here as well. First and foremost you must avoid rewarding any employee for mere volume of new customers. Paying for volume will net you butterflies, whereas the key to loyalty and sustainable growth is your volume of barnacles. Loyalty leaders create incentives for growth in profits and cash generation, not for new account volume. Chick-fil-A does not reward new customer counts; instead, it pays operators a share of the profits. Ditto for Enterprise Rent-A-Car. In the insurance industry, most salespeople get front-end-weighted commissions, so they care too much about new sales and not enough about whether customers stay. State Farm bucks the trend. Their agents care deeply about retaining customers, not just because of the company culture, but because direct compensation and bonuses are heavily correlated with customer retention success.

Loyalty leaders find ways to encourage sales and marketing channels to focus on enticing the right customer. As a result, their organizations get the numerous benefits of superior customer selection, including superior

growth and cost efficiencies. And because there is a finite pool of customers, every time a loyalty firm attracts a barnacle or avoids a butterfly, the
competition is weakened. It pays to be picky.

PICKING YOUR WAY TO THE HIGH ROAD

We have seen that companies that are highly discriminating in selecting
their business associates can afford to take the high road by investing more
in each person's success and sticking with him or her through any tough
times. This same logic applies to vendors, customers, and the entire network of business partners. Three additional examples will illustrate both
the reciprocal nature of good business relationships and the benefits of
being picky.

Enterprise Rent-A-Car decided to outsource all document processing
to Xerox Business Systems. Scott Doney of XBS recalls the initial bidding
process:

> Those guys were far more rigorous in their selection process—they
> really put us through hoops. . . . They wanted to know much more about
> our business and our economics than our other customers did. . . .
> [They] really did their homework and were very demanding on pric-
> ing. But once we won their business, they started treating us like insid-
> ers—sharing all their information with us. They made it clear that they
> wanted me to succeed. For example, I share my profit target with them,
> and we sit down together to see how we can both achieve our mutual
> objectives.[18]

Because loyalty leaders such as Enterprise are so picky in selecting the right
vendors, it makes sense to invest in their vendors' success and to do what it
takes to strengthen the relationship. One tragic incident illuminates the
nature of these loyal commitments. A young Xerox employee who was working on the Enterprise account was killed in a weekend car accident. Members of the employee's family, who lived out of town, rushed to St. Louis and
were surprised to discover not only a note of sympathy from Andy Taylor and
a floral arrangement for the funeral, but a complimentary van to shuttle
them around St. Louis. Enterprise had become a committed partner.

Loyalty leaders set such high standards that their partners are proud to be associated with them. John Nagorniak of Franklin Portfolio Management Company is an outside investment manager hired by Vanguard to run some of its funds. He describes the satisfaction he gets from his relationship with Vanguard:

> We are part of the family—a very demanding relationship—but we can count on them to stick with us. I was sitting at a table of eight or nine executives from the investment management industry last year and mentioned that Vanguard was our largest customer. You can't imagine how proud it made me to hear the positive comments from these other institutional managers—and to hear that almost all of them were Vanguard customers with their own personal investment portfolios.[19]

One final story features an executive who found himself at loggerheads with his wife in an acrimonious divorce. The judge declared a cooling-off period during which all the couple's assets were frozen. The couple had two bankcards, one from MBNA and the other from a large, New York–based competitor we'll call ProfitsFirst Bank. When a phone call came from ProfitsFirst asking why an overdue bill had not been paid, the executive explained about the divorce and the temporary freeze on assets. The ProfitsFirst employee curtly advised him to pay off the balance right away and work out the details with his wife later; otherwise, his credit record would be penalized. Over the next few weeks, the executive received a series of increasingly threatening calls from ProfitsFirst representatives who attempted to intimidate him into paying. They warned that unless he paid up immediately, he would be considered an unacceptable risk and would not be able to get credit in the future. The urgency of available credit in today's world was already painfully evident to the executive, who couldn't even buy lunch for his colleagues unless he paid cash.

A phone call came from MBNA several days after the ProfitsFirst call. Again the executive explained the situation, but this time he was taken aback by the sympathetic tone of the MBNA representative, who reassured him that his situation was not as unusual as he might think. She acknowledged that divorces do result in greater risk for credit card companies, but she wanted to offer him at least a little help since he had been a loyal MBNA customer for years. So she offered to issue a new card in his name alone. It could have only a small credit line of $1,500, but that would help him through this difficult period.

The executive did get his life back together, paid all his bills, and has given all his credit card business—and dozens of testimonials—to MBNA. He has also made hundreds of negative references to ProfitsFirst Bank. This is a story of pickiness at work on several levels. Because MBNA is choosy about its customers, it had a clear picture of the executive's true risk profile. In addition, the firm's superior retention gives it operating margins that can allow it to take occasional losses, so that it could afford a certain amount of generosity toward a loyal, longtime customer. MBNA is also selective about its employees, hiring college graduates and starting them in the credit and collections department. So the MBNA representative likely had more formal and on-the-job education than did her counterpart at ProfitsFirst. And she was no doubt far happier to be allowed to help someone instead of being trained to threaten him. Thus the odds are increased that she will stay with MBNA for many years and that her experiences will help her make ever wiser decisions about credit lines and customer service.

Consider the impact of this story on people touched by ProfitsFirst Bank. The collections people could hardly feel proud of their treatment of the divorcing executive. It's more than a coincidence that turnover rates at ProfitsFirst are double those at MBNA and that ProfitsFirst has a hard time attracting college grads to work in its collections department. Nor is it coincidental that MBNA has much higher average balances per customer and a 10 percent customer retention advantage, both of which contribute to an enormous economic edge.

Furthermore, executive turnover is also a problem at ProfitsFirst, which was acquired by an even larger financial services firm with a similar history of valuing profits more than people. A former ProfitsFirst executive who corroborated the story shared this lament: "ProfitsFirst's senior leadership just doesn't understand loyalty. They think that you can create customer loyalty with airline mile rewards, and employee loyalty with stock options."

The moral of this story is that of the entire chapter: By maintaining the most rigorous standards for choosing your business partners—your employees, your customers, your suppliers, and your dealers—you will be headed for the high road of loyalty leadership.

ACTION CHECKLIST

■ **Examine the Loyalty Acid Test Survey results**
Focus on the responses to these three statements: *The company attracts and retains outstanding employees and partners; The company treats me like a real partner;* and *I always know where I stand with the company.*

■ **Refine your recruiting strategy**
Assign this chapter (and chapter 4 of *The Loyalty Effect*) as required reading for your recruitment team.[20] Appoint a senior leadership task force to identify the best tactics for finding and attracting the candidates most worthy of joining your ranks. Begin with the following steps:

1. **Profile your ideal recruits.** Ask your task force to clarify what distinguishes your ideal candidates from those of your competitors (especially in terms of character traits and personal values) and to determine how your organization can offer such candidates a truly superior career experience.
2. **Study the best practices of loyalty leaders.** Examine recruitment at the top retention firms for ideas that might fit your business.
3. **Include family members in job interviews whenever possible.** Understand that family dynamics often reveal a job applicant's most deeply ingrained character traits, and that family members belong in your network of mutually supportive relationships.
4. **Rank your recruiting programs and recruiters.** Evaluate recruiting initiatives and personnel on the basis of their yield rate of successful candidates who stay more than five years. Eliminate the bottom half, and reallocate resources to the most effective strategies.
5. **Chart your employee retention rates, and learn from the best.** Rank your branches, plants, and departments on their two-year and five-year retention of high-performance employees. Hold workshops to establish retention targets and to share best practices.
6. **Learn from your failures.** Analyze employee resignations and dismissals to spot patterns and root causes; defections in the first year or two typically result from faulty selection or flawed initial experiences.
7. **Make the most of downturns.** Recruit during downturns in industry business cycles, when the best candidates are most easily won to your team. Steady hiring delivers the highest-caliber recruits.

■ **Make recruiting an executive priority**
By taking an active personal role, emphasize that nothing is more basic to your success than the employees you hire. Insist that top management stay involved in recruiting. Review schedules regularly to ensure that time allocations accord with this priority. Be sure that your best (and busiest) young

stars are involved in the interviewing process by making it an honor and, perhaps, a requirement for promotion.

- **Redesign the first forty hours**
  Assign a senior task force to lay out the ideal initial work experience, attending to every detail. Examine loyalty leader best practices. Then insist that every new employee gets this experience.
- **Promote only loyalty leaders**
  Ensure that successful candidates embody corporate values. Gather 360-degree feedback, and weight this input heavily in promotion decisions. Reinforce your corporate values in promotion announcements; for each promotion, write up illustrations of how the newly appointed leaders role-modeled company values.
- **Rigorously distinguish barnacles from butterflies**
  Make sure that your senior leadership team can answer the following questions:

  - ❐ How can our frontline employees identify a target customer?
  - ❐ What percentage of our new customers represent prospective barnacles?
  - ❐ What should be our target yield of barnacles, and how can we reach that target?
  - ❐ What are the economic consequences of reaching that target?
  - ❐ What are the top three root causes of early defection among our new customers, and what should we do to fix them?

- **Balance volume with quality incentives**
  Ensure that your sales teams and marketing channels receive richer rewards for acquiring more barnacles than the competition does, and levy stiff penalties on anyone who attracts too many butterflies. Consider commission or bonus claw-backs if customers defect before eighteen months.
- **Reallocate marketing investments**
  Systematically rank all customer acquisition programs on the basis of their barnacle-to-butterfly yield. Eliminate the bottom half, and reallocate resources to the most discriminating programs. Prevalent early defectors signal customer-acquisition problems that need attention.
- **Make sure that every partner appreciates that membership is a privilege**
  Be very clear about the performance standards required to maintain membership privileges. Raise the bar every year. Set targets for the percentage of partners who agree with the Loyalty Acid Test statement: *I am proud of my association with the company*. Reward performance, not tenure.

Keep It Simple

■

Complexity Is the Enemy of Speed and Flexibility

Clarify the simple values and rules that must govern all decisions. Organize into small teams to maximize responsibility, flexibility, and accountability. Be sure that all partners understand the link between loyalty and responsiveness so that everyone will embrace the changes required to sustain mutually beneficial relationships. Loyalty is about the future, not the past.

Like it or not, the world today runs at Internet speed. So like it or not, organizations must have the capacity for rapid learning and rapid response if they are to remain effective and relevant. To build loyalty in today's highly competitive world, you and all your people must be capable of continuous change and adaptability to meet the needs of your partners.

The link between loyalty and your capacity for speed and adaptability, however, may not be apparent to everyone in your organization. In fact, most people tend to invoke "loyalty" to old structures and old practices in an attempt to resist change and progress. Employees may even question your loyalty to them when you ratchet up your demands for rapid response and perpetual learning. But they are confusing loyalty with nostalgia. As a leader it is your job to convince them that loyalty is not wistful adherence to outdated traditions. You must convince them that the future can never be as good as the past—it must be far better. You must convince them that the proof of loyalty is the ability to change and adapt as necessary to continuously serve the best interests of all partners and to continuously create superior value for customers—even when the required pace of change feels uncomfortable. Loyalty leaders must maximize people's welfare, not their comfort.

Great leaders know that the best business, like the best machine, is so reliable and so adaptable that it does the best possible job in the fastest and simplest way. So to be an effective leader you must resist the world's inevitable drift toward complexity by simplifying your organization's structure, systems for measuring progress, and rules for decision making. You must pare away the distractions and focus on the relatively few principles and practices that make a vital difference in creating superior value. These are the loyalty principles and practices that define high-road leadership.

SIMPLE RULES ARE GOLDEN

Almost nothing reduces flexibility and slows organizational progress as severely as uncertainty and confusion about core values and operating principles. By clarifying how the high road leads to personal and professional success and how treating others right is the basis for growth and profits, you will simplify the lives of all your partners. Loyalty to a clear and simple set of principles is the basis for flexibility and speed.

Treat Them Right

Northwestern Mutual provides a good case in point. Life insurance is not an inherently simple business. It rests on reams of regulations—different for every state in the union—enforced by a variety of mildly coordinated state and national regulatory bodies. It also involves tax codes, trust and estate laws, and a host of sophisticated investment management techniques. Even more confusing, the rules seem to change every year. It is in this setting that Northwestern Mutual has grown to become the largest issuer of individual life insurance in the United States. With ordinary life insurance policies in force approaching $650 billion and a field force of 7,500 financial representatives, the company quietly marches up the high road as chaos roils its industry.

Financial services deregulation has now brought hundreds of new competitors into the marketplace, with a plethora of new products: not just life and disability insurance, but mutual funds, variable annuities, trusts, wrap accounts, and more. And Northwestern's acquisition of the Tacoma, Washington–headquartered Frank Russell Investment Management Company adds still another layer of complexity to the Milwaukee-based company. Despite all the potential for confusion, Jim Ericson, Northwestern's

CEO from 1993 to 2001, has managed to stay a straight and steady course by keeping his organization focused on one simple rule: Do whatever is in the customers' best interest.

> When my people come to me with new product ideas, or investment ideas, or suggested changes in pricing structure, I just ask them these simple questions: "Is this in our customers' best interest? Will we be treating people right?" As long as they are asking these questions of themselves and their colleagues, they are going to make the correct decisions—and they are going to make them faster.[1]

The effect of these clarifying questions can be seen in the way that some Northwestern Mutual people responded to a tragic situation several years ago, when a father tried to buy a life insurance policy for his newborn daughter. Northwestern Mutual's financial representative submitted the completed application and first payment to the company to begin the underwriting process. Everything proceeded smoothly until the family's doctor failed to supply the baby's medical records. Northwestern tried repeatedly to prod the physician's office, but to no avail. Finally, the underwriter advised the financial rep that the application would have to be dropped.

On the same day that she heard from the underwriter, the financial representative also received a call from the client. The rep began to explain the problem, but the client cut her off to say that it was too late now—his daughter had died that morning from sudden infant death syndrome.

The financial representative was devastated, not only because of the tragic death but also because the doctor's neglect had prevented the company from issuing the policy. She conferred with the company's claims analyst, who in turn conferred with her manager to reach a decision that some might find surprising. They decided that since the parents had done everything they could to insure their daughter's life, Northwestern should try again to obtain the necessary medical records, and if a routine underwriting review subsequently approved the policy, the company would honor it. This time the doctor provided the required records, which indicated a healthy baby, so the company issued a policy to the deceased infant and paid the claim.

Jim Ericson didn't have to get involved to make this remarkable decision. He never even heard about the situation until after the fact. His employees felt comfortable responding on their own because they already knew how he would respond. He would ask them a couple of simple questions: "Is this in our customers' best interests? Is this the right thing to do?" Having already asked these simple questions of themselves, they had acted quickly and efficiently on their own.

A remarkable feature of this story is that Northwestern Mutual has one of the lowest mortality costs in the industry. How can a company that is willing to pay death claims on people with no valid policy be so profitable? The answer has much to do with the economic benefits from the loyalty and commitment generated when a company is known for simply doing the right thing.

Simplify Your Purpose with Intuit-ive Clarity

As noted in chapter 2, Scott Cook, Intuit's founder, knows that the key to fast and efficient decision making is a clear understanding of the simple values and mission of the company. When Intuit was still a one-room start-up, decisions were made at lightning speed and the values of the group were manifest in routine interactions. But with expansion, daily operations became more complicated. Cook observed that it had become far more difficult to act with the clarity and speed that had distinguished his original small team. The 1993 codification of Intuit's Vision and Operating Values helped recapture the focus and efficiency of the old days. It is centered on the primary value that guides the firm, the fundamentally and sublimely simple injunction to "Do right by the customer." It's a phrase that you hear often from Cook, and you will see it at the top of the list in the company's statement of principles and practices. It is the philosophy by which all the company's major decisions are gauged. Why does Cook consider it so important to clarify and reinforce the company's simple values?

> People must know what we stand for. It's not so much that this will help us make the big decisions any better—because I easily give my personal input on the big decisions. It's all the other decisions that you want to influence, the decisions that get made every day by people throughout the organization which never rise to my attention—never rise to top-level strategy. These are decisions like how a customer gets treated on the phone, or which projects should be put on the top of the stack today. When people throughout the company understand

the values clearly, they are going to make these little decisions faster and better.[2]

Sometimes the power of simplicity is most obvious in times of crisis, as was the case at Intuit one February morning in 1995. Just before Cook was to board a flight to Los Angeles for a speaking engagement, he learned that there was a bug in the company's TurboTax software program. With the April 15 tax deadline just around the corner, February is a bad time to discover a problem in a tax program, but to discover the problem by reading about it on the front page of the *San Francisco Chronicle* business section made the situation even worse. There was no time to cancel the speech, so Cook resolved to trust his executive team to make wise decisions in this potentially high-profile disaster. By the time he arrived in Los Angeles, he found that his team had already released a press statement to explain the bug, its history, and precisely what customers should do to fix it.

After delivering his speech, Cook checked in again and learned that his team had also offered to send a new copy of TurboTax to any customer who requested it, even though the bug affected far fewer than 1 percent of Intuit's 1.65 million customers. To minimize further inconvenience to customers, no proof of purchase would be required, although this decision meant that Intuit would be sending free upgrades to many people who had never bought the program and were simply using "borrowed" copies. And Intuit offered to pay any IRS penalties incurred by customers as a result of the bug. Contrast the speedy resolution of Intuit's problem with the prolonged crises at Intel over the Pentium bug, or at Coca-Cola over the tainted bottles in Belgium, or at Firestone and Ford with their tire failures, or at many other companies facing product performance problems, and you will see the benefits of living by simple values and simple rules. Such crises typically last for months, create public relations disasters, incur millions of dollars in legal fees, and seriously diminish organizational pride and confidence in leadership.

At Intuit, the entire decision cycle—from discovering the problem to deciding on the solution, to training the phone reps, to issuing a press release—took less than a single workday, and the decisions were made while the boss was out of town. How did Cook feel about this rapid-fire response? "I was delighted that my team acted with such speed and clarity—and I think the reason they could do it so well is that they knew the simple rule that should guide all of our decisions at Intuit—do right by the customer."[3]

Simplify 'til the Cows Come to the Spelling Bee

A celebrated Chick-fil-A story shows how simple rules can unleash creativity and generate speedy decisions, particularly in thorny situations. The story begins when the company introduced its award-winning advertising campaign centered on cows. These cows took over the barnyard and created their own advertisements that implored people to "Eat Mor Chikin." This tongue-in-cheek campaign became a huge success. Customers chuckled at the creative arguments cooked up by the one constituency that cared most about herding fast-food customers in the direction of chicken restaurants and away from the traditional burger shops responsible for the demise of the cows' ancestors. The bovine stars carried signs, painted billboards, and even created their own TV spot for the Chick-fil-A Peach Bowl. Stuffed toy cows were a big hit at the restaurants.

Everybody loved the ads—well, almost everybody. One group of local schoolteachers, frustrated that the cows were misspelling words, argued that the illiterate cows were a bad influence on students and that the campaign should be canceled. At most companies, the executives would scoff at such criticism. After all, you can't keep everybody happy. But Chick-fil-A leadership has always tried to operate by the Golden Rule; in fact, the injunction to treat others as you would have them treat you is essentially the basis for all win/win strategies. While taking this rule seriously simplifies most business decisions, it doesn't leave room for easy answers. It certainly didn't allow the leadership to ignore or disparage the local schoolteachers who felt that the company was neglecting the best interests of their students.

The employees of Chick-fil-A understand that the company is committed to serving its local communities, so they helped search for a mutually agreeable solution. And that solution was developed not at headquarters but by a store employee responsible for local marketing. Carol Thomas sat down with the teachers in her town and came up with the idea of using the cows to help the children improve their spelling. She developed a promotion that encouraged the children to "help those poor cows learn how to spell." Any child who found a misspelled word from the cows—in a print advertisement, on a Chick-fil-A bag, or in promotional material—could circle the word, spell it correctly, and earn a free Chick-fil-A sandwich. This promotion was such a hit with the students and the teachers that Thomas developed a continuing program for the local schools, in essence a spelling curriculum for primary graders based on the cows. Her ideas sparked a win/win success story and spread around the country like wildfire.

Chick-fil-A continues to enjoy the benefits of the cow campaign—and the company is creating even more value for its customers and their communities. The reason for all this success was not that a brilliant executive at headquarters devised a solution to a thorny problem or hired a change-management guru; the reason was that the leadership at Chick-fil-A has kept it simple for its people and taught them the simple rules for doing business.

KEEP SCOREKEEPING STABLE AND SIMPLE

If you want your partners to act according to simple rules, you must help them track their progress with simple scorekeeping systems that can be trusted to remain stable over time. Keeping score is one of a leader's most powerful tools for clarifying the rules and focusing the energies of his or her people. Therefore, loyalty leaders try not to change company rules, because this creates confusion and complexity. That's why Andy Taylor has never changed the fundamentals of the Enterprise incentive system. That's why Chick-fil-A has never changed its basic deal. Jimmy Collins comments on how important simple, stable scorekeeping has been to his organization's success:

> Lots of people come to talk to me about the deal we have with our
> store operators. They think there's something magical about the fifty-
> fifty split of net profits we have with operators—but they are wrong.
> There's lots of different deal structures that could have worked just as
> well for us. The secret to our success is not the deal; it's that *we have
> never changed the deal!*[4]

When Truett Cathy opened his first Chick-fil-A mall store in 1967, he offered Doris Williams, the high school cafeteria worker who became his first store operator, basically the same deal that is offered to new store operators today. Each operator is guaranteed a base draw and receives 50 percent of the store's net profits. The world has changed a lot since 1967, but the only change in the Chick-fil-A operator deal is that the base draw has been increased in proportion to inflation. Operators don't waste time dickering with the numbers, lobbying for a pay system that better suits their specific needs, or worrying that management will cut back on their percentage because their incomes have grown so dramatically. They simply dig in and concentrate on building their store's profit pool by providing customers with the best possible value and service.

Slick Scorekeeping Yields Muddled Decisions

Contrast the simplicity of this scorekeeping system with the system employed by Boston Chicken, the flash-in-the-pan chain of restaurants that was the darling of Wall Street between 1993 and 1996. The firm went public in 1993 and was hailed by analysts as the restaurant concept of the 1990s. Robust reported earnings rose for three years, and the stock sky-rocketed to a peak that valued the company at $3.2 billion. But the company's financial scorekeeping system was so complex that Wall Street never quite understood what was going on—and neither did the founders or their franchisees. The parent company reported earnings by selling bonds and then making loans to its franchisees, who then used the cash to pay fees to the parent company. Book losses were absorbed by the franchisees, who cared little about reported earnings since they were private. This system made the company's profits look plentiful and provided the stores with plenty of cash as long as the parent company could sell debt.

The problem was that all this obfuscating of the real underlying economics confused company management and store personnel. They couldn't determine which individual stores were profitable or even whether the restaurant concept itself was profitable. The effects of experimental changes in menu, pricing, or physical layout were hard to decipher because of such complex scorekeeping. So, rather than simply and quickly sharing the results of field experiments across the system, store managers and investors remained muddled. In the end, the chain declared bankruptcy and was sold to McDonald's for a fraction of its debt's face value.

Boston Chicken may be an extreme case, but many companies have adopted similar approaches to reported earnings. They fiddle with their scorekeeping to impress Wall Street analysts. The decision to "adjust" the way that a firm books revenues, stretches out depreciation periods, or implements any of the dozens of tricks that enable it to smooth earnings may seem relatively minor, but the costs can be enormous. First, it tells a firm's partners that fudging the numbers is an acceptable practice—which means they will feel entitled to take similar license with the numbers under their control. Second, it escalates complexity as managers and partners try to anticipate changes in the scorekeeping system and manipulate them to their own advantage. Instead of focusing energy on creating superior customer value, the approach redirects energy to accounting and budgeting gamesmanship.

It is important to recognize that there are inherent forces that can fool managers about the true underlying economics of their business. The reality of the cost-accounting process in most companies is more of a political science than an economic science. For example, internal accounting systems usually understate the true profitability of the most lucrative businesses and product lines and overstate the profits from weak or problem businesses. To minimize the squeeze on already meager profits, managers of low-margin product lines naturally fight harder to cut allocations for overhead expenses.

On the other hand, managers of high-performance product lines are less inclined to fight these bothersome political battles since their economic superiority affords them plenty of opportunities in the marketplace. Over time, costs get insidiously reallocated to the best lines of business, where they can go unnoticed until their cumulative effect eventually leads to bad resource-allocation decisions. With every change of the scorekeeping rules, with every reallocation of overhead, with every fudging of reported earnings, the true economics become further buried in this complex web, and accurate analysis, rapid response times, and real-time learning are compromised.

The Thirty-Year Exception

Of course, a business must sometimes change its scorekeeping system even at the risk of complicating operations during the transition period. Chapter 3 described how State Farm Insurance discovered that its agent compensation system needed to be updated after thirty years of stability. The system, which paid a fixed rate of commission on premiums, had become too costly for the customer. Auto insurance premiums had risen by more than 50 percent, largely because of litigation expenses, yet the amount of work involved in processing an application and servicing a customer had not grown proportionally. Too many agents were being superbly compensated for doing a less-than-superb job of creating value for customers.

Nevertheless, State Farm leaders remained steadfastly committed to the success of their agents and wanted to maintain as much stability as possible. After all, their agents had always been their partners, so any change had to represent a win/win solution and be simple to put into practice. Finally, after several years of careful analysis and planning—including countless hours of executive time spent communicating with agents and a panel of advisers—the company created its new agent contract. State Farm has been painstaking with the new contract because it knows that every change creates more complexity for its partners, who already have their plates full coping with changes in technology, competition, and customer needs.

SIMPLIFY WITH SMALL, FLEXIBLE TEAMS

Loyalty comes naturally in a small town or in a small company. People know each other and each other's families. They treat one another as neighbors who will probably see a lot of each other through the years ahead. And there is little confusion about accountability and responsibility—people's reputations aren't built through media or spin control, but through their daily behavior.

Think Small

Dave Illingworth, the first general manager of Lexus U.S., used the small-town car dealership as his model for the Lexus system. He knew that small-town dealers can't afford to alienate customers through abusive or deceitful treatment—almost everybody in town would hear about it, and there just aren't enough additional customers around to replace any defectors. Consequently, small-town dealers understand that their job is to cultivate personal relationships and to provide superior service. This simple, straightforward philosophy has created enormous success for Lexus. The company's resulting customer retention advantage has accelerated sales volumes to levels that match or exceed those luxury import brands that have been around for decades. Lexus has no plans to go along with the industry trend toward high-tech megadealers. It knows that its success in redefining customer loyalty in the auto industry has been based on a network of local partners for whom loyalty comes naturally, just like dealers in a small town.

Loyalty also comes naturally within a small team—or within a large organization that is composed of small teams. Thus many loyalty leaders utilize small teams as the molecular structure of their organizational design. Jeff Bleustein attributes many of Harley-Davidson's productivity and quality improvements to the reorganization of its large manufacturing plants into work groups of four to twelve members. The company's management team struggled for years to convince unions, employees, and managers of the major benefits when small teams are accountable for the costs and quality of their own production. But the resulting steady improvement in plant performance made clear to everyone the wisdom of the small-team organizational design.

Bob Herres at USAA, the preeminent insurer of military personnel and veterans, agrees with this approach. Herres inherited an organization with six large regional units, each comprised of large functional departments (claims, underwriting, policyholder services, etc.). Today, these six units have been broken into 110 teams so that each team can now focus on the specific needs of a smaller and more uniform segment of customers. Team members know the regional idiosyncrasies of the insurance business; they know their customers and each other better. And cross-training across functional lines also fosters better understanding and faster decision making. Within these 110 teams, the thousands of phone reps are segmented even further into small teams of ten to twelve people. The members of each team work out their own schedules and vacations, solve problems together, and are evaluated together. Herres believes that this small-team structure is a key reason that USAA has been able to grow while simultaneously shrinking bureaucracy:

> Our goal is to be a large company but to have a small-company touch and feel. With these smaller teams, we give better service, we make fewer mistakes, we're more responsive, and we avoid the information silos which are such a typical problem in functional organizations.[5]

USAA continues to win service excellence awards, to appear on every list of best places to work, and to be considered a benchmark of excellence. Herres and his organization have demonstrated the power of simplicity. Even in a bureaucratic industry like insurance, there is enormous potential in creating small teams with local leadership.

The branch office network at Enterprise Rent-A-Car obviously reflects Andy Taylor's belief in small teams with local leadership. His company consists of more than 4,400 of these teams, a number that is expanding at the rate of nearly one a day. He explains why he is such a fan of small teams and simple organizational structures:

> The reason we have been able to grow so fast for so long is that we aren't really one big company; we are really a confederation of small businesses, a network of entrepreneurial partnerships. We could never have achieved this kind of success if we were trying to make all the decisions at headquarters.[6]

One decision did get made at headquarters, however. Whenever an Enterprise branch grows to a specified size (usually between 100 and 200 cars), it is split in two and a new branch manager is appointed to the new location. Branch managers who successfully grow their branch receive favorable consideration for the next promotion; rather than bemoaning their loss of revenue, therefore, they continue to expand their business as rapidly as possible. Even in new airport locations, which are larger than the existing home market locations, Taylor keeps branches much smaller than those of the competition. He values the simplicity. Branch results are easy to see, accounting is less complex, there is no question about who is responsible for driving the results, and the team itself seems to gel better when there isn't room for scapegoats. Problems get recognized and fixed promptly; personal relationships are built faster and become stronger.

The drive toward simplicity is evident across the board at Enterprise. Whenever a promising new business opportunity comes along, it is quickly spun out as an independent entity. For example, Enterprise's used-car sales business was split apart from the rental branch system in its infancy, its management and profit-and-loss accounting kept separate from the start. This way no manager has to choose between growing used-car sales and growing the core rental business; there is a separate manager to focus on each mission. This approach provides more entrepreneurial incentive and enables the rapid growth of new businesses without sapping the strength of the core rental business.

By assigning the used-car business to a separate set of management teams, Enterprise has created many additional management opportunities for its workforce. The energy and creativity of these separate teams have helped build Enterprise into the largest seller of used cars in the United States, without draining energy from the expansion of the core rental business, which continues to grow and divide at rates more commonly observed in petri dishes than in the car rental industry.

Additional benefits accrue when separate teams are simply split off to run with new opportunities. Different businesses require different skills and different cultures, each of which can be accommodated. Building a used-car sales business is basically different from building a branch rental business, and the ideal teams require different kinds of people. Furthermore, it becomes clear very quickly whether the new team's efforts are succeeding, and there is little risk that the small unit will inadvertently be subsidized by draining resources from the core business. But the biggest advantage is that forcing the hatchling out of the nest and into the sunlight increases its odds of success. Small teams with a clear and challenging mission, and no safety net, usually figure out how to fly.

Not only entrepreneurial firms such as Enterprise but also large institutions such as Northwestern Mutual favor simple organizational structures. Northwestern Mutual's nationwide agency system is based on 100 or so independent general agents, each responsible for building a local team to hire, train, and develop new agents. Because all distribution costs are handled by these general agents, who pay the costs out of their own revenues, the system is remarkably efficient and flexible, especially for a big company in an industry notorious for its bureaucracy and inflexibility.

Even at the home office, Northwestern Mutual has learned how important it is to split off separate teams whenever possible. A good example involves disability insurance, which had originally been a segment of life insurance when it was a new product line. Over time, however, it became apparent that disability insurance was significantly different from life insurance. These differences presented great challenges in the 1990s, when the disability industry as a whole began to incur major losses. Although Northwestern, the country's second largest issuer of disability insurance, did not lose money on disability, its profitability was threatened. The problem was quickly righted, however, when Jim Ericson split out the disability department as a completely separate and independent team, free to build the culture and systems required for success in this niche of the insurance business.

To Fight the Large-Team Bias, You Might Need Dynamite

There are so many obvious advantages to building networks of small teams that you may wonder why all companies don't use this structure. You may think you already operate with small teams, but don't be too sure unless you have tracked the average team size in your company over time. Growing companies usually end up letting their team size increase even though in the natural world successful organisms grow and adapt through cell division, not by creating bigger cells. Why, then, do most companies evolve in the direction of larger and larger team units at the inevitable cost of accountability, flexibility, and speed? Scott Cook asked himself the same question and learned some important lessons about organizational philosophy from his consulting experience:

> Back in my days as a consultant at Bain & Company, I was struck by
> the speed and the flexibility with which our case teams got the job
> done compared to most of our client organizations. We could do
> things over a weekend that might take the client a month, despite their
> massive resources and industry experience. The lesson I took away
> from those experiences was the enormous power inherent in a small
> team. When that team has a leader who has been provided with the
> appropriate resources, and when the team accepts responsibility for a
> clearly defined and challenging mission, it can achieve outstanding
> results quickly and efficiently. This is why I have tried to incorporate
> small teams as the basis of our organizational design at Intuit.[7]

In the early years at Intuit, this small-team philosophy came naturally. After all, every start-up begins as a small, cross-functional team. But as the firm grew, Cook saw team sizes also begin to increase and functional specialization begin to creep into the structure. He observed the same human tendencies that had created the slow, inflexible, change-resistant organizations at some of his Bain clients. This insidious drift will spell almost certain failure in the fast-moving software industry. Scott knew that his leaders understood the logical advantage of small teams, yet they were veering away from this simple design precept. Cook came to recognize two basic obstacles that he had to overcome if Intuit were to enjoy the speed and flexibility advantages of small-team structure.

The first is a series of oft spoken, enticingly logical arguments against small-team structure. Allegedly, functional expertise should be pooled and consolidated; software engineers want to work for other software engineers who can train them and understand their career needs, not for some marketing person in a remote team out in the field. Conventional wisdom holds that big teams can transfer resources more easily to high-priority projects; a large functional group can deliver ten software engineers next week, whereas it might take a small team months to hire and train a similar group. Then there is the argument that if you want to create a body of real expertise, you must centralize experts so that they can pool and share knowledge. Scale supposedly provides cost efficiencies, and the critical mass of expert brainpower supposedly unleashes creative breakthroughs. Size is also supposed to offer deeper bench strength and recruiting clout, an argument applied to sales and marketing groups as well as to engineers. And, finally, isn't it sensible to keep the various teams consolidated since they may be dealing with common customers and channels? In combination, these rational arguments seem to make a pretty strong case for large teams.

Cook observed another obstacle that works against small, simple team structures—a political issue. Leaders who successfully build a large group under them have very little inclination to split their followers into small teams independent of their control. He or she hired the followers and trained them; the leader's job status, compensation, and power are directly proportional to the size of the team he or she leads. Therefore, most leaders with vainglorious aspirations don't want small teams.

For Cook, these compelling forces explain why most companies evolve into centralized bureaucracies in which projects no longer have one clear owner, decision making often grinds to a crawl, and the most talented young employees opt out of the organization to go where they can have a real impact. Work in large-team organizations is frustrating because too much activity consists of political posturing to please the higher-ups. Senior functional leaders will have opinions or well-meaning advice, but nobody has individual accountability for results—nobody except the leader at the top of the pyramid.

For all these reasons, the leader at the top can most clearly see the need for smaller teams, and Cook has concluded that it is the person at the top who must take responsibility for the organizational design. In 1999, he split his Small Business division into twice the number of teams, and many other divisions at Intuit will be similarly blown apart in the future. The rest of the organization will have rational and selfish and emotional arguments against creating an organization of small, decentralized teams. He has found only one approach that works: "I use dynamite to break up large teams into smaller teams."[8]

Dell Computer has taken the identical approach to simplifying its organization by dividing it into finer and finer cells as the company has grown. The sales force at Dell is constantly being divided into more focused units on the basis of geography, product line, and customer segment. Similarly, the manufacturing operation has been divided into separate teams for every product line. As the company continues to grow, Michael Dell will undoubtedly continue to carve up the firm into more and more teams, as many as it takes to create the accountability, responsibility, flexibility, and responsiveness required for success in the digital age.

One last example illustrating how loyalty leaders utilize small teams more effectively than do their competitors is Southwest Airlines. Southwest maintains one supervisory employee for every ten workers because this team size has proven to be the most effective. Other airlines have tried to reduce their costs by increasing the span of control of each supervisor, resulting in an average ratio of twenty employees for every supervisor.[9] While these bigger teams may look more efficient on an accounting spreadsheet, they are not. Southwest maintains the highest productivity and lowest costs in the industry.

SIMPLIFY BY OUTSOURCING

One of the greatest opportunities to simplify in the interests of organizational speed and flexibility is to outsource all functions for which you cannot provide uniquely outstanding customer value. Most of the model leaders in this book woke up to this reality early in the development of their organizations, and they are strong advocates of outsourcing. Earlier chapters have already highlighted Enterprise's preference for outsourcing non-strategic activities; its decision to outsource document processing to Xerox Business Systems is a case in point. Such partners have invested far more in leadership technology and business processes than Enterprise ever could or should. The advent of the Internet has opened up even more opportunities to outsource effectively. Cisco Systems, for example, has outsourced 75 percent of its manufacturing to companies like Jabil and Solectron.

The Vanguard Group has gone so far as to outsource the investment management for the majority of its actively managed equity funds. John Bogle and Jack Brennan have always believed that the company could provide better value to customers by structuring the right kind of partnerships with the best-in-class outside managers rather than struggling to build similar capabilities in-house. Most of Vanguard's competitors, however, consider the very idea of outsourcing their "hallowed" investment laughable and proof that Vanguard is not truly a full-service competitor.

Competitors once made the same arguments about Dell Computer. Industry insiders held that real computer manufacturers hired lots of engineers. Dell, which broke rank with these traditional, integrated competitors and outsourced all basic components, was seen as merely an assembler—not a true full-service competitor. But Vanguard, Dell, and many other loyalty leaders have shown that by weaving together the best network of partners and then creating the right set of metrics, incentives, and information flows, they can provide a far more flexible and responsive organization that can deliver customer value faster and better.

In fact, Dell's partner relationships with the best component suppliers both saved the firm from having to pour precious capital and management resources into areas in which Dell could not create distinctive customer value and led to a far simpler organization. Dell didn't have to worry about managing all the various administrative and overhead functions for outsourced areas. Furthermore, it was easier to structure contracts, performance metrics, and accountability standards between independent organizations than among internal departments.

Dell didn't stop at the outsourcing of component manufacture. The firm also outsources most of its field service. Of the more than 10,000 service technicians who service Dell products, only a few are actually Dell employees. By dealing with third-party service providers, Dell saves time and energy but sacrifices nothing in terms of coordination and integration, thanks to the superior information systems it has created to manage its partner network.

When a customer calls Dell with a problem, two electronic messages are automatically generated—one to the manufacturer to order any needed parts and the other to the service company to schedule the visit. Dell insists on knowing the cause of every problem, so it has the service rep return the flawed component to Dell for analysis; the final diagnosis is sent back to the vendor that manufactured the part. Obviously in a system such as this, the fewer the partners, the simpler the communications challenge. Therefore, Dell's basic rule is to have as few partners as possible in order to keep its network as simple as possible. Michael Dell explains why outsourcing provides such an advantage in speed, flexibility, and simplicity:

> There are fewer things to manage, fewer things to go wrong. You don't have the drag effect of taking 50,000 people with you. Suppose we have two suppliers building monitors for us, and one of them loses its edge. It's a lot easier for us to get more capacity from the remaining supplier than to set up a new manufacturing plant ourselves. If we had to build our own factories for every single component of the system, growing at 57% per year just would not be possible. I would spend 500% of my time interviewing vice presidents because the company would not have 15,000 employees but 80,000.[10]

SHRINK HEADQUARTERS

Loyalty leaders love small teams, especially small headquarters teams. In many cases they have the smallest headquarters operations in their industry. When you build an organization of decentralized, locally managed teams and outsource all nonstrategic functions to best-in-class partners, you have little need for a large headquarters organization. Leaders such as Andy Taylor like to keep decision making out in the field—as close to the customer as possible. They rely on creating a talent advantage over competitors at the local level, and the best talent in the field doesn't want lots of supervisors overseeing local decisions.

Too many companies routinely promote talented field employees into headquarters jobs. This is a disastrous mistake. It diminishes the talent facing the customer, slows decision making, reduces flexibility, and undermines local ownership of decisions and results. Taylor comments on his experiences in managing headquarters at Enterprise Rent-A-Car:

> There is a tendency for managers at headquarters to take things away from the field organization as we get bigger. But I have always resisted that. We should only do things in St. Louis that the branches can't even

come close to doing as well. We believe and preach that the best ideas come from the field dealing directly with customers. The real job of headquarters is to help the branches be the very best that they can be. Outside of our information technology staff, which we consider a strategic weapon, we have a very small group of people here at head-quarters. And all corporate officers have real jobs to do.[11]

With a national and regional headquarters staff of 1,500 (including technology workers) serving a total workforce of 45,000, Enterprise's productivity ratio of only 1 headquarters employee for every 30 field employees sets a benchmark of excellence. Nevertheless, Taylor keeps headquarters small. In fact, he accompanies his chief financial officer on visits to regional headquarters, which must justify the levels of overhead they take out of branch profits each year. The field's inherent skepticism about centralized spending provides a good counterbalance to the headquarters staff's inevitable tendency to increase spending each year. Taylor finds that savvy insiders who are being paid out of the profit pool provide far more effective discipline than any outside board of directors. Moreover, paying most of the headquarters staff out of the same profit pool also imposes a degree of self-restraint.

The best talent in the Enterprise system is not obsessed with the desire to move into headquarters. Employees can earn great money running their own regional business efficiently, so why move to St. Louis? Most of Enterprise's large competitors don't show such loyalty to local and regional teams. The more standard game is to find a way to get promoted to head-quarters, where there's potential for unbridled power and compensation. Usually, large companies create organizational incentives for a person to keep moving up, so the challenge to keep headquarters small and efficient is nearly impossible. Since a large central staff clogs up decision making and is inimical to speed and flexibility, most large companies need to rethink their organizational design and incentives.

STAY ALLERGIC TO HIERARCHY

High-speed, responsive companies have no patience for complicated hier-archies and soaring organizational silos. When Rich Teerlink and his Harley management team began their climb from near bankruptcy, one of their first moves was to eliminate executive vice president positions. Shortly after the management buyout, they eliminated executive perks such as front-row parking spaces. This vestige of a corporate class system has no place in the new organization, in which all employees share responsibility and account- ability for implementing change and improving results. Today, when Jeff Bleustein goes to a HOG rally, he works alongside a team of production workers and field staff, not an entourage of executive chefs and personal trainers. Similarly, when Harley decided to locate local union reps in the same office as that of the Kansas City plant manager, the company was sim- ply following the belief that hierarchy and organizational barriers get in the way of fast, flexible decision making.

Harley introduced another procedure—one more typical of a profes- sional service firm than a public company—that has broken down func- tional silos. Rather than giving the CEO sole power to appoint managers to serve on the Leadership and Strategy Committee, the committee members are elected by their peers. All twenty-four vice presidents vote for all the slots, so obviously only the leaders who show a good understanding of and sensitivity to all the functions get elected to this powerful and prestigious group. The tendency toward powerful silo mentality is greatly diminished.

Jim Ericson has busted up the silos at Northwestern Mutual. Most of his direct reports have been required to rotate jobs. It is a very challenging and humbling experience for a career investment manager to have to manage a sales force, or for the general counsel to lead human resources, among other new areas. It forces all the top leaders to expand their knowledge of the functions and teams under them and to build more effective relation- ships across traditional lines of expertise and authority. And it provides Ericson with a clearer picture of who would do the best job as his successor.

Vanguard's Jack Brennan is forever searching for ways to reduce hierar- chy and organizational barriers:

> One of the ways we beat bureaucracy is by developing as many leaders
> as possible who can take on accountability for results. We don't need to
> add extra layers to the organization when we have more talented and
> accountable leaders. Dividing into small teams has allowed us to grow
> to over nine thousand employees with only three organizational levels.[12]

One of Brennan's successful red-tape-busting programs encourages employees to identify any bureaucratic procedure that is driving them crazy. Brennan then assigns responsibility for finding a solution and gives the employee a badge of honor to stick onto his or her computer monitor. It should not be surprising that Brennan, like many other loyalty leaders, also has a fondness for cross-functional teams. He regularly gathers managers from several departments to tackle big challenges with short time fuses.

> We picked six of our best and brightest young managers and gave them the assignment [60–70 percent allocations] of creating an online environment for our customers within one year. They had five months to develop the plan, one year to get us results. We made sure they had the resources, and we made it clear that the team would dissolve when the mission was accomplished. We never would have met this goal if we had put the project inside an existing department or a division.[13]

SIMPLIFY BY SHOOTING HIGH

It probably wasn't reasonable for Brennan to request six young managers to take 70 percent of their time and get Vanguard online in less than a year. But you will see many loyalty leader executives splitting off small teams of talented young managers and then giving them breathtaking challenges with short deadlines. In fact, this strategy may be the single most important step you can take to simplify organizational focus and to create rapid and flexible responses in your own business.

Scott Cook, for example, seemed equally unreasonable when he asked one of his engineers with no general management experience and a young, seemingly underqualified M.B.A. to build Intuit into a force in the online mortgage business—in a little over a year. This team's job was to build the business from the ground up and split the group off from the existing divisional structure.

The M.B.A., a Harvard Business School Baker Scholar, had been one of Intuit's biggest recruiting coups the previous year. She had joined Intuit so that she could have an immediate impact, but had quickly become bored with her role in the larger division and had begun to look elsewhere for greater challenges. However, once freed from the bureaucratic and political decision process as well as the need to negotiate for resources from the current divisions—thanks to Cook's personal intervention to ensure that the right resources were available—she and her small team did the impossible.

They built Intuit into one of the leading providers of online mortgages in a matter of months. Not bad for a company that until 1997 was solely a producer of shrink-wrapped software products.

When a small team accepts ownership of a sufficiently challenging mission, a wonderful dynamic emerges. Everyone stops worrying about who gets credit or whether this is the perfect career step or whether personality clashes might disrupt the team. There is just no time for such petty distractions. Nothing clarifies the mind quite as well as the acceptance of the right kind of challenge, one so high and so ambitious that people have no alternative but to stave off distractions and focus only on the issues vital to its solution.

One reason that so many leveraged buyouts perform so well is that the same forces are at work. A management team seems to achieve far better results when split off as an independent entity that must survive on its own. Politicking, accounting gamesmanship, and budget sandbagging are swept aside by a simple, crystal-clear set of challenges and opportunities. Part of the adrenaline rush comes from the enormous financial upside that typical leveraged buyouts offer for successfully improving performance levels, and part comes from the pressure of eye-popping interest charges and debt repayment deadlines. Loyalty leaders achieve much of the same excitement and focus—without the need for a leveraged buyout—when they create simple, small, high-powered teams and charge them with the right kinds of challenging missions.

All teams, no matter how carefully chosen, are rife with the potential for politicking and infighting. One benefit of providing a major-league challenge is that the team must minimize any such misdirected time and energy. Just as political leaders have been known to embrace conflict with a foreign rival in order to unite warring factions within their own borders, loyalty leaders understand the benefit of focusing their people on an external threat or challenge. Sometimes the focal point of the threat is a competitor, but outstanding firms eventually outpace most competitors and require further, more worthy challenges to keep their energies channeled productively. Great leaders don't rely on building contempt for the competition. Rather, they ensure that their teams set such challenging goals for delivering value to customers and partners that all energy must go toward meeting these important targets.

The axiom of loyalty leaders is to keep it simple, because they know that loyalty depends on simplicity and that simplicity does not come naturally in most human organizations. So they constantly reaffirm the company's simple values and operating principles. They obliterate hierarchy. They break teams into small units with local leadership and direct accountability. They initiate simple, breathtaking challenges that concentrate minds, focus energy, and inspire their people to achieve more than they ever dreamed possible. Thoreau's nineteenth-century Walden Pond venue bore little resemblance to today's high-tech corporate world, but his exhortation to "Simplify, simplify" still rings true. This is your simple challenge.

ACTION CHECKLIST

- **Examine Loyalty Acid Test scores**
  Compare your results with those of the loyalty leaders for the following statements: *We keep organizational structure simple by utilizing small teams,* and *I understand the values and principles that guide company leadership.*
- **Create a golden rule for your firm**
  To help your employees make quick, wise, independent decisions, identify a simple goal or guideline to drive all decisions. Ensure that everyone understands this rule: Incorporate it in training, reward those who follow it, and explain how critical decisions support it. Encourage questions and challenges from your partners any time they don't see how certain actions square with your golden rule.
- **Obliterate hierarchy**
  Reduce the number of levels in your organization to no more than three or four. Abolish hierarchical distinctions that are inimical to broad-based accountability and responsibility for results. Get rid of executive privileges like private dining rooms, front-row parking, and executive rest rooms.
- **Break down silos**
  Put the best young talent on cross-functional, mission-specific teams. Give these teams very challenging targets, short deadlines, and appropriate rewards. Rotate and reposition your talented, experienced employees so that they are less inclined to become stale or to rely on their organizational power instead of their ability to get results.
- **Cut incentives that reward leaders for the size and power of their departments**
  Reward leaders throughout the company for promoting candidates to positions outside their chain of command. Make sure that none of your rewards encourage growing department size.

- **Ensure that headquarters staff grows at a slower rate than field staff**
  Compare your ratio of headquarters to field personnel, and develop a plan to become the best in your industry. If you are already the best, then shoot for beating Enterprise's ratio of 1 to 30. Insist that overhead managers justify expenses to field executives, not simply to corporate executives. Let field executives vote on budgets.
- **Pare down functions to only those in which you can be the best in the business**
  Outsource all nonstrategic functions to a best-in-class partner, and keep the number of outsource partners to the absolute minimum.
- **Form small teams with clear, simple responsibilities**
  Determine the ideal team size, then analyze how many teams exceed this ideal. Develop a standard process for dividing all teams that exceed this target. Place the burden of proof for not subdividing on the large team.
- **Split off separate businesses early**
  Simplify your focus and accounting by assigning new business opportunities to separate, independent teams. Provide small teams with the necessary resources, and then hold them accountable for results.

6

Reward the Right Results

■

Worthy Partners Deserve Worthy Goals

Align performance targets so that partners reach for the stars—not into each other's pockets. Share value generously with partners responsible for its creation. Help everyone stretch to his or her full potential, taking special care that star performers are rewarded with additional opportunity to grow and develop. Let no one confuse value with profits, nor loyalty with obedience and tenure.

Most companies are shooting themselves in both feet with their rewards systems. They pay on results that are easy to measure rather than on the right results. Incentives are misaligned, so individual interests trump team goals. Distinctions between profits and value are muddled, so grabbing value and creating value are rewarded equally. Worst of all, employees and customers are not rewarded for loyalty; in fact, loyalty is often penalized. High rates of defection are the norm for star performers since few firms provide sufficient growth opportunity or financial incentive. Ambitious employees conclude that the best way to get ahead is to defect to another company. "Loyal" employees are perceived as lazy, satisfied with modest compensation, and content to aim far below their full potential.

Most of today's corporate rewards systems are philosophically antithetical to the principles and practices of loyalty leaders. Most systems are designed to be reasonable and, therefore, easy to justify to the board of directors or to an outside auditor. But the problem is that loyalty is not generated by *reasonable* performance; it is generated by *overachievement*—and this level of performance requires outstanding teamwork by partners who trust one another's commitment to win/win results. Today's compensation schemes rarely align partner interests; they create zero-sum games in which one player can win only at another's expense.

Chapter 5 underscored the need for a simple and stable system for keeping score and for distributing rewards, but you don't earn the right to keep any system simple and stable until you get it right. Consider the reward systems crafted by our model companies to reward loyalty appropriately and to help all partners reach for the stars. Then examine your own system. Ask what you must change to attract and retain the kind of partners your organization needs to grow and prosper.

MEASURE THE RIGHT THINGS

Your partners are smart enough to know that anything you truly care about, you measure. What you decide to measure clearly reflects your values and your priorities. You can talk all you want about creating value, building loyal relationships, and putting customer interests first, but if the vast majority of your scorekeeping efforts go to measuring profits, then your customers and other partners will get the unspoken message. To show them that loyalty is at the top of your leadership agenda, make sure that your central metrics gauge the value you are creating for all your customers and partners. Measure the health of key relationships and the level of loyalty you are earning. Only by tracking the full dimensions of performance can you bust the myth that the purpose of business is merely profits.

Clarify the Difference between Value and Profit

Even from the point of view of investors, it is too simplistic to claim that the sole purpose of any business is to generate profits. Accounting systems that focus only on profits blatantly ignore another equally important factor that drives investor value: the cost of the capital that is implicitly being borrowed from them, as investors, for the company to operate and grow the business. Many businesses today book huge accounting profits and pay fat bonuses to executives. But many of these same companies are creating little if any real value for their investors because their profits, though substantial in absolute dollars, are extremely modest in proportion to the investor capital employed by the business. When profits don't provide a reasonable return on equity, investors would be much better off putting their money into an index fund. For this reason, if leaders truly care about creating value for their long-term investors, they must incorporate into their calculations a reasonable interest charge for their use of equity capital. Profits in excess of this hurdle rate can then be considered to have created investor value.

Some academics and consultants have devised a complicated solution to this basically simple problem. They have calculated a sophisticated, risk-adjusted cost of equity for every business line, and then subtracted the implied costs from profits. Some even go a step further and presume that the most recent period's result will be perpetuated in the future, and they calculate the implied "market value-added." Wall Street analysts love this approach, as do the consultants who spend thousands of billable hours recalculating your internal financials, allocating equity to each product line, training your employees in sophisticated financial theory, and realigning your management incentive schemes.

Loyalty leaders prefer simplicity. Putting so much effort into refining the measurement of value creation for the investor can only send out the wrong signal and misrepresent their priorities, so they skip the complicated calculations and simply charge a reasonable interest rate for any cash used by each business team. At Enterprise Rent-A-Car this interest cost is included in the calculation of branch profits. At Chick-fil-A, real estate and equipment charges capture the preponderance of capital costs in the calculation of store profits. At Dell Computer, each business team is ranked on its return on invested capital. Clearly, value is created for investors only when their rate of return exceeds some base rate of interest for the use of their money. Any bonus pool to be shared by you and your employees should be funded only with this excess return, not with total profits. This idea is really not very complicated since everybody understands the need for some base rate of return for money invested. Find the simplest way possible to incorporate this basic cost of doing business into your accounting, and then get on to the tougher measurement challenges.

The most challenging scorekeeping issues for most businesses are not related to investor value, but to the measurement of value creation for customers. And many loyalty leaders have developed a clear metric for customer value. Northwestern Mutual, for example, compares the real costs and rates of return for policyholders with similar data for policyholders at the competition. This is a fundamental metric of success for Jim Ericson's organization and a source of immense pride as Northwestern dominates its competitors year after year. The organization understands how its superiority in delivering customer value translates into a customer retention advantage, which drives the company's growth, lowers its costs, and fuels its compensation opportunities.

Measure Retention—Carefully

Ericson is not content with merely keeping score of today's standard dimensions of customer value. He understands that customer value is a constantly shifting concept as competitors' capabilities and customer needs evolve. So he insists that the organization take the ultimate step and keep score of customer retention, the most accurate gauge of whether the company is truly delivering the best value to its customers. Ericson's leadership team has developed rigorous systems for tracking customer retention rates, differentiating between various customer segments such as new and mature customers. Through routine surveys, Northwestern also develops a clear picture of its market share for each individual customer (share of wallet).

Corporate leadership at the *New York Times* provides another good case in point. Executives at the *Times* track retention in three separate buckets: new subscribers (have subscribed for less than twelve months), middle-aged (thirteen to twenty-four months), and mature (longer than twenty-four months). Even though the paper's 94 percent retention of mature subscribers is by far the best in the business, the *Times* wants to continue improving performance in all areas. Scott Heekin-Canedy, senior vice president of circulation, comments:

> We've been using subscriber retention as our measure of success for a variety of improvement programs, including service quality initiatives and a more focused subscriber acquisition marketing effort. Measuring new subscriber retention is how we judge our acquisition efforts, while mature subscribers are a better gauge for many of our service initiatives.[1]

The New York Times Company management team evidently does not consider its stellar 94 percent retention rate a sufficiently worthy target, even though the average retention rate in the newspaper business is in the range of 60 percent and the closest competitor hovers just above 80 percent. The paper continues to invest aggressively in Web pages and other Internet-based customer services and in improved home delivery service in markets across the country. The *Times* is intent on being better than the best.

Build a Better Dashboard

Loyalty leaders must customize the right kind of dashboard for steering their company up the high road. Standard accounting metrics such as profits must be supplemented with gauges that monitor the creation of partner value and, what is even more important, customer value. With the growth of the Internet, increasing numbers of companies are capable of tracking individual customer purchases—not just retention rates, but average purchase size, frequency of purchases, and the like. Even so, my consulting work at Bain & Company, as well as the many surveys that I conducted in conjunction with keynote speeches and executive seminars, reveals that fewer than 20 percent of leaders rigorously track customer retention, even in industries for which these measurements are already feasible.

Although this statistic is a discouraging comment on the general culture of the business world, it also flags a golden opportunity for you and your firm. As a champion of the principles of loyalty, you can quickly outdistance the other 80 percent if you get serious about monitoring how well your organization is delivering customer value. Paul Bell, senior vice president at Dell Computer and a member of its Customer Experience Council, concurs: "Every public company tells shareholders how it's doing every quarter, but few companies have a set of metrics that measure the customer experience from month to month, quarter to quarter."[2]

For some industries, such as newspaper publishing, mutual funds, and life insurance, measures of customer retention are straightforward and relatively easy. The greater challenge awaits those companies—yours may be one of them—for which retention is equally critical but measurements are more elusive. Even when purchase cycles are irregular (auto rentals) or when individual customer purchases are difficult to track (fast-food restaurants), there are still important scorekeeping lessons to be learned from loyalty leaders. For most companies, customer value is determined through a complex formula that incorporates such factors as relative price, service, quality, reliability, and convenience. The trick is to home in on the relatively few dimensions of performance that truly matter to your target customers, and then to track performance with the same rigor that most companies apply to their profit statements.

The Dell leadership team has developed a customer dashboard that focuses on the three key dimensions of the company's customer experience: order fulfillment, product performance, and service support. The team picked what it considered the best summary statistic to represent each dimension. For order fulfillment, it chose "ship to target," which captures the percentage of orders delivered to the customer on time with complete accuracy. For product performance, it selected "initial field-incident rate," which measures the frequency of product problems encountered by customers. For service support, it singled out "on-time, first-time fix," which measures the percentage of problems fixed on the first visit of a service rep who arrives when promised. There are, of course, many other dimensions that Dell tracks in order to sort out problems, root causes, and solutions, but by focusing on these three summary measures, it has targeted and met goals for improvement in excess of 15 percent per year in every one.

Another favorite customer metric of loyalty leaders is the calculation of lifetime ownership cost. For this calculation, Dell includes all the costs—both those fees paid to Dell as well as any others incurred by the customer—involved in shopping for, ordering, installing, operating, servicing, and disposing of computers. By keeping score on this vital aspect of customer value, Dell management has been able to prioritize investment projects. The DellAuction site, where customers can receive full residual value for their equipment, is an excellent example of a mechanism that improves the lifetime cost of ownership.

Lexus also considers lifetime ownership costs an important element of its performance dashboard. Members of the Lexus management team work hard to keep residual values high for used Lexus cars. Foremost, they have always insisted on the highest quality design and avoided high-fashion components that might quickly become devalued in the next wave of auto fads. Next, they developed the Certified Pre-owned Auto Program so that used Lexus autos could be reconditioned by the dealers and guaranteed by the manufacturer for up to 100,000 miles of operation. This program has boosted residual values of used Lexus autos and thereby has reduced the actual cost of ownership for the customer. Toyota, the parent company of Lexus, has long known the importance of superior lifetime ownership in creating customer value and loyalty. In fact, Toyota's scorekeeping metrics have given the firm a significant advantage over other car manufacturers, which are just beginning to get the message.

Historically, most car companies have focused their scorekeeping on traditional profit metrics. They have given superficial attention to customer loyalty by measuring satisfaction scores, though these satisfaction metrics have hardly been central to their decision-making process if the experience of the auto critic at the *Boston Globe* is typical. The *Globe* writer discovered that the remote control of his keyless entry system failed to open the lock. When he took the problem to his local dealership, he duly noted the banner over the door boldly proclaiming "Customer Satisfaction Is Job #1." The bad news from the parts desk was that the device could not be repaired and a replacement would cost $100. Skeptical that there was no other recourse, he visited the local Radio Shack for a second opinion. In a matter of minutes, a helpful clerk took out his penknife, pried open the plastic case, replaced the batteries, and recommended sealing the seam with a little rubber cement in case it ever got wet. The grand total for the parts and advice: $4.95. Mr. Critic was very satisfied with Radio Shack—and very satisfied that he could wreak his revenge on the car dealer in a story for the *Sunday Globe's* half million readers.

The lesson is clear. Any company that designs products and pays incentives that undermine customer loyalty is not going to improve retention through a customer satisfaction campaign. The engineers who designed the keyless entry would have included a resealable gasket and provided instructions for simple, inexpensive battery replacement if serving the customer's lifetime needs had been their priority. The dealer's parts department could have sent the customer to Radio Shack but instead tried to maximize commissions. Automobile manufacturers don't need more satisfaction surveys; they need to fix their deeply flawed network of relationships and rewards. Their atrocious defection rates (averaging over 50 percent for new-car purchases) should provide a wake-up call. Furthermore, 70 to 80 percent of post-warranty service is performed by mechanics not associated with the dealership where the car was purchased. For loyalty, it is not only how satisfied you keep your customers, but how many satisfied customers you keep.

ALIGN INCENTIVES

Once you have designed the right gauges for your dashboard, the next step is to make sure the gauges correctly influence the route your organization takes. The essential problem in the preceding story was not the way the automobile manufacturer tracked customer satisfaction; the problem was that leaders did not link this gauge to their driving strategy. Gauges will have the correct influence only when incentives are consistently aligned across the network of partners. Then everyone will seek out win/win solutions and concentrate on improving customer value.

Typically, companies' efforts to improve rewards systems are limited to realigning the incentives of senior managers with those of investors. Of course it is always laudable to improve the alignment of interests of any partners within a company—and many of the profit-sharing, stock purchase, and stock-option programs being introduced today are steps in the right direction—but aligning the interests of employees with investors is relatively uncomplicated. Loyalty leaders take an equally simple yet more comprehensive approach to aligning investor interests with the interests of other partners, and especially with customers. Keep in mind, however, that the greatest challenge for any leader is to align everybody's incentives in a way that resolves the tension between short-term profits and long-term value creation.

Reward Value Creation, Not Value Grabbing

Some executives dismiss the Taylor family philosophy at Enterprise Rent-A-Car—"Put customers first and employees second, and profit will take care of itself"—as disingenuous or naive, but they obviously don't understand that a fundamental component of the Enterprise formula is to pay employees a share of the profits they help generate. With this reward system, profits do tend to take care of themselves. But Jack and Andy Taylor have learned that paying on profits alone is not wise, because some employees will take shortcuts that boost current earnings but diminish the assets needed to boost future profits. Pure profit incentives need to be balanced with incentives to build long-term assets such as customer and employee loyalty.

Andy Taylor became concerned that some Enterprise customers and employees were being shortchanged by overly zealous branch managers who were maximizing short-term profits instead of focusing on customer service. Taylor's first step was to develop a reliable gauge for customer service, which evolved into ESQI, the Enterprise Service Quality Index. Each month, sample customers from every branch are surveyed by phone and asked to rate their rental experience and their intentions to use Enterprise again. With only two questions on the survey, response rates are high and results quickly available. Branch scores are posted electronically within two weeks of month's end.

It took more than creating and fine-tuning this gauge to have the desired effect, however. Leaders also trumpeted the value of customer loyalty, demonstrating that customers who are completely satisfied express an 85 percent likelihood of returning. Next, branch profit statements were redesigned so that ESQI was listed right alongside branch profitability on all the management reports. ESQI was highlighted at management meetings and business review sessions. But one vital step remained. The Enterprise leadership team adopted the policy that no employee would be promoted if his or her branch had below-average ESQI scores, and the leaders formalized the four criteria used to rank all promotion candidates: (1) branch ESQI score, (2) branch growth, (3) branch profitability, and (4) the number of promotable management candidates developed at the branch.

By incorporating customer satisfaction and employee development into the manager promotion process, Enterprise improved the alignment of interests across several partner groups. Branch managers eager to reap the substantial rewards of promotion to area and regional offices know they must not only grow a profitable branch, but also vault their branch into the top tier of customer satisfaction and attract employees who will grow into managers. The compensation system remains simple. Managers get a share of the real cash generated by branch profits, but their financial future is linked to development of both customer and employee assets for the company.

This effort to align profit incentives more directly with customer and employee interests did not bubble up from the bottom of the organization or from a staff group assigned to measure satisfaction. It happened because Jack and Andy Taylor and their most senior executives took the lead. Their perspective as long-term owners and their organizational clout were essential to success. Very few companies will manage to improve the alignment of partner interests simply by assigning a staff group to build more gauges for the dashboard, yet this is precisely what most do. The key is not more gauges, but better, more relevant gauges that link directly to compensation and promotion systems.

CEO Jack Brennan played a central role when rewards at The Vanguard Group were realigned in 1993. Since scorekeeping at Vanguard is primarily focused on the returns earned by its customers relative to returns earned by its competitors' customers, if Vanguard's customers don't win better returns, then Vanguard's employees don't win. Brennan designed this bonus system when he saw that employee efforts to continue to reduce costs and work harder were flagging. Disgruntled employees, feeling over-worked and underpaid, claimed that Vanguard's strikingly low costs had come at their expense. Today, customers essentially share a portion of their excess return with the employees who helped create it, and at the same time employees are motivated to create even more. This Partnership Plan has aligned the interests of every Vanguard employee with those of customers. Each employee's share in the pool of excess value is based on his or her own performance and number of years with the firm; the average payout has been 20 percent of base pay and can occasionally rise as high as 40 percent for longtime employees. Vanguard's base pay levels are adjusted by geo-graphic region, so by delivering superior value to customers, employees earn 20 to 40 percent above market. And remarkably, Vanguard continues to operate at cost levels only a fraction of those at the competition. When leaders correctly align the interests of their employees and their customers, they can be exceedingly generous while still keeping costs low.

Despite these impressive results, such well-aligned rewards systems are threatening to many executives because they contradict the basic paradigm underlying conventional thinking. Since most executives want to be con-sidered responsible and cost-conscious managers, they feel obliged to keep a lid on compensation. But clearly Vanguard, Enterprise, and many other loyalty-based firms show enormous cost advantages even while they com-pensate their people well beyond market rates. Take heed of this paradox. Your current system of rewards has quite likely been developed on the flawed paradigm and needs serious realignment if you want to build loyal relationships. Remember that both productivity and loyalty grow whenever there is opportunity for greater rewards. And whenever your employees create exceptional value for your customers and for your other partners, they deserve exceptional rewards.

Fix the Misalignments

There are far too many examples of employee interests in conflict with cus-tomer interests: The car salesperson's commission is based on how much he or she can gouge the customer; the stockbroker's commission is paid whenever a customer churns holdings; the claims representative's reward is for minimizing reimbursements. Even inside the great loyalty companies, there are sources of misalignment, but they are soon corrected.

At USAA the scorekeeping system once went awry and emphasized metrics that were not in the customers' best interest. Always sticklers for top-quality service, the managers had invested in a device to measure the average wait experienced by customers calling in to the phone teams. A digital scoreboard mounted high above the office cubicles tracked this statistic for each team and even spurred employees to run back from the washroom or from lunch when the wait got too long. Phone reps endeavored to shorten their calls any time the digital readouts began to climb. But eventually it became clear that something was wrong. Phone reps began focusing more on getting their customers off the line quickly—even when their questions weren't completely resolved—than on providing the best possible service. Even worse, the service rep dealing with, say, a customer who had just suffered the accidental death of a spouse could feel considerable pressure although the next call in the queue might be only a change of address.

When Bob Herres and his leadership team realized the potential effect of this inherent problem in their system, they moved quickly to stop tracking the wrong measures. They took down the digital signs and assigned a team to determine what the right measure should be. That measure, the far better criterion for level of service, is the percentage of customers who complete their business on the first call, with no need for follow-up. By minimizing callbacks, errors, and miscommunications, this metric has enhanced productivity and improved customer satisfaction. Most important, the use of this metric has motivated the phone reps, who know that it is a useful measure. Because the new measurement connects to real customer value, the phone reps feel more committed to provide world-class levels of performance.

Herres applies the same kind of rigorous scrutiny and standards to the evaluation process for USAA's executive team and for himself. He has always believed that customer retention rates are the best measure of the firm's success in delivering the best value to its customers, yet the board of directors had only traditional, profit-based measures to judge the executive team. Today that system has changed, and the most important metric used for executive performance is customer retention. To get board approval now, budgets must contain a presumed level of excellence in customer retention, and when executive bonus levels are determined, it is customer retention that provides a heavily weighted gauge of performance. No wonder USAA enjoys one of the highest customer retention rates in the world.

A further sampling of the numerous techniques utilized by loyalty leaders to align incentives and rewards may suggest improvements for your own system.

- **Cisco:** At least 20 percent of employee bonuses is driven by performance on customer satisfaction scores. Targets are raised each year and widely published, so everyone knows that to win individually, and for the company to win, the customers must be well served.

- **MBNA:** The results of customer-oriented performance metrics are posted daily outside the company cafeterias, and employee bonuses are funded every day that 90 percent or more of the targets are hit. Cooperation across departments is legendary. Employees know that their bonus is tied to more than the efforts of their own department; at least 90 percent of the departments must meet their goals.

- **Lexus:** One of the most successful Lexus dealers decided to hold back a portion of the sales commission until the customer came in for a first service visit. Not only did the sales force ensure that customers were appropriately introduced to the service department, they even helped schedule visits for customers who did not respond to the computer-generated "time for your checkup" postcards.

- **State Farm:** By avoiding the front-load sales commissions typical of the insurance industry, State Farm ensures that its agents will care more about keeping customers and selling to the right kind of new customers.

- **Mary Kay:** This cosmetics firm pays its agents an ongoing commission on the sales of everyone they recruit. This incentive not only encourages aggressive hiring, it also focuses on hiring the kind of people who will be happy and succeed. The incentive also encourages partners to invest in each other's success.

Straightening Teeth and Rewards the Reichheld Way

No matter what the size of your business, you will likely have some opportunity to improve the alignment of customer and employee interests. These principles can benefit even small-scale operations, such as the one of an orthodontist with the unlikely name of Reichheld, *John* Reichheld. Although in the 1970s, I did not know of John Reichheld or, for that matter, any other branch of the Reichheld family in the United States, I noticed a sign for Dr. Reichheld, Orthodontist, posted next to the Boston restaurant where Karen and I had our wedding rehearsal dinner. Twenty years later we found John, as well as several other Reichhelds, on Cape Cod and finally got in touch.

By the time we met, John Reichheld had built a successful practice with multiple offices. He had also read *The Loyalty Effect* and was already intellectually—if not genetically—predisposed toward loyalty. He recounted how he had struggled through some very lean years, when fluoride and the aging of the population challenged orthodontist practices in the 1980s, and he credited his survival in large part to a timely restructuring of his system of rewards. Reichheld had learned that administrative salaries in a typical office—for secretaries, hygienists, and dental assistants—ran about 30 percent of total revenues. Continuing to pay in the traditional way would have led to cutbacks and layoffs, so he struck a deal with his administrative team, which agreed to split 30 percent of whatever office revenues were generated.

The change was dramatic. Instead of griping about being overworked, staff members found ways to get more work done with no increase in the number of employees. Customers received superior service, so customer referrals skyrocketed. Dental assistants and secretaries had business cards printed up and marketed the practice at PTA meetings, supermarkets, and churches. The administrative teams became much more discriminating about new hires, recruiting only top-quality candidates who could help boost productivity rather than anyone who might absorb some of the workload.

The business grew, unlike other practices nearby; his people were happy; the doctors who led each office pocketed more money; and with his equity as the owner of these practices, Dr. Reichheld bought a grand vacation home on the ocean. When frontline employees are paid not for their hours but for generating customer demand and serving it profitably, their jobs are enriched and the entire network of partners can prosper. Incidentally, Dr. Reichheld did protect his long-term employees whenever revenues stumbled by paying them a base amount, but only rarely did such a circumstance arise.

REACH FOR THE STARS

Most reward systems today are far too generous to mediocrity and far too stingy in rewarding superior performance. They set reasonable performance goals and define minimum levels for acceptable performance. As a leader, you can't establish minimum performance standards for your organization. Minimum performance standards are created *for* you by your customers, your competitors, and, if you let them, your superstar performers. Your stars will be the most intolerant of mediocrity because it drags down team results and is unworthy of their commitment. Moreover, it is the people out on the front lines who are in the best position to judge true standards of excellence as they observe customer reactions. The right targets evolve and shift far more quickly than any top-down goal-setting system can anticipate.

Forget the Floors, Get Rid of the Ceilings

Think of the countless hours being wasted in the negotiation of budgets and performance thresholds to determine bonus payouts that range from you-get-to-keep-your-job all the way to maximum payout. Think of all the organizational creativity and energy spent convincing bosses, owners, and partners that targets should be set low enough so that the vast majority of people will hit them. In the process, employees sandbag both their bosses (and investor/owners) and themselves. There is a little Malthusian pessimism in all of us, ready to prove how little progress is really possible. The budget-setting process at most companies fans this pessimism and focuses employees on the seemingly insurmountable barriers and challenges to achieving outstanding growth and profits.

Loyalty leaders consider this whole process not only destructive to the creation of economic value but also destructive to the human spirit. Encouraging people to aim below their fullest potential is no favor to anyone, yet most rewards systems do precisely this. They encourage everyone to keep a little buffer in reserve since maximizing performance now will only serve to ratchet up the budget floor later. Wise leaders have learned that their job is to help their people aspire to goals higher than ever believed possible, not to squirrel away performance-boosting possibilities. It doesn't take a genius to figure out minimum performance standards. Loyalty leaders don't waste their time on floors. Andy Taylor pays people according to the real profits they generate, not some predetermined budget. There is no ceiling on how much they can earn. The result: Enterprise has the highest compensation in the industry, along with the highest productivity and the lowest costs.

So how can you inspire your people to shoot for higher goals? Successful leaders have found that browbeating and threats don't work—at least not for very long. A better approach is to inspire employees to shoot for world-class performance targets by surrounding them with other employees with similar ambitions. Home Depot's program for Olympic athletes provides job opportunities with flexible hours to accommodate their training. Since 1994, the company has had more than 200 Olympic hopefuls working in the stores and stands out as the leader in the U.S. Olympic Games jobs program. Of course, the company receives some public-relations benefits for its support of the Olympics, and for its employees' success (fifty medals, including twenty-five gold). But the bigger benefit comes from the coworkers' exposure to the world-class standards and dedication embodied in their athlete colleagues.

Sometimes the key is simply to expose your employees to the true standards of excellence achieved by your competition. When management needed to lead the Harley-Davidson organization away from the brink of bankruptcy, it didn't commission a consulting study or market research to inform headquarters executives about the quality and performance goals that the troops had to meet to take back share from the Japanese. Instead, management sent production employees and frontline staff into the field to learn firsthand why customers preferred competitors' bikes. And the staff visited top-quality manufacturers so that they could see what kind of targets they needed to match to become competitive.

Now it is Jeff Bleustein's job to inspire his successful Harley team to shoot for the stars. Bleustein's challenge, one shared with leaders of any high-performance business, is to find ways to stave off the arrogance and complacency that eventually overtake so many successful organizations. One of his most powerful tools is simply to ensure that every Harley team gets to compare its performance to historic standards and improvement objectives. He knows that it is human nature for teams to contrast their results with all the others teams. Superior performers will always find ways to raise standards of excellence.

Loyalty leaders don't waste their time on minimum performance standards;

they do everything in their power to help their people accomplish astonishing levels of performance. Consider these examples:

- Enterprise's intranet provides instant access to every branch's performance. Chick-fil-A's internal computer system does precisely the same thing. Both companies celebrate major accomplishments and make the best case studies available to everyone in the organization so everyone can apply the lessons of success to his or her own situation.

- Charlie Cawley at MBNA encourages his people to learn more about the best companies in the world, knowing that the MBNA employees will try to match that performance and then go one step better. He doesn't try to set performance goals top-down. Instead, he asks his managers what level of performance would make them proud.

- Vanguard's Jack Brennan encourages people to establish their own goals, and he is regularly shocked at the audacious targets they set. "My team in data processing recently instituted a new set of systems to handle customer transactions. Rather than focusing on the competition, or even on our own best stretches of performance, the team decided to target cutting the error rate in half every year. And they are doing it!"[3]

- Chick-fil-A holds annual seminars attended by all its operators in which "Symbols of Success" awards are presented to operators who grow sales up to 30 percent (versus the industry standard of 5 to 10 percent growth). In 1998, for example, 91 of the 536 Chick-fil-A store operators received the coveted award, a new Mercury or Ford that they drive for the next year at Chick-fil-A's expense. Symbols of Success operators who win two years in a row are presented with the permanent title to the car. In 1998, thirteen car titles changed hands.

Don't Confuse Loyalty with Tenure

Low base pay is a just as important a strategy as high average compensation in most loyalty leaders' companies. The base has to be low enough so that very few people who are not generating superior results for customers and other partners will want to stay unless they are very confident that they can build their success over the years. Otherwise, leaders run the risk that employees will mistake tenure for loyalty and think they get paid just for showing up. They will begin to believe that they are entitled to a job at an attractive wage just because they have stayed with the company for a long time—irrespective of whether they are creating value for customers and partners. Loyalty demands a two-way street; employees must hold up their end of the bargain by finding ways to contribute to the creation of real value. There is nothing loyal about retaining an employee who can't contribute beyond the cost of his or her salary and benefits. Such a retention policy doesn't treat employees with the dignity and respect they deserve. It pulls them off the path to their full potential and is unfair to the rest of the employee team, whose performance is weighted down with deadwood.

Enterprise Rent-A-Car avoids this situation by guaranteeing managers a base salary of no more than $35,000. Managers must earn every dollar of bonus by serving customers and partners successfully. For typical managers who have been with the firm six or seven years, the base pay is a small fraction of total compensation, so their focus on generating value and profits is unrelenting. At Vanguard the compensation of frontline employees will plunge by 20 to 40 percent if the firm fails to deliver better value to its customers than does the competition; for senior executives, compensation will fall to a fraction of current levels. No wonder Vanguard teams are so responsive to changes in the marketplace.

Contrast these loyalty-based rewards systems with the typical system in corporations today, under which managers—from CEOs on down—continue to be well compensated whether or not they create real value for customers and other partners. At the same time, these corporations usually limit the upside of the rank-and-file bonuses to protect themselves from investors' accusations of sloppy cost management. What this system really ensures is that the star performers will be encouraged to defect while the deadwood continues to decay at the company's expense.

Help Your Stars Shine

You can try to find less costly ways to hold on to your star performers than by letting them earn thousands of dollars without putting up a dime of risk equity. Don't kid yourself. The truism that you get what you pay for is equally valid for employee compensation—though not all compensation is monetary. Andy Taylor never cuts back on his basic deal with star performers, despite the astoundingly high paychecks some receive, because he feels they have earned their compensation, and indeed they have. He knows that his top performers are the people who can lead the company to future growth and success—precisely the people whose loyalty he needs most. He has grown the organization and invested in new business opportunities in part to ensure that the stars see plenty of potential for growth and development. Many of his best people will want to run their own business, so Taylor does his best to ensure that those businesses are in the Enterprise federation of partnerships.

Similarly, Chick-fil-A tries to accommodate its star performers, even allowing a few of the best operators to take on a second store when the original unit has no more opportunity for growth. Of course, if the star operators can't sustain strong results, not just in profits but in customer satisfaction scores, then they must cut back to a single store. But the company works hard to promote their success. For example, when the company enters into a concession arrangement with a local college, airport, or hospital, instead of hiring a headquarters staff member to oversee the operation, Chick-fil-A awards a consulting contract to the best local operator, who is then paid a royalty of 15 percent on concession revenues. Chick-fil-A's college, airport, and hospital locations regularly outperform the competition largely because their interests are aligned with a star performer who knows the area and has a vested interest in the new location's success. The company wins, and its star performer store operators continue to grow and learn—while earning annual compensation that can exceed $300,000 per year.

Retaining and motivating your stars means offering them the opportunity to earn outstanding compensation. In the long run, however, it is not the money alone that keeps most of them motivated. Huge compensation can even have the opposite effect and encourage premature retirements. The real incentive is the gratification that comes from using their gifts to their fullest potential and from creating truly extraordinary value for their customers and partners.

The stars stay because they have been given the opportunity to build something of significance and because their team members have come to depend on them. They stay because they can continue to learn, to grow, and to have greater and greater impact. That's why Harley-Davidson will reimburse four years of college tuition for its workers. USAA has a similarly generous program for investing in any of its people who are motivated to grow and develop. This emphasis on personal growth may make the weaker players in your organization uncomfortable. But if you align the financial interests of the stars with those of the rest of the team, as loyalty leaders do, you can achieve the best of both worlds. Any resentment toward those rate-busting stars is quickly diminished when the team gets to share in a portion of the value it creates.

The Dark Side of Stock Options

Lots of companies now endeavor to retain their stars by offering them stock options, often with vesting periods of several years. Given today's accounting rules and tax laws, options are a very efficient way for public companies to align the interests of employees with those of shareholders. Many firms, however, are falling into dangerous options traps. First, they award options with strike prices so low that mediocre performance is too generously rewarded. Five-year options issued at today's stock market price should be in the money even if the share price rises at only a fraction of the broader market rate of appreciation—a rate of return that would represent a failing grade in terms of true value creation. Historically, investors put money in stocks only when they expect an inflation-adjusted return of 7 to 8 percent. It seems clear, then, that strike prices would need to exceed this minimal rate before any option value is created. Why pay bonuses to managers when the investors would have been better off invested in a stock index fund? If you do use options, be sure that share price appreciation targets are sufficiently demanding. Only then are interests truly aligned.

Then there is the opposite side of the coin. When stock market price/earnings multiples ramp up across the board, a manager usually can do little to avoid market corrections that wipe out the value of options issued at such peaks. Or sometimes the overall market is not priced too high, but the market simply prices a company's stock too optimistically, presuming that enhanced performance will extend into the future even if the partners who created it decide to leave. If you create such wealthy employees that they leave to practice Zen in Tahiti or to do charitable work in the nonprofit sector, then you had better be in a business in which you don't need your best people to build a successful future. The cutthroat competition and rapid changes facing most businesses today, however, signal a desperate need for the ongoing commitment, enthusiasm, and dedication of those same managers whose options have made them rich. Make sure that you are not mortgaging your future and that in the years ahead you can afford to offer prospective stars equally outstanding opportunity and to up the ante for your existing stars who remain loyally productive.

Many loyalty leaders who use options face other potential liabilities. In periods like 1998, when stock prices soar, Dell must deal with the likelihood that some of its Dellionaires will prefer golfing or boating to staying on the front lines to create ever more value for the firm's demanding customers and partners. And in those periods like 1999–2000, when Dell's stock dropped by almost 70 percent despite a broad consensus that the company remained the healthiest of the personal computer manufacturers, stock options don't do much for team motivation.

Meg Whitman at eBay certainly appreciates the role that stock options can play in the war for talent, but she warns, "If you let stock options become the center of gravity for employee loyalty, you are headed for trouble."[4] She has seen firsthand how stock market gyrations can swing employees' net worth and distract them from their daily responsibilities. For this reason, she regularly reminds her colleagues of the more fundamental elements—such as pride in what they can accomplish and in how they treat partners and one another—that must become the foundation of employee retention.

Several privately owned, loyalty-based companies have developed rewards structures that seem to work even better than options. These plans allow employees to share in any excess cash they help generate—but only for as long as they are playing an important role in generating it. For example, the strongest executives at Enterprise Rent-A-Car have the greatest incentives to stay on board and to ensure that the outstanding profit stream they have built remains healthy and vibrant. Their bonus is based on the actual profits realized under their leadership, not on a hypothetical perpetuity that capitalizes these estimated flows into the future.

State Farm's agents don't sell their customer books back to the company at some enormous multiple of earnings; the books belong to the company. The real incentive is the strong sense of fulfillment that comes from working with the best company in the business—a company structured as a network of mutually beneficial relationships and dedicated to high-road principles. In any service business that relies on the intellectual capital of its employees, it is a mistake to reward them in any way that diminishes their commitment to building an even better future.

Focus on the Front Line

Most companies' efforts to align rewards systems focus on senior management teams. In some ways these systems are the easiest to change since the relatively few people affected are already used to having performance-based bonuses account for a large portion of their total compensation. Yet when you study the loyalty leaders, you usually find that the most radical departures from the norm involve restructuring frontline rewards. The front line is where your customer's experience can be most dramatically affected. And in most firms, it is frontline compensation that seems to have drifted furthest from the basic partnership structures that share excess value.

There are plenty of historical precedents for paying people the right way. For example, on the old New England whaling ships, officers and crew signed on knowing that food and lodging would be provided but that the real compensation would be a prearranged percentage of the gross revenues earned by the voyage. Somewhere along the line, however, companies shifted to paying by the hour rather than by results. One of the worst business decisions ever made, it has continually eroded the potential for real partnership with frontline employees.

Chances are that fixing these frontline incentives will boost your performance faster than any other step you can take. Establishing a partnership structure will help attract and retain the best talent and encourage star performers to stretch for startling levels of success. It will generously reward employees both with a share of the economic value they create and, more significantly, with opportunities for further growth and development. It will give them a rational incentive to remain loyal.

Cisco Systems reserves at least 40 percent of its stock options for non-management employees. When its stock price plummeted in 2001, option prices were reset across the board, not just for senior executives. This approach fosters teamwork across the organization. It provides an enormous edge in attracting new talent to the firm and an even more important enticement for acquired talent to remain on board after an acquisition. As mentioned in chapter 2, Cisco calculates the cost per employee acquired between $500,000 and $3 million, so it is no surprise that rewards are structured to retain and motivate the employees of acquired firms. With forty companies acquired between 1995 and 2000, Cisco is considered by many to be number one worldwide at acquiring and integrating talent. Voluntary attrition runs in the low single digits over the first two years, versus 40 to 80 percent for a typical high-tech acquisition. Similarly, Dell Computer has awarded options to every one of its employees—which may explain why it could grow so rapidly in a very tough recruiting market. While option-based compensation holds risk, the more widely those options are spread across an employee base, the more the risk is minimized and enthusiastic commitment is maximized.

REWARD LOYAL CUSTOMERS

Although most of this chapter has focused on employees, the same rules apply to all your other partners. To build loyalty across all your business relationships, you must track what's important, align incentives, and reward the right results across the entire network. You must be sure that those partners who create the most value receive the most benefits. Sadly, most companies make just as many errors with other partners as they do with employees—perhaps even more.

Don't Shortchange Loyalty

The pricing strategies of many, if not most, companies shortchange loyal customers and reward the most disloyal ones. Customer trust is rewarded with abuse whenever the most loyal customers pay the highest price. A classic example of this approach can be observed in the cellular telephone business. Most cellular companies experience enormous customer churn (30 to 40 percent is common) despite their voracious use of satisfaction surveys and service training programs. Cellular executives are painfully aware of the spiraling cost of customer defection, but they continue to address chain-saw wounds with Band-Aid programs. The real problem is that the partnership with their customers is fundamentally flawed. Instead of rewarding customer loyalty, they abuse it. For instance, they favor new customers with subsidized handsets of the latest technology and calling plans at rock-bottom rates. Loyal customers, on the other hand, must pay full ticket to upgrade their equipment, and they get those low rates only if they take the initiative to call and complain. Over time these abusive practices encourage all customers to defect. The few companies that have redressed this wrong by offering loyal customers at least as good value as new customers have seen customer defections plummet and employee morale rise. Growth and profits at these firms have surged.

The long-distance telephone companies have made similar mistakes over the past decade, as they have tried to build the loyalty of their customers in the aftermath of deregulation. With market prices plummeting, corporate executives have felt enormous pressure to boost profits by retaining as much business as possible at the highest prices. They've felt backed into a corner, forced into relying on used-car-dealer tactics. So they give the lowest price only to those customers who know enough and are assertive enough to demand it. Instead of winning the loyalty of their best customers by focusing on providing truly special value to them, the companies invest in win-back programs designed to bribe switchers back to their companies. Some of the most trusted brands in the United States, most notably AT&T, have lost credibility when customers have learned that they have been victimized by such practices. The ultimate irony, of course, is that by putting profits ahead of their customers' best interests, these companies are undermining their very own growth and profits, which eventually leads to a collapse in their stock price.

Many of these companies have invested in powerful, new customer relationship management tools that offer unprecedented opportunity to analyze customers' product and service usage patterns and to ensure that each customer is placed on the optimal pricing and service plan for his or her needs. However, most customers still discover that they are on the wrong plan only when the competition offers them a better deal. Despite the language of loyalty used to justify investments in customer information tools, companies use these tools less to ensure that each customer gets the best value than to identify which customers seem most susceptible to a cross-sell sales pitch. Customers identified as less price sensitive are ignored and left on high-priced programs. The philosophy of extracting maximum value from each customer rules the day. One-to-one marketing technology has the potential to raise loyalty to a science, but it is too often used in the science of betrayal.

You Can't Fool Customers

The archetypes of this philosophy—utilize sophisticated technology to extract maximum value from each customer—are the yield management systems developed by the airlines to get the highest possible price for every available seat. And these methods seem to make perfect sense from an accountant's viewpoint. Computers continuously recalculate the odds that seats will be available on each flight, based on advanced booking patterns. Prices are adjusted according to algorithms designed to maximize profit on each flight. As a result, a customer can get a quotation for $250 on a round-trip to Cleveland and call back an hour later to find that the best price available is now $325. What will the price be next week? Maybe $199, or perhaps $450.

This price gaming does little to build customer trust or improve convenience. It definitely does not enhance the job of the employees, who are constantly trying to explain the seemingly capricious computer system to their customers. One of the few airlines that has avoided this approach is Southwest, which concluded that the yield management systems are unfair, complicated, and expensive to administer. So Southwest has one price for advance purchase and one fare for unrestricted purchase. Customers know that they are getting a fair deal. The accountants at the competition probably believe that Southwest is leaving a lot of money on the table with this unsophisticated pricing strategy that emphasizes fairness and simplicity over extracting maximum value from every customer, but they cannot deny that Southwest is the only consistently profitable major airline.

Share Economic Advantages with Loyal Customers

Loyalty leaders consistently follow Southwest's lead. Consider how State Farm uses its customer information. State Farm has also invested millions in technology in order to track customer profitability and loyalty. Its loyal, profitable customers enjoy price reductions every three or four years. By the tenth year, State Farm not only offers its lowest rates, but in most states also guarantees coverage for as long as the customer holds a valid driver's license. In other words, the company shares the superior value generated by loyal customers with those same customers.

Or consider how Vanguard's pricing is set up to reward customer loyalty. In many of its funds, investors pay a one-time fee up front, which goes into the fund itself to compensate all the existing investors for the administrative costs of selling new shares. In essence, this fee subsidizes long-term, stable investors and penalizes those who remain in the fund only a short time.

Always on the lookout for ways to reward loyal customers, leaders at

Vanguard developed a novel approach with the introduction of its Admiral shares. Admiral shares are available to customers who have $50,000 in a fund account held for at least ten years, or $150,000 for at least three years, or currently have a balance exceeding $250,000. The benefits of the shares are substantial. For example, Admiral shares of the Vanguard 500 Index Trust would pay expenses of 0.12 percent per year, whereas ordinary shares of the fund now pay 0.18 percent a year.

Dell Computer provides another window into the pricing philosophy of a loyalty-based firm. Dell targets a constant profit margin and then aggressively searches for ways to give its customers a better value. Even for a new product line for which the competition has not yet forced rock-bottom margins, Dell charges only the basic margin required to earn reasonable returns. And Dell constantly seeks ways to shave costs from its system and then passes these savings on to customers. Understandably, customers are willing to work with Dell to develop more and more improvements. They trust Dell to pass on the savings—to reward loyalty. Dell doesn't overcharge on spare parts or service contracts as many firms do, yet it is clearly the most successful computer firm in the industry.

REWARD LOYAL VENDORS

By now you can hardly be surprised that loyalty leaders apply the same set of principles to rewarding vendors. At Enterprise, Andy Taylor teaches his managers to help vendors meet their earnings targets whenever they deliver superior value to Enterprise and its customers. The testimony of one Xerox Business Systems employee is a good case in point:

> They really make an effort to get to know you and to show they appreciate your relationship. For example, Andy Taylor has a box at St. Louis Cardinals games set aside for Vendor Appreciation Day, a day when Enterprise entertains and recognizes its loyal vendors. You know that lots of companies do those things for their customers—but I haven't seen many who take such good care of their suppliers.[5]

Dell Computer also wants its vendors to succeed. The computer company is extremely demanding about cost and quality but looks for ways to reward vendors that consistently deliver value, including increased order volumes and tighter integration into Dell's planning process. Dell executives meet regularly with their vendors to build relationships and to ensure effective communication.

Another excellent model is the deal that Vanguard struck with its external investment managers. A substantial percentage of any management firm's compensation is tied to actual portfolio returns relative to a negotiated performance benchmark. Although many mutual funds claim to use this approach, most tie only a nominal amount of the fee to performance. At Vanguard, 50 to 75 percent of the fee is based on real investment performance, that is, on real creation of value for Vanguard's customers. Just as a low base salary works wonders in motivating employees, this compensation structure for independent fund managers truly aligns the interests of the partner with the interests of Vanguard's customers. The net result of this well-aligned system has been a remarkable track record of success for all Vanguard partners, including, above all, the customers.

Consider the following checklist of practices that you can employ to reward your most loyal vendors:

- Invite trusted vendors on-site to review possible efficiencies between your operations. Share 25 to 50 percent of the benefits you realize with the vendor.

- Take your engineers to the vendor's site to help vendors find profit enhancements for their own operations.

- Help your best vendors build their business and reduce their sales and marketing expenses by providing introductions and referrals to non-competitive customers.

- Invite vendor leadership to off-site retreats where you can jointly create the most effective mutual scorecards and review performance against those scorecards.

- Consider temporary job rotations across your companies.

- Share your best customer and employee loyalty programs with top vendors, and review their best practices.

All these ideas seem so basic, so intuitive, whether they are applied to customers, employees, vendors, or any other business partner. Keep score of the right things, align interests so that partners who create value share in the success, set the right targets, and reward star performers with opportunities for growth and development. Despite the commonsense nature of these ideas, most companies are stuck in a misguided paradigm of measures and rewards that precludes real partnership. As a result, smart employees have no alternative but to defect to get ahead, and only foolish or lazy customers remain loyal to the same supplier. No wonder business loyalty has become an oxymoron at so many firms today.

ACTION CHECKLIST

- **Examine Loyalty Acid Test scores**
  Pay particular attention to these items: *The company sets the standard for excellence in its industry; How likely are you to be working here two years from now?* and *Customer loyalty is appropriately valued and rewarded at the company;* and *Employee loyalty is appropriately valued and rewarded at the company.*
- **Modify your dashboard to feature reliable gauges for customer and employee value and loyalty**
  Connect those gauges to organizational behavior through compensation and promotion systems.

  - ❐ **Pull out all the stops to keep your star performers**
    Examine the root causes of premature departures. Set up a task force to figure out ways to increase retention, and keep most of your first rank enthusiastically committed to the team's success. Customize career options and expand alternatives for your best people.
  - ❐ **Build and monitor loyalty metrics for every customer segment**
    Determine which dimensions of value are critical to your customers. Chart purchasing behaviors and retention, and analyze any differences between new and mature customers. Establish the best metrics and target the best performance in your industry.
  - ❐ **Establish clear and equitable measures of value for all other key partners**
    Search out and correct any misalignments of incentives. Keep this process public and open; invite partner input and feedback.

- **Benchmark loyalty and value metrics across your firm**
  Recognize and celebrate star performance. Disseminate team performance results throughout the organization. Create forums in which stars can shine by sharing best practices. Compare your performance metrics with those of world-class performers across industries.
- **Clarify what loyalty means**
  Charter a broad-based task force to define what it means to be a loyal employee and to recommend changes to the current system so loyalty is appropriately rewarded. Even loyalty leader organizations should consider

this action; based on Loyalty Acid Test Survey results, only half of their employees agree that employee loyalty is appropriately valued and rewarded.

❑ **Reduce base pay and increase the earned share of excess value for all employees**
Be sure that your average compensation exceeds that of the competition but that your base pay is lower.

❑ **Stop paying bonuses on performance versus budget**
Shift away from hourly compensation and toward performance-based bonuses that align employee interests with customer interests. Don't put ceilings on pay. Instead, using the models provided by loyalty leader firms such as Enterprise and Chick-fil-A, simply share with your partners the value that they help create.

❑ **Reconsider promotion criteria**
Utilize promotion criteria to reinforce important asset-building and relationship efforts. Formalize and publicize these criteria.

■ **Stop shortchanging loyal customers**
Ensure that your loyal customers receive the best pricing and service. Quantify the value of customer loyalty, and make sure that loyalty rewards are structured proportionally. Create new programs (such as Vanguard's Admiral shares) to acknowledge and reward loyalty. Where appropriate, review and adopt loyalty leader best practices in the area of loyalty incentives. Make sure that none of your rewards systems penalizes loyalty or takes it for granted (review the Loyalty Acid Test Survey results to be sure that you've gotten this right).

7

Listen Hard, Talk Straight

■

*Long-Term Relationships Require Honest,
Two-Way Communication and Learning*

**Loyalty is impossible without trust. Trust is impossible without
accurate, reliable information. Develop state-of-the-art communication tools and listening skills so you and your partners can
reach deeper levels of understanding that yield clearer priorities,
coordinated actions, and superior results. Nothing magnifies the
loyalty effect like the trust engendered by open, honest, and
direct exchange of information and ideas.**

The immediate market potential for e-commerce may initially
have been overrated, but you would be equally mistaken to underestimate
the Internet's potential for revolutionizing communications. The ability
to communicate in real time with any or all of your constituencies, to
maintain dialogues throughout the network of partnerships that define
your business, to gain and provide virtually unlimited access to vital information, twenty-four hours a day, 365 days a year—these are truly revolutionary capabilities. The capacity to connect your operations with those of
customers and suppliers in a seamless web of digital communication can
create enormous efficiencies and profit opportunities.

The Internet is redefining competitive economics and raising the standards of excellence, but the basic rules of good communication remain
constant. You cannot simply layer new communication tools on top of a
fundamentally flawed, low-trust communication culture. The result will be
simply more communication. Your people will drown in a torrent of beep-
ing pagers, warbling cell phones, superfluous e-mails, and glitzy Web
pages—and levels of trust will remain abysmal. The key to better relationships, better businesses, and better lives is not *more* communication, but
better communication.

Just what is better communication? It's the kind of open dialogue among partners that builds stronger, more trustworthy, and more productive relationships. It is forthright communication that honors people's dignity by respecting their time as a precious asset. Better communication helps partners focus more efficiently on the vital, few priorities for which they can truly improve the value provided to their customers and to each other. It helps partners understand the big picture and coordinate actions. It candidly assesses their performance and shows them how to create better results. It builds trust by ensuring that information received is reliable, and that information shared will be used to build a better relationship, never abused for selfish gain.

To participate in the Internet revolution, you must first enlist in the loyalty revolution. As in the physical world, connecting with customers, suppliers, dealers, and investors via the virtual universe demands totally trustworthy, transparent relationships. Information transparency means breaking down the barriers between companies. It means breaking down walls between departments within companies and dissolving hierarchical barriers that separate frontline workers from senior managers. Information from customer surveys can no longer remain the sole property—and the power base—of your marketing department. Customer complaints, product quality metrics, and supplier performance statistics can no longer stay hidden away in manufacturing or purchasing departments; the information must become public, accessible to your customers and partners alike. The same goes for parts availability, service lead times, and specific prices and terms for individual customers. In other words, if you want to take advantage of all the Internet has to offer, then you had better get ready to bare all and to hear all.

FOLLOW CISCO'S LEAD

For a role model of communications excellence in the Internet era, look to John Chambers at Cisco Systems. Few leaders have so effectively integrated Internet technology with the basics of good communication. From their first day, Cisco employees are totally immersed in an Internet-centered communications culture. Their training and integration are Web-based, and all their benefits are explained and administered online. So how do employees develop trust in leadership when digital interaction is the norm? For starters, the leadership clearly puts a lot of trust in them and values win/win strategies. For example, employees file time and expense reports online and are reimbursed within two days—well before their hard-copy receipts are processed. Along with saving employees time, the online method provides significant productivity benefits for the company; it takes only a handful of staff members to process more than 20,000 filings each week.

Trust is at the core of all Cisco's communication, and it has created an extraordinary environment. Internal politics and turf battles are minimal, while candor and openness are routine. Teamwork and cooperation are fundamental cultural values that Chambers has carefully reinforced and that encompass Cisco's customers and suppliers as well. For example, Cisco reveals all its product bugs on a public Web page as soon as any problem is reported. This bug database, available to anyone, helps customers and programmers avoid infestations and discover common solutions. Cisco's online bulletin board is a genuine network, with e-mail and chat group components so that customers can interact with one another to share problems and best practices. And Cisco technicians can intervene with help when needed. Clearly it takes courage and confidence to be so forthright— to encourage customers and dealers to talk about the problems you have created and the ways to solve them.

By moving beyond electronic brochureware and designing its Web site as an open communication network, Cisco has benefited all its partners. Customers' impressions of quality, reliability, and responsiveness are based on the truth, not on public relations efforts or a salesperson's persuasive patter; the company's technical engineers can focus on the biggest headaches; and senior management can learn how to improve competitive strategies. Bugs are caught in their infancy and fixed faster. Cisco engineers have an added incentive to strive for the highest-quality work, since any mistakes will be broadcast to the entire community of stakeholders. Through all these open-communication innovations, Cisco has saved many millions of dollars: Although the company's revenues have grown exponentially, its customer-support staffing has not. More than 70 percent of all nontechnical customer communications have now been shifted to the Web. Without its superior communications network, Cisco estimates that it would have had to hire as many as 10,000 more engineers to keep up with its call center's growth.

The Internet can play a major role in speeding you along the high road to success. But it can't replace "old-fashioned" avenues of communication like face-to-face dialogue. Even though Chambers wants Cisco to model state-of-the-art technology, he estimates that he spends more than 70 percent of his time face-to-face with employees, customers, and suppliers.[1] To talk with his employees and to hear their reactions and concerns, Chambers regularly tours company offices pushing an ice cream cart. He also holds monthly meetings for everyone whose birthday falls in that month. Although employees know he has an open-door policy and they can e-mail him directly, Chambers chooses to interact in person. He wants to show others how to listen effectively. He wants all his employees to strive for outstanding communications with each other and with all their partners—especially with their customers. In fact, Cisco's management team sets individual goals for their own personal interactions with customers and follows up with customer surveys so that employees can continually improve.

Chambers also chooses other low-tech, traditional communication channels when appropriate. For example, every night, he gets personal updates on fifteen to twenty major customer accounts via voice mail, which, like e-mail, respects the personal time of his account reps and of his own family. "'Sure, e-mail would be more efficient,' he says, 'but I want to hear the emotion, I want to hear the frustration, I want to hear that person's level of comfort with the strategy we're employing. And you can't get that through e-mail.'"[2]

At other times, however, e-mail is most effective. Chambers always uses an urgent e-mail to tell employees of an acquisition or another major corporate event before notifying the media. For routine communication with employees, he and his senior management team utilize conventional channels. He also has a personal Web site that provides an overview of his most recent articles and speeches as well as a clear statement of his own values, objectives, and priorities.

Chambers works equally hard to communicate openly and to build trust with government regulators, who could protest the substantial market share that Cisco has garnered in many of its business lines. He spends time with them personally and has established a Washington office to maintain constant channels of communication. Furthermore, the company invests heavily in teaching its executives about antitrust laws and emphasizes that it intends to play by the rules. Chambers tells regulators that he would be disappointed if antitrust were to become an issue for Cisco: "If I'm ever doing anything wrong, let's just talk about it and I'll fix it."[3]

Loyalty leaders recognize that good communication is more about trust-worthy actions than about communication technique. Chambers never confuses state-of-the-art technology with state-of-the-art communica-tions. He does indeed effectively use all the channels that technology has made available. But you need more than technology to follow Cisco's lead in your own communications strategy. You must integrate the Web with your other channels of communication in a manner that plays to the strength of each. Perhaps what is most important, you must establish the candor and trust that underpin all effective communication by always using what you learn to serve the best interests of your partners and your customers. Great communicators are defined by their great results.

NOTHING BUT THE TRUTH

Too many executives define great communicators as masters of spin who can twist the truth to their own purposes and charm any audience. These polished speech readers rely on scripts generated by so-called communi-cations departments charged with engineering messages to reflect well on the company rather than with disseminating accurate information or cre-ating more open dialogue among the community of stakeholders. Unfor-tunately the term *communication* has drifted from its original meaning, based on the same root as *communion*, which denotes an intense, two-way sharing or exchange—a coming together of thoughts and ideas. Real com-munication has to do with careful listening, observation, and dialogue, and it is founded on the truth.

One reason that loyalty leaders have been able to integrate the Web into their operations so rapidly is their inherent commitment to the highest standards of honesty and candor. They know that secrets are damaging to relationships. Manipulative control of information will keep any relation-ship unstable and will leave anyone on the short end of the truth feeling insecure and hesitant to make decisions. Partial truths and selective report-ing are as intolerable as bald-faced lies since any cover-up or distortion sug-gests insufficient confidence to deal with reality. So loyalty leaders are willing to tell partners everything they might need to know, including truths they might not want to hear.

Let All Partners Know Where Things Stand

Loyalty leaders want all their partners to understand the organization's strategy, its core principles, its priorities, and even its problems. They want the partners to know performance expectations and the partners' individual standing so that they can make wise decisions and trade-offs in their daily work. When partners engage in a totally open, honest exchange of reliable information, they maximize the potential for creativity and growth. When your customers tell you where you truly stand with them, you can focus on serving them better. When employees and suppliers share their real concerns and aspirations, you can be a partner in helping them succeed. Similarly, when you explain your goals and report the facts to your customers, colleagues, and other partners, you establish the basis for coordinated teamwork and mutually beneficial relationships. To be a loyalty leader, therefore, you must go to great lengths to be forthright in all interactions. By trusting partners to use candid information in the best interest of the company and each other, you send an empowering message that builds a sense of security and teamwork conducive to the highest level of creativity and energy.

When auto manufacturers started buying up rental companies in the late 1980s, Andy Taylor decided to share with his employees his uncertainty about Enterprise's ability to compete as an independent company. Could Enterprise still acquire cars at a competitive cost if the other firms were owned by manufacturers? Could the privately owned Enterprise afford to compete against the deep-pocketed, massive public companies like Ford and General Motors? Taylor and his executive team wondered, "Would car rental companies only be concerned with buying cars to satisfy their manufacturer owners? Would rent-a-car companies no longer care about a profit? As a privately held company with a finite amount of cash to invest in growth, would we be able to keep up?"[4]

Some of Taylor's senior executives and many of his advisers worried that revealing these concerns would distract employees from their daily jobs and risk mutiny, or at least a surge in turnover. But Taylor wanted to be sure to tap all the best thinking in his organization, so instead of keeping the strategic assessment of sale or merger options a closely guarded secret, he expanded deliberations to include all employees:

> Believe it or not, we stuck to our philosophy of treating our employees like family, and thus shared our concerns about our possible strategic weaknesses. . . . [W]e even told our employees that we were conducting talks with potential purchasers of our business. . . . Frankly, the candid and open approach to employees paid off. No one jumped ship, people openly talked about the strategic issues for the business, and obviously, the right decision was made as the rest is history. . . . Sharing information, news whether good or bad, . . . will always win.[5]

Taylor was more confident in the decision to go it alone as an independent company when he saw how confident his people were in their ability to beat the competition—and how committed they were to making this strategy work.

Loyalty leaders' penchant for forthright communication applies not just to employees but to customers and all other stakeholders as well. For example, vendors to Enterprise Rent-A-Car feel like part of the family and communicate with trust accordingly. Scott Doney of Xerox Business Systems testifies to the unusual level of openness in his dealings with Enterprise:

> Once Enterprise chose us as their partner for billing and document processing, they started treating us like insiders. They openly share internal information about their own objectives and performance targets and their ratings of our performance versus other vendors. As a result of their openness, I know I can trust them. They are one of the few accounts where I share my own profit targets and personal performance goals. I know they want us both to succeed. Communication and trust is a two-way street.[6]

It takes courage to set the standard of information transparency—to give vendors full access to your intranet system and such data as profit margins, shipping deadlines, and volume forecasts. But this level of candor is the norm at loyalty companies like Dell Computer and Cisco Systems. The use of the Internet—which minimizes costs and inventories while maximizing coordination and responsiveness—requires an open-book relationship. Michael Dell explains his thinking about vendors:

> Sharing plans and information openly and freely makes a measurable difference. So few companies do this because, generally, the buyers are so busy trying to protect themselves that the best the seller can do is fill the order. You can't be a partner if you don't know what your buyer's goals are. You need to replace the traditional "bid-buy" cycle with a relationship based on ongoing communication and a huge amount of shared information.[7]

We have already seen how Dell cultivates a similar relationship with customers, who can readily get information about costs, order status, delivery schedules, and technical problems online. In fact, information transparency is unavoidable if you are going to link into your customers effectively. There's no fudging about delivery times when customers have access to schedules. And specific pricing information available electronically to a corporate customer's employees essentially becomes available to all customers everywhere as employees change jobs or simply forward e-mail attachments. Gone are closed-door pricing negotiations and terms. In today's Internet world, pricing and terms for every customer have moved out of locked files into the public domain. Kevin Rollins, Dell's vice chairman, applauds this development, noting that instead of creating value, pricing negotiations just shifted it from one party to the other. What's more, this win/lose process of price negotiations would soak up enormous amounts of executive time. Now, with prices on the Web, all customers will get a fair price, and executives can concentrate on win/win strategies to reduce cost and improve quality across the board. Sunshine not only acts as a good disinfectant, but also helps things grow—things like value, creativity, trust, and loyalty.

Doesn't this honesty and openness among all of your stakeholders come at a cost? If you open your bug database or marketing data to customer and supplier, isn't it also open to journalists and competitors, who can use it to exploit your stumbles? Of course. But journalists are looking for news, and it's hard to find a scoop on a database already open to the world. And competitors who might publicly criticize your mistakes may hold their fire, knowing that savvy customers would turn the spotlight on them as well.

Partners invested in each other's success have to talk straight with each other. Dell Computer constantly grades the performance of each vendor on a supplier report card that includes targets for quality (defects per million parts), logistics excellence (on-time delivery), efficiency, availability of technology, inventory velocity, and integration of its Internet operations with Dell's. Vendors can check online anytime to see how they are stacking up against other Dell vendors. Dell shares everything, from customer feedback on products to inventory management practices, so that suppliers can muster the creativity of all partners and stretch for even higher performance targets.

Most of the top loyalty firms are equally forthright in telling employees precisely where they stand. One of Home Depot's best tools for employee feedback is its 360-degree interview process. Fifteen to twenty employees—bosses, peers, and subordinates—are polled so that each manager receives constructive criticism about his or her performance effectiveness and consistency with the firm's values. At Cisco Systems, John Chambers applies this same rigorous evaluation to his own management team. Each quarter, he ranks all vice presidents and senior vice presidents by the number of their customer visits and the evaluation scores they receive from those customers.

Naturally you must also welcome straight talk when it comes to evaluating your own performance. When Dell was in the middle of one of its toughest stretches at the end of 1992, stock analysts were looking for Michael Dell's head. The company had stumbled during the introduction of its notebook computer line and was way off financial targets. Its stock declined by 68 percent between January and June 1993, and many wondered if Dell could recover. Rather than trying to hide from the problems, however, Michael Dell was extraordinarily candid with his partners, his customers, and even the press:

> One of our sayings is "Don't perfume the pig." By that we mean "Don't try to make something appear better than it really is." Sooner or later the truth will come out, and you are better off dealing with it head on.[8]

The lesson Dell learned from this experience is axiomatic for loyalty leadership:

> Communicating is one of the most important tools in recovering from mistakes. . . . Because we laid out our plan to correct the problem in a clear, straightforward manner, we never lost [the customer's] trust. . . . What we were saying to our customer was, "You're not a customer for just one transaction. You're a customer for life."[9]

Keep the Big Picture in Focus

Loyalty leaders will tell you that establishing a two-way process of candor and openness is just the beginning of effective communication. The principal goal of all your communication must be to help everyone connected with your business spend his or her time, energy, and resources in the most meaningful and productive way possible. You must take the time to explain the big picture and your firm's vision and strategy. Without a clear view of company goals, a full understanding of his or her own role, and reliable information about all that's going on, no one can confidently gauge priorities or make the myriad daily decisions required to generate the loyalty effect. John Chambers recognizes that with thousands of new employees entering Cisco each year—many from acquisitions—effective communication is vital. As the company speeds ahead, all the moving parts must know how they fit together. As previously mentioned, a credit-card-size piece of plastic is attached to each employee's ID card with the objectives for the current year on one side and the objectives for the next three to five years on the other. One fiscal year 2000 objective read "leadership in Internet capabilities in all functions." At meetings throughout each year, Chambers routinely refers to the cards and asks managers what they are doing to shift more of their department's function onto the Web.

Chambers also talks with the media so that his customers, suppliers, and investors can better understand the company, its philosophy, and its objectives. But he never wants the employees to get secondhand news through media channels. Therefore, he Web-casts a thirty- to forty-five-minute management update every few weeks for employees to view—and respond to with questions or comments—at their convenience. The key topics covered help employees understand how the big picture has changed and what challenges now deserve their urgent attention. A marketplace evolving as fast as Cisco's can't wait for hierarchical decisions to cascade down the various levels of management. Chambers is trying to ensure that his people at every level can explain how their actions help the firm achieve key objectives.

Herb Kelleher of Southwest Airlines belongs to this same school of management. In his business, in which customers regularly join employees in a hermetically sealed metal tube that launches into the upper atmosphere at hundreds of miles per hour, trust is paramount. Customers must trust Southwest's employees, and employees must trust its leadership. Kelleher works hard to ensure that everyone understands the firm's strategy and why it makes economic sense. If they don't understand it, they can't believe in it and they won't know how to improve and adapt to changing conditions.

One of Kelleher's managers tells of waiting for a flight and overhearing several other passengers grumble about Southwest's policy of no assigned seating, which often results in long lines to board planes. One passenger asked in exasperation, "When is Southwest going to get around to boarding planes like all the other major airlines?"

Before the manager could comment, a young flight attendant pleasantly explained that one reason for the company's low prices is its strategy of no assigned seating. She went on to outline the economic advantages—how much it saves in reservation systems and in superior capacity utilization—and noted that the airline would have to add seventeen new planes at a cost of over $35 million each just to serve its existing business if it switched to preassigned seating. The passengers were impressed with her grasp of company strategy, and they knew she had a point, since Southwest's average nonstop, one-way ticket price is less than $70 systemwide.

Contrast this incident with one on a competing airline, an airline that had just trumpeted that it would be improving legroom in coach by reducing capacity. When a flight attendant was asked whether there would be any corresponding changes in first class, she explained that she had no advance knowledge and had heard about the new program on the local news—just like everyone else. Later, she was overheard exclaiming to a fellow employee, "I don't know how they can afford to cut the number of seats in coach when they don't even have a contract with our union yet!"

Unless your employees understand your strategy and its economic rationale, they can't be very effective in making it work. They won't know how to respond to changes in the competitive environment, or in technology, or in customer needs. And they are unlikely to be as committed to its success.

LISTEN-LEARN-ACT-EXPLAIN

If you aspire to building a business community of enduring relationships, you can't simply hone your own communication skills. You must help everyone in your firm's entire network of relationships become more effective communicators. The communications networks at high-loyalty firms are based on four components essential to superior business relationships: listening, learning, acting, and explaining. As a loyalty leader, you must both learn and teach the art of communication and how these four essentials work in a dynamic, self-sustaining, perpetual cycle.

- **Listen:** Good communication begins with good listening. Create the culture and the tools necessary to insure maximum efficiency and accuracy in the exchange of cogent information. As a natural part of dialogue, reiterate in your own words what you've heard to confirm its accuracy. Remember that what you've heard is not always what was said, and that what was said is not always what was meant. Listen hard to negative feedback; combat the tendency of ears to close with defensiveness and mouths to open with excuses. Listen with your eyes as well as your ears, and scrutinize behavior that often says more clearly than words which priorities need attention if relationships are to thrive. Loyalty leaders know that the ideal ratio between listening and talking is reflected in our having two ears but only one mouth.

- **Learn:** After you've listened, you need to learn through reflection and analysis. Step back to separate appearances from reality and to determine the significance of what you are hearing. Have you considered the source of criticism? Is it constructive advice from a leading customer or simply the grumblings of a chronic curmudgeon? Is praise genuinely insightful or designed merely to stroke the egos of supervisors? Does feedback reveal a consistent pattern or an aberration? Does feedback square with high-road priorities and the big picture? Are problem behaviors unique to a single individual or potentially systemic and chronic? The best communication networks help partners pool their observations and insights. They use not only experience and judgment, but also statistical analysis to search out the high-priority problems so that investments in solutions will truly create more value.

- **Act:** One benefit of effective listening and learning is that everybody feels better—at least for the moment—when you and your network of partners care enough about your relationships to listen to each other. But the kind of communication and learning that builds loyalty demands much more of each partner than a nod of the head and an "I hear you." The test of effective listening and learning is the resultant action. Trust and openness are reinforced only by consistent, mutually beneficial responses. If partners don't see their communication leading to productive results, they will stop making the effort and taking the risk to speak the truth. So poll them routinely to be sure they understand the link between their feedback and your actions. And insist that they be responsive to the feedback they receive.

■ **Explain:** As organizations and their networks of partners grow larger and more dispersed, it becomes increasingly important that you take the time to explain the rationale for your actions—why they are consistent with input, with company goals, and with the best interests of all relationships. An action that rings loud at headquarters may easily be missed or misinterpreted out in the field unless you complete this final step.

Once you have explained your actions, the cycle launches again with your listening and observing to see if the actions and explanations are having the desired effect, and to make any adjustments or amendments, which, in turn, must be explained, and so on.

One of the best examples of the listen-learn-act-explain paradigm can be seen at USAA. It's no surprise that an organization whose leaders typically have military backgrounds views communication as a vitally strategic issue. Bob Herres, USAA's CEO from 1993 to 2000, joined the firm after retiring from a military career that culminated as a four-star general and vice chairman of the Joint Chiefs of Staff. What consistently set him apart, both in the armed services and at USAA, was his outstanding listening skills. People who have worked with Herres know that he cares about people and their success—not just from his sympathetic listening style but from his follow-through with practical action that improves their lives.

One of Herres's first steps at USAA was to review every customer and employee survey form. Like many organizations concerned with improving customer and employee loyalty, USAA had developed a variety of increasingly lengthy survey forms to capture feedback. Herres agreed with the objective, but he knew that one key to effective communication is to keep it simple. He pared the surveys down to the four or five essential questions and left plenty of space at the bottom for additional comments. These simpler forms were easier to complete, so more were returned. They were also easier to interpret, so customer and employee needs came through loud and clear. Between satisfaction surveys, defection analyses, letters to executives, and service reps' documentation of customer comments, there were more than 300,000 inputs per year; Herres made sure that he saw the analysis of all this input himself on a weekly basis. He had recognized the tendency—common to many firms—of survey results to stay within their own departments, slowing learning across organizational boundaries. With this in mind, he charged a small, central team with gathering, analyzing, and summarizing the data every month so that management could take action on vital issues. Subsequent monthly statistics revealed whether solutions were on track. And Herres opened the information to everyone.

Herres particularly valued the letters addressed to his office. Rather than routing them automatically to customer service, he made time to review and respond to about half of them himself. In this way he not only remained plugged in to unfiltered customer input, but also taught his entire organization the strategic importance of good communication. He taught his people that listening and reacting to customer problems is worthy of a leader's time and that he wants to hear the bad news when customers lay it on the line.

Coax Out the Bad News

No one likes to be the bearer of bad tidings, particularly when it means reporting them to a boss. Many senior managers try to protect their leaders from bad news, considering it their responsibility to screen such news and fix the problem before the boss hears about it. But no part of a communications network can afford to be cut off from any other; leaders need more feedback—unfiltered, unadulterated, candid feedback—in order to set the right priorities and to build better relationships.

During his military career, Bob Herres learned to listen hard for the bad news. When he visited posts under his command, he knew that it wasn't smart to spend time only with commanding officers. He made it a point to talk with enlisted personnel as well, often over lunch or dinner. Listening to people at both the top and the bottom of the organization is the only way to learn what is really going on. Herres's involvement with customer letters and defector interviews was similarly motivated; few people will be as candid about problems as will customers so disappointed with the value delivered that they decide to walk down the street and do business with strangers.

Routing bad news from employees to their bosses can be more of a challenge, so Herres utilized an existing intranet-like system to simplify and improve processes at USAA. The system, called ODOCE (Online Documentation, Employees), was used to collect employee entries (compliments, criticism, complaints, general suggestions, and the like) electronically and process this feedback for analysis. A centralized unit forwards every comment to an appropriate person for action. Employees can route their feedback to fellow employees, to supervisors, and even to the members of the executive council and the CEO if they see fit, and a personal response will be provided if requested. Most inputs are signed voluntarily, but Herres insisted that the system enable employees to remain anonymous. This true network of communication allows anyone to get a message up to the most senior leaders of the organization, whether it be about an idea continually stifled by management or about an abusive boss.

The venting is therapeutic, but the greatest benefits accrue when leaders acknowledge what they have heard, learned, and done. So, at major management meetings, Herres reviewed inputs of broad interest to employees, prioritized them by frequency and urgency, and reported on subsequent actions. He cites one example:

> We had made a change to our retirement system that benefited over 96 percent of our people and left the rest neutral. But we obviously didn't communicate it very well because on the day of the announcement, the ODOCE system started lighting up like a Christmas tree. I put this in front of the management committee the next day, and we worked out a plan to resolve the confusion. If it weren't for our feedback system, it could have taken days, or weeks, for all the grumbling to reach us. Think of all the wasted worry, confusion, and time that we saved.[10]

Of course you can coax out some of the bad news from frontline employees without a state-of-the-art automated system. Scott Cook at Intuit, for example, schedules luncheon meetings with a variety of employees and lets them set the agenda. His one request is that all attendees write at least one serious issue or question in advance, on unsigned three-by-five index cards. Until Cook hit on this device, people rarely opened up about what was bothering them. And when he thought about it, it wasn't reasonable to expect junior employees to confront the company founder with problems in such an intimidating setting. Similarly, Jack Brennan regularly joins various groups of frontline employees at Vanguard's cafeteria; they know they must come prepared to talk about problems if they want to get invited again. Brennan's thank-you note to each participant detail the actions taken since their meeting. Herres's, Cook's, and Brennan's skill at coaxing out negative feedback helps fix problems and teaches the organization how to listen, how to learn what deserves action, how to take the right action, how to explain the action taken, and how to sustain the flow of constructive criticism. Herres put it this way:

> If employees feel like they are throwing pennies down a bottomless well and they never hear a splash, they are going to stop throwing the pennies. We have got to show them that we are listening and that we are taking action if we want them to make an effort and keep the communication flowing.[11]

Use Call Centers Strategically

Bob Herres didn't view USAA's call centers and Internet help desk as mere cost centers or obligatory public relations. He saw them as strategic listening posts, potential gold mines of information for charting the company's future. The challenge was to convert thousands of daily conversations between frontline service reps and customers into lessons learned and actions taken. With ODOCE as a successful digital model for processing employee feedback, USAA's management team developed a comparable system for customer feedback that enables senior management to tap into the flow of information between customers and phone reps. Like any good military team, the managers came up with an acronym for the name of the system, in this case a particularly apt and philosophical one: ECHO, for Every Communication Has Opportunity.

The ECHO system ties the computer terminal of every property and casualty customer service rep into a central data warehouse. Whenever phone reps encounter a customer problem or a request that they cannot handle routinely, they log it in to one of the categories on the ECHO screen, such as service, complaints, or ideas. A second screen then allows them to input necessary details, to do a quick root-cause analysis of any negative feedback, and to add brief comments. The system is so simple that phone reps can use it while they are interacting with customers—and, indeed, there are more than 2,000 entries every week. A tap of the "send" key immediately alerts an "action agent" at the central data warehouse that there is feedback for processing, action, or resolution.

The system is completely transparent. Anyone can watch how well and how quickly messages are resolved, since they are digitally time-stamped. The open nature of the system, with senior management reviewing all unresolved items, increases the likelihood that each item will get appropriate attention. Its key-word search capability helps everyone learn what types of problems are developing and how they are best solved. In addition, the system allows two-way learning. Management can issue an ECHO advisory on specific issues so that reps can flag any relevant feedback. A more refined analysis of categorized input is appropriate for senior managers, who can gauge the relative frequency and importance of data. For instance, instead of having to wait until quarterly reports show that competitors have aggressively gained share in a specific Alabama zip code, executives, using ECHO, learn of the threat immediately and implement a rapid response. To ensure that phone reps appreciate the results of their inputs and keep generating more, Herres reviews the ECHO analysis with the appropriate staff. His explanation of what actions are being taken completes one communication cycle and triggers the next.

Like Bob Herres, John Chambers at Cisco treats his company's call centers and help desk as strategic learning centers, not simply as cost centers. Earlier in his career, he saw what can happen to companies such as IBM and Digital Equipment Corporation when they fall in love with their own technological prowess and stop listening to customers. He has ensured that his organization learns from these customer inputs. Chambers insists that the root cause of every customer call for help be categorized in a weekly management report, and that each category be rank-ordered by frequency of occurrence. Every week, he is briefed on action plan specifics, including who is accountable for resolving each of the top three culprits. This system mobilizes the entire corporation to focus on problems bothering the most customers.

Because Chambers puts a premium on customer satisfaction, he also uses an online survey to ask a few key questions of customers after they have dealt with his organization. Any score of three or below on a five-point scale is automatically routed to senior management. Learning how to satisfy customers better has become a core element of the system because all management bonuses are tied to the company's published satisfaction goal for the year—4.20 in 1999, 4.23 in 2000, and 4.30 in 2001.

Other loyalty leaders have also found that the phone center or the Web help desk offers a prime opportunity to plug senior management head first into the listen-learn-act-explain loop. The leaders encourage senior management to staff these areas themselves on a regular basis. Vanguard's Jack

Brennan joins the company's so-called Swiss Army to work the phones during any trading surges. Charlie Cawley, MBNA's CEO, has long had his senior managers work the customer support lines or at least listen in for several hours each month. Chick-fil-A has a similar policy for its headquarters executives. Even Michael Dell, who already spends an enormous amount of time face-to-face with customers, likes to communicate with customers on his firm's Web site, and he participates anonymously in various chat rooms focused on Dell products. There he is exposed to a hardcore truth he could not otherwise experience, because, as he likes to say, "On the Web, nobody knows I'm a CEO."

Use Fewer and Better Surveys, and Link Them to Actions

You might expect companies committed to building better communication networks and stronger relationships with customers and partners to be among the heaviest users of surveys. Obviously surveys can help you understand the health of key relationships and spot key issues; that is why I have included a loyalty survey tool in the appendix of this book. Loyalty firms, however, tend to use fewer, shorter, and far simpler surveys than do most other firms. They do not want to waste their partners' time. Therefore, time spent crafting better surveys is well invested since it yields higher rates of response and clearer calls for action.

You can't get much simpler than the two-question survey that Andy Taylor uses at Enterprise (see chapter 6), but Taylor continues to work toward further simplifications, including simplifications through the use of Internet technology. And as also mentioned in this chapter, one of Bob Herres's first acts as CEO was to simplify and further automate the multitude of surveys at USAA. Remarkably, despite being regularly highlighted as one of the best places to work in the United States, the firm conducts employee surveys only infrequently. Its first companywide survey of employees took place in 1994; the second came in 1998, although short, follow-up surveys on specific issues were conducted in the meantime.

Remember that it takes a lot of time and energy for your employees and customers to respond thoughtfully to surveys and that it also entails a serious investment of time for you to respond with appropriate actions and explanations. Too many companies blithely conduct long surveys but then fail to report what was learned and what actions were taken. At Southwest

Airlines, Herb Kelleher knows how to minimize the intrusion of surveys into his customers' lives and to maximize their value. He insists that every input be personally acknowledged with a letter explaining what action will result. In fact, this connection between learning and action may be the most distinctive feature of any loyalty leader's survey system. Response rates to Cisco's customer satisfaction survey are high not only because the automated interaction is simple to use but also because customers know that complaints generate action; tying management bonuses to survey scores provides considerable incentive. Enterprise links promotion to survey results. Everyone at Enterprise knows that the CEO regularly reviews the rank-ordered listing of area and regional management based on survey metrics. SAS lets customer surveys drive budget allocations for product development, and the top 20 percent of favored enhancements get funded.

By contrast, in most companies the survey results end up in a dusty file drawer of some departmental functionary who has neither the strategic perspective nor the organizational clout to make changes that would truly make customers happier. So why would rational customers waste their time providing thoughtful feedback to such a system? They shouldn't bother, and they usually don't. People take the time to communicate well only when they believe that both sides have a vested interest in improving the relationship.

Create the Right Forums

In their quest to communicate better with customers and partners, most loyalty leaders have created new forums that directly connect senior managers in a two-way flow of communication. Harley-Davidson prides itself on the deep and intimate connections between headquarters personnel, customers, and dealers, yet its market research and survey budget remains minuscule. The HOGs (Harley Owners Groups, see chapter 2) have proven to be remarkably effective forums for communications, not just with customers and dealers, but also within Harley's corporate hierarchy. Joining forces to build local chapters for Harley riders has improved relationships across the board since everyone participates in the fun and sense of community. Sponsored by authorized Harley-Davidson dealers, these motorcycle affinity groups elect local leadership. They host rallies, take tours together, organize camping trips, share information about biking fashion trends, and even create their own communication channels with newsletters, chat rooms, and the like.

Compared to its enormous value, Harley's cost of running the HOG programs is modest, with only a small department at headquarters to support local dealers. The program provides high-impact listening and learning opportunities for Harley leadership. Like Rich Teerlink before him, Jeff Bleustein personally attends at least three or four HOG events each year and strongly encourages every senior executive to follow his lead. The executives always invite a cross section of other employees to come along, so the experience itself becomes a broad-based forum for talking about key issues. The leaders get a chance to teach everyone their own approach to effective listening in real time. Then at the HOG event, the entire team gets a chance to exercise its listening skills in conversations with HOG members and dealers. Whether flipping burgers for local members, participating in bike rallies, or judging a contest for the best customizations, the team looks, listens, and learns firsthand what Harley customers care about and where the company can do a better job.

The trip back to Milwaukee provides a chance to debrief and brainstorm about follow-up options. And, while there is no formal plan, when team members return to their jobs, HOG feedback naturally filters further throughout Harley's organization—at staff meeting discussions, during locker room kibitzing, and in lunchroom conversations. At the same time, Harley can monitor feedback from HOG newsletters and Internet chat rooms. All told, Harley has engineered a model communications network at minimal cost with maximum benefit. And executives feel they have only begun to tap its full potential.

Leaders at USAA felt a similar need to connect directly with their customers, so in 1997 they created a customer advisory board, called the Member Advisory Board in recognition of the company's structure as a mutual. The twelve board members, who serve staggered three-year terms, are carefully recruited for their vested interest in the company and to ensure accurate representation of USAA's customer population. So what's the big deal, you ask? Aren't consumer advisory panels a dime a dozen? The answer is both yes and no. Though common in the industrial world, they are quite unusual in companies like USAA, which serve millions of individual, independent customers.

The advisory board meets regularly with executives twice a year and whenever the chair, who is also the vice chair of USAA's board committee on personnel and membership, calls extra sessions. The personal relationships that develop during these face-to-face meetings—and are nurtured throughout the year via telephone, mail, and the Internet—inspire candid, thoughtful discussions and insight into the nuances of each other's questions and answers. Not only do executives probe customer reactions to USAA's existing products and services in greater depth, they also test new ideas and let the advisory board help prioritize and fine-tune management strategies. This group is decidedly more than a sounding board; it is responsible for raising issues about USAA's business operations, financial goals, market performance, and relevant corporate objectives. Moreover, USAA management has promised to report on actions taken in response to each agenda item. Clearly Herres and his team have created a forum for intimate dialogue and learning that far exceeds the scope of any survey or traditional market research.

Yet another format for listening to and learning from customers has been instituted by the *New York Times*. Company executives were dissatisfied both with the limited understanding that can be gleaned from traditional surveys and with the group-think process that often pollutes focus groups, yet the managers needed customer insights to help guide new growth strategies. They opted to conduct intensive, one-on-one interviews with carefully selected loyal readers, defectors, and nonreaders whose values closely resembled the loyalists'. An interviewer trained in root-cause analysis took each individual through an in-depth analysis of the evolution of his or her reading patterns and looked at any pivotal lifetime events that had built or diminished loyalty to the paper. The questions also covered the reader's broad assessment of content, customer service interactions, and the reliability of home delivery. Because the same facilitator performed every interview—more than 1,000 over several years—she developed a keen sensitivity for the business issues at stake.

The executives could see the customers' reactions for themselves by observing the interviews through a one-way window or on video. Managers from the business and news departments agreed that they learned far more from this process than they had from any previous surveys or focus groups. Predictably, though, the editorial staff of the *Times* initially had more mixed feelings about listening to customer feedback. While editors acknowledge the economic necessity of writing news that people will pay to read, their professional ethic demands greater loyalty to journalistic independence and integrity than to readership counts or marketplace success. When the editors actually observed the interviews, however, they were sufficiently impressed with the readers' logic, knowledge, and sophistication that they began to listen as they had rarely listened to prior market research. They heard readers vent frustration not at writers who argue contrary points of view—in fact, readers appreciate healthy disagreement—but at any whiff of unfair treatment of issues or individuals. *New York Times* readers clearly do not like to be grabbed by the lapels and told what to think. They want fairness and intellectual honesty, and they cherish the *Times* for providing these things.

When the editors listened to their readers, they heard them defending higher, not lower, standards of journalistic integrity. These people were not yahoos threatening to defect if the newspaper refused to add comics and horoscopes; they were intellectual peers whose views deserved attention and who might actually teach the journalists a thing or two. The joint attendance of journalists and business managers at customer interviews helped both sides of the house make better decisions about the direction of the paper. The emphasis on loyalists, true-blue *Times* fans, also fostered far better working relationships across functional lines.

Back to Basics

Most companies deserved failing grades in the basics of communication before they ever heard of the Internet. With the digital revolution, they are falling even further behind. Remember that the fundamental requirement for good communication is trust—and that trust is the result of what you do with information, not just how efficiently you broadcast it. Be sure that you are a role model for the open, honest, and direct exchange of information. Teach others how to utilize the listen-learn-act-explain framework so that they will remember that real communication is not about spin, but about learning how to get results. Make sure that you are utilizing the Web to its fullest potential, but remember that traditional channels also have valuable roles.

Be sure that your communication system treats partners with dignity and respect; taking five days to reply to e-mails—typical for Web sites today—does not pass this test. Time is everyone's most precious asset.

Good communication not only utilizes the channels that each partner finds most efficient, but helps the partner focus precious time on the few things that really matter. The digital revolution is essentially all about communication. Its seismic impact is indeed comparable to the invention of the printing press; the world has forever changed and will continue to change more rapidly than ever before. But some things have not changed and will never change.

ACTION CHECKLIST

- **Examine Loyalty Acid Test results**
  Pay special attention to these items: *The company communicates openly and honestly; The company listens well and responds quickly to feedback; I always know where I stand with the company; The company provides me with the information I need to make good decisions;* and *Leaders respect my time and help me manage my time effectively.*
- **Make openness and honesty the linchpins of your communications**
  Tell the world what you're doing, why you're doing it, and how you're doing it. List the key elements of your vision, your strategy, and your current priorities on your corporate Web site; consider embossing them on employee ID cards. Organize all major communication around these priorities.
- **Make the goal of your communication to clarify ideas and motivate actions, never to deceive or manipulate**
  Emulate John Chambers and quiz managers, employees, and other partners to ensure that they can explain how their current priorities relate to company goals. Define good communication as an exchange of fully accurate, reliable information. Encourage your employees and other partners to challenge your actions when they don't understand how the actions square with the principles of loyalty. Schedule an off-site review with your partners after they have read this book so that they can help you identify improvements required to match the communications excellence of loyalty leaders.
- **Aim for information transparency**
  Move toward the open-book structure modeled by loyalty leader firms. Put the onus on your partners to prove why any information should be secret in your organization. Earn their trust by entrusting them with detailed information about your operations—made easily available through your Web site.
- **Utilize the best of both low- and high-tech communication options**
  Invest resources strategically to stay ahead of the competition, but remember that good communication is determined more by basic values than by electronic gadgetry. Respect your partners' time as a precious commodity. Create a customer advisory board to operate like the one at USAA, and

establish a routine of face-to-face gatherings with employees. Create customer and employee Web sites for sharing feedback, problems, solutions, and best practices. To coax out the bad news, enable the participants to send feedback anonymously.

■ **Monitor key metrics for excellence in customer communications**
Measure your turnaround time in the resolution of all e-mails and phone requests, and measure the percentage of requests fully resolved without any follow-up required.

■ **Test all your existing surveys for simplicity and linkage to action**
Consider cutting the number of your surveys in half and cutting the length of the remaining surveys in half. Then double or quadruple the effort you put into taking the right actions based on survey feedback and explaining these actions to the constituents surveyed.

■ **Keep senior management in touch with frontline issues**
Assign senior managers to work phone lines and help desks on a regular basis. Encourage your top managers not to screen their phone calls.

■ **Adapt HOG programs to your company's culture and customer base**
Take cross-functional groups (including senior executives) with you to visit customers where they use your product or service. Be sure to probe for the root causes that account for shifting loyalty and purchase patterns.

■ **Turn call centers and help desks into strategic listening posts**
Using USAA's ECHO system as a model, automate feedback and create action and report-back linkages. Build a system to track call-center and help-desk volumes and to categorize requests by root cause. Establish regular senior management reviews of the top culprits and the action plans for their resolution. Assign responsibility for the resolution of the top-priority items; give deadlines for their resolution.

■ **Tell partners exactly where they stand**
Develop annual report cards for customers, suppliers, dealers, and employees with as much care as you now give to annual reports for investors. Consider publicly posting a grade for how successfully each partner is integrating with your Internet solutions. Test a 360-degree feedback system, starting with senior managers and rolling out to all employees.

■ **Rate managers on the four dimensions of communications excellence, listen-learn-act-explain**
Make the paradigm central to your corporate training programs, and demand an accounting of actions taken and explanations made in response to feedback from customers and employees. Review your own communications effectiveness along these dimensions. Ask your partners for feedback, and develop a plan for improvement. Share the plan with your partners so that they can help ensure its success.

8

Preach What You Practice

■

*Actions Often Speak Louder than Words,
but Together They Are Unbeatable*

**You can neither practice nor preach effectively until you have
clarified your principles. Write down your guiding principles, and
then preach them with passion. Only then can you and your network of partners truly understand what it means to be loyal. Only
then can those principles become the gravitational center for
organizational loyalty.**

Each of us is preaching a sermon with our life. If building loyalty
is to become a central theme in your sermon, then you had better brush
up on your preaching skills. You can't go quietly about your business and
presume that your results will speak for themselves. Loyalty has become too
radical a proposition. Unless you preach loyalty's wisdom with power, clarity, and conviction, your actions and your words will be drowned out by the
chorus of digital-age dogma that maintains not only that loyalty is dead but
that its demise is cause for celebration.

The world abounds with people who believe that commitment to loyalty
principles is antithetical to competitive excellence, superior profits, and
personal success:

■ *Fortune* proclaimed in 1996, "Corporate loyalty will probably cease
to exist."[1] *Fast Company* advises workers in the new economy that
they must join the "free-agent nation." The 1 November 1999 cover
story of *U.S. News and World Report* trumpets, "Loyalty Shmoyalty.
. . . In today's job market, staying put gets you nowhere."[2] Executive
recruiters proclaim that a résumé revealing stints of more than four
or five years at the same company clearly signals limited experience
and a lack of ambition.

- Tom Peters advises new-economy workers: "Forget loyalty. Try loyalty to your Rolodex." Futurists Jim Taylor and Watts Walker warn that loyalty takes the fun out of work: "Work can be fun, [if you] shed the notion that any loyalty is to be given or received in a business relationship, realize that you are a freelancer moving from deal to deal even when you are in someone else's employ, and understand that there is only one person you are working for: yourself."[3]

- From management classrooms to boardrooms, heads nod reflexively as these putative truths roll off the presses and ring out across the airways: "the purpose of business is profits," and "the primary responsibility of business leaders is to maximize shareholder value."

- With annual investor churn approaching 100 percent, typical shareholder horizons today are measured in just months, or even hours. In such a short time frame, many paths to investor value creation have nothing in common with the high road and loyalty principles.

- And self-help, business success literature, with its advice about gratifying greed, hit-and-run get-rich-quick schemes, and profiting at the expense of others, adds to the Machiavellian din.

For new-economy workers, such Dilbert-style cynicism seems justified because their corporate leaders emphasize that there can be no expectation of a long-term career within a single company. At best, bosses may feel some obligation to help people stay employable—somewhere. Therefore, as an aspiring loyalty leader you cannot afford to presume that your results will speak for themselves. If you want to be taken seriously, you must climb into the pulpit and preach the principles of loyalty loud and clear.

Previous chapters have underscored the need for loyalty leaders to live their principles if they want to inspire others. You must become a role model, a living example of how your principles can be put into practice. Your company policies and procedures must be fully aligned with your loyalty principles. "Practice what you preach" has become a cliché precisely because it rings with the truth. Loyalty leaders know that their actions, however large or small, speak volumes. Cisco employees, for example, are quick to cite John Chambers's standard-issue, windowless office and his personal frugality when asked whether their leader practices what he preaches. They note that Chambers always flew coach class until he became convinced that a corporate jet made sense for him and paid for it with his own money. (He'd concluded that if the jet boosted his own personal productivity, it would boost his own bonus and ultimately pay for itself.) At ServiceMaster, employees still talk about the time CEO Bill Pollard took the cleaning solvent from the janitor, got down on hands and knees, and scrubbed a coffee spill on the new boardroom carpet to spare the janitor humiliation in front of board members. And far from relying on a corporate jet, Herb Kelleher joins Southwest Airlines customers in coach class and even helps flight attendants hand out peanuts in an effort to reinforce the principle that management is there to serve frontline employees, not vice versa.

Yes, loyalty leaders realize that they are delivering a sermon every minute of their lives. They never forget that their primary responsibility is to be a role model. But they are just as clear that they must preach what they practice if their actions are to be interpreted correctly and achieve their fullest impact.

TALK THE TALK

Another chief responsibility as a loyalty leader is to articulate and clarify how your core principles are in concordance with the rules of loyal relationships presented throughout this book. You must also clarify how these same philosophical foundations are the practical principles behind competitive and economic success, not just feel-good platitudes. Then you must preach your principles with courage and conviction and power. Your message must be so clear that your audience will understand why loyalty makes eminent sense, even in an Internet world full of fast-paced changes and technological and competitive revolutions. When most players in the game of life are concluding that the only winning strategy is the relentless pursuit of self-interest, you must convince them of precisely the opposite—that by setting aside short-term, selfish interests, by committing themselves to the right principles and the right relationships, they will lead happier, more successful, and ultimately richer lives.

If you are reluctant to assume the pulpit and preach about the values at the core of your life and your relationships, you are not alone. Most loyalty leaders have a healthy dose of humility and are painfully aware of how often they fall short of their ideals. But they recognize the power of clearly articulating their principles and ideals for themselves and for their partners. For it is words that establish the standard of excellence toward which leaders and their partners can aspire. Some criticize Thomas Jefferson for not always living up to the principles he set forth in the Declaration of Independence, but we should all be thankful that he and his compatriots had the courage to set down those fundamental principles. In so doing, they accelerated a nation's progress toward narrowing the gap between principles and actions.

You need not match Jefferson's eloquence, but to build relationships worthy of loyalty you do need to follow his courageous lead. You must lay out your convictions for all to see and hear, fully cognizant that you yourself won't always live up to them. No leader is perfect, and most people don't want perfect leaders. People want leaders with integrity—leaders who constantly seek out inconsistencies between their actions and principles, acknowledge them, and then work to correct them.

Is it really sensible to spend your time preaching? Most effective leaders are action oriented and want to spend their precious time in practical ways. But few endeavors are more practical than putting your principles into words for the entire world to see and critique. Only then can you be sure that you've got it right, that you've revised and refined until everyone understands your message. Only then can you ensure that you are attracting the right partners and that together you can build relationships that will live up to those principles.

Get It in Writing

Whether etched in marble, penned on ancient parchment, or laminated in plastic, the inspirational words that echo over time are those captured in writing. The best preachers always write and rewrite their sermons. The discipline involved in the process of writing will deepen your own understanding, compelling you to define your terms precisely and to recognize and resolve any inherent inconsistencies in your logic or discrepancies in your message. Until you make the effort to write down the principles underpinning your own relationships, chances are they won't consistently drive your own decision making, let alone create the requisite foundation for building loyalty throughout your broader community of partnerships. If you haven't taken the time to articulate your principles, then you probably don't understand them as well as you think—and you can bet that your organization and partners won't understand them sufficiently either.

Jack Brennan and Scott Cook have already testified to the importance of writing down a firm's principles and values, particularly as the organization grows. Brennan says of Vanguard's growth, "When you are hiring two thousand people in a year, writing down your values becomes a very big deal!"[4] Because he considers it one of leadership's primary responsibilities to clarify and perpetuate the ethics and values of the organization, he authored a pamphlet on the principles of leadership for his Vanguard crew and routinely cites them in his speeches and daily interactions. As discussed in chapter 2, Scott Cook at Intuit shut down the entire company for a day to initiate the process of codifying the firm's mission and principles. Looking back, Cook still considers this decision—to write down the gospel from which Intuit's sermon would be preached—to be a seminal step in the firm's progress. "It has played an enormously important role in helping us grow the company and successfully evolve our business model to compete on the Internet."[5] At Harley-Davidson, MBNA, and Cisco Systems, plastic credo cards are the order of the day. Charlie Cawley prefers to see MBNA's precepts not only on small cards but also writ large, where hallway walls and floors become oversized tablets. Though the format may vary, the vast majority of loyalty leaders have made it a priority to codify the core principles as a blueprint for leadership and relationship management.

Many loyalty leaders have taken the inscription of their principles so seriously that they have published books to provide deeper and richer explanations as well as more detailed case studies of how their organizations have put them into practice.[6] John Bogle, Vanguard's founder, has written three books to clarify the moral and economic superiority of Vanguard's approach to the mutual fund business. Bill Pollard of ServiceMaster laid out the immutable principles of his firm in his 1996 book, *The Soul of the Firm*. They may sound familiar:

- Truth cannot be compromised.

- Everyone has a job to do, and no one should benefit at the expense of another.

- We should treat everybody with dignity and worth.

- Our combined efforts are for the benefit of our owners, members, and customers, and not for some select group.

- We must always be willing to serve.[7]

Michael Dell wrote *Direct from Dell* in an effort to crystallize the leadership principles that created Dell's extraordinary success and to help future generations extend the track record. With a published book, there would be no need for speculation or journalistic interpretation. The core principles that have made Dell so special, and the business philosophy that has guided the firm, are laid out in black and white by the original source. Truett Cathy has published a similar book about Chick-fil-A. Rich Teerlink couldn't find the time when he was leading Harley but used the first year of his retirement to coauthor *More than a Motorcycle: The Leadership Journey at Harley-Davidson*. Andy Taylor, too, has commissioned a book, *Exceeding Expectations*, and closely supervised the creative process to be sure that the content accurately reflects the organization's guiding principles.

The best of these books are not puff pieces designed to attract new customers to the firm or tributes to outsized CEO egos; rather, they read like carefully crafted sermons that clarify the principles that have made the firm what it is. These books also serve as a reminder of why these principles still make sense in today's world. Perhaps these models will inspire you to begin by drafting a letter to yourself to articulate the core principles that you believe in, that is, your own gospel. You might decide to share the first draft with your immediate colleagues and partners, and, after reflecting on their feedback and advice, share a revised version with a broader circle of your relationships, including some customers.

If you find the prospect of writing an entire book too daunting, even with the help of a professional writer or coauthor, then you might consider the approach used by Herb Kelleher at Southwest Airlines. He carefully crafted a speech for his colleagues about the core principles of leadership and created an archival videotape to communicate these ideas to future generations of Southwest leaders. The medium is secondary. What's important is that gradually you will gain a deeper understanding of your own principles and of any gaps between your actions and those principles, and you will have begun to recruit a community of partners committed to helping you bring that sermon to life.

PREACHERS MUST TEACH

Once you have crafted your sermon, the real work of preaching begins. Now you have to breathe life into your message by teaching all your partners what you stand for, how to put the principles into practice in daily activities, and, in turn, how to spread the message to others. Loyalty leaders don't delegate this critical task; they assume personal responsibility for teaching the core principles to the rest of their organization at the very least. Many are inspired to broadcast their sermons across the globe.

Lead Classes and Case Studies

At Harley-Davidson, Jeff Bleustein teaches a class on leadership development. One of his teaching tools is a case study based on the development of the new consumer e-commerce Web site for Harley dealers. Students role-play dealers, marketing executives, and everyone else involved in order to consider all the points of view that must be taken into account. Someone inevitably argues that the company could have developed a better Web site cheaper and faster without involving the dealers—and maybe even spun the unit out as a separate operation at an enormous valuation. But in class discussion it becomes clear that this option, though it likely would have boosted profits in the short run, would have been inconsistent with the firm's core philosophy of treating partners fairly and building lasting, mutually beneficial relationships. The best case studies for teaching the principles of loyalty simply lay out the facts in some of the toughest situations faced by senior management so that a much broader audience can wrestle with the trade-offs—and practice developing win/win solutions.

Despite a dizzying schedule, either Andy Taylor or Don Ross (Enterprise's chief operations officer) manages to set aside time on those Saturday mornings when a training session for new managers is held at Enterprise Rent-A-Car headquarters. Speaking at the sessions provides them the chance to influence personally more than 2,000 employees each year. And their appearance clearly demonstrates the seriousness of their commitment to perpetuate the firm's culture and values. Similarly, Vanguard's Jack Brennan has made it a policy that no management training class will graduate until it has heard from him, in person, on the subject of putting the core principles into practice.

Widely known as both a preacher and a teacher, John Chambers of Cisco maintains that when he retires from the business world, he will probably become a full-time teacher. He is fascinated with questions like "How do you teach culture?" and "How do you teach ethics?" and "Do you teach integrity earlier on?"[8] Of course, it is precisely these concepts that he is teaching so effectively to his own leadership team at Cisco.

Chambers uses the case study of the government's antitrust litigation against Microsoft to teach his senior leadership team about the right way—and the wrong way—to compete. He makes it very clear to the group that, as committed as he is to beating competitors, it is never acceptable to disparage them either to customers or within the company. He explains how the goal should be to outperform competitors, but not to eliminate or crush them; strong competition is good for Cisco and keeps the company on its toes. Everyone must remain focused on serving customers better, not on destroying competitors, Chambers asserts: "Never do anything to competitors that you wouldn't want them to do to you."[9] The Microsoft case also clearly illustrates why holding to this lofty principle is good business in the long run. Whenever customers or partners—or even competitors—feel abused, odds are that they will find a way to get retribution, whether through public opinion and the media, through the political process, or through the courts.

Practice the Art of Storytelling

For thousands of years wise leaders have known that the best way to teach lessons about values and principles is through stories. It is still true in today's digital age. In fact, speakers on virtually any topic typically capture their audience's attention at the start with a joke or story. And when the eyes begin to glaze over, it's time for another. It is always helpful to nail down abstract concepts and logic with an example or two; the richer the descriptive or narrative details, the more deeply they become embedded in our memory. Precisely because stories are entertaining and memorable, they are a highly effective way for you to preach your gospel. The holier-than-thou, finger-wagging moralizer is easy to tune out, whereas a good storyteller commands rapt attention. Some people seem born with the gift, but we can all hone our storytelling skills by studying the masters and by practicing ourselves. It is well worth the effort. To communicate how the principles of loyal relationships work, begin building your own collection of colorful stories and telling them every chance you get.

Every six weeks or so, Dan Cathy, Truett's son, teaches a Chick-fil-A history lesson to the incoming class of store operators. He organizes a bus trip around Atlanta with stops at the original restaurants, the old headquarters building, a new mall location, and the latest restaurant concept, called Truett's Grill. He plays tour guide and narrates the journey with stories that provide a strong dose of the culture he absorbed while growing up with the business. He always includes a visit to his father's original restaurant, the Dwarf House, and recounts the lessons that Truett Cathy learned in his early years as well as how those lessons have been translated into today's operating principles. One of Dan's stories tells how his father always invested in the success of others and how that philosophy often helped the business in unexpected ways:

> Forty years ago or so, my dad had an employee by the name of Eddie White at the Dwarf House. Eddie couldn't afford to go to his senior prom, so Dad gave him a little money to join the rest of his class. Then, when Eddie decided he wanted to go to college, Dad gave him enough money to fulfill that dream. Though Eddie never came back to work at Chick-fil-A, he has always remained an enthusiastic supporter of the company. He just retired as the superintendent of schools for Clayton County. Of course, Dad's generous treatment of Eddie had another benefit. His brother, Henry White, became our kitchen manager. Henry had some problems from time to time, but my dad never gave up on him. Because of Dad's loyalty to Henry during the rough times, Henry was not only grateful, he ended up working here for thirty-four years. Now Henry has become the pastor in a church south of Atlanta in College Park.[10]

Dan doesn't need to explain how many new employees have come to Chick-fil-A over the years because of direct referrals from Eddie and Hank White and indirectly because of the prominent and influential positions they grew into. He does explain that today's college scholarship program evolved from the gift Truett made to help Eddie further his education, and he explains that because of this philosophy of investing in the success of others, fully 52 percent of new store operators come to Chick-fil-A originally as hourly employees in the chain's restaurants.

Dan Truett wraps up the Dwarf House visit with stories about Annie, the kitchen worker who just retired after thirty years with the company. Over that time, he chuckles, performance issues, personal crises, and rude customers caused plenty of stresses and strains in the relationship between Annie and his dad; each had good grounds to be upset with the other many times. Nevertheless, their tolerance, forgiveness, and their mutual commitment to a long-term relationship got them through the rough spots, and both had prospered. Dan reflects on his father's leadership philosophy: Whereas many bosses hope that the people around them stay out of trouble and avoid performance problems, Truett knew that few lives are so charmed. He viewed difficult times as opportunities for him to do something special for his partner. No wonder Truett has built so many loyal relationships.

The tour bus next drives to a franchise located in a modern shopping mall, where Dan describes the major sociological changes in shoppers and their preferences during the years that Chick-fil-A has been in business. Here he also tells the story of the very first mall-store operator and how her financial deal was similar to the formula for rewarding operators today. Finally, the class concludes with a visit to Dan's own home, where he cooks dinner for the crowd, with a little help from his wife, Rhonda, and their sons, as a reminder that personal service and hospitality are leadership responsibilities no matter how senior the executive.

Ask any loyalty leader why one of his or her principles makes sense, and you are much more likely to hear a story than abstract logic. Leaders at Southwest Airlines are particularly notable. One favorite tale dramatically conveys the message that everyone touched by the company deserves to be treated with dignity and respect. When Midway Airlines closed its Chicago operations, it left many employees jobless. Several of the big airlines participated in a recruiting free-for-all at the airport, where crowds of unemployed workers inched forward in lines that snaked around the terminal in hopes of getting an interview. Southwest, in stark contrast, gave everyone interested in talking with the firm a specific appointment to spare them the indignity of long unemployment lines and to avoid wasting hours of their time. The importance of treating people right is the message of this story, and Kelleher and his colleagues preach it every chance they get.

Create Heroes and Heroines

A culture's choice of heroes—and villains—communicates a lot about its values, and leaders must be careful not to let their organizations be unduly influenced by outsiders. Herb Kelleher has steadfastly refused to permit Southwest Airlines to apply for the Malcolm Baldrige Quality Award, not because he doesn't believe his company is worthy, but because he is averse to having others define the standards of excellence for his business. By buying into the award process, he would be placing Baldrige winners on a pedestal as the heroes who should inspire his organization. He would rather select his own heroic models and tell their stories.

All the loyalty leaders have found ways to create heroes as role models. At its annual operator meetings, Chick-fil-A's Symbols of Success program spotlights store operators who have accomplished outstanding growth, not only rewarding them with a free automobile, but also publishing biographical sketches of each winner, emphasizing those qualities and actions that best reflect the company's core principles. At this annual operator meeting, executives can also tell the stories of other heroes, like the marketing rep whose "teach the cows to spell" program is a stellar example of a win/win solution (see chapter 5).

Andy Taylor searches out some of the best examples of heroic customer service and then has these case studies written up in the company magazine. Sometimes he simply publishes thank-you letters from customers who have received outstanding treatment from branch employees. Other heroes and heroines have their stories told at the Enterprise annual gathering. Such was the case for a young branch employee who modeled caring concern for customers. She not only had accompanied the wife of a customer stricken with a heart attack to the hospital, but had stayed with her for hours until relatives arrived on the scene.

Charlie Cawley of MBNA is similarly committed to honoring the heroes in his organization. For example, of the senior managers in charge during the difficult period preceding MBNA's initial public offering, only one was not rewarded with stock options, options that eventually made multimillionaires of all the others. That exception was Ken Bowman, who had served the company for years and had been a model of loyalty. At a tragically young age, and shortly before the company was spun out as an independent entity, Bowman died from a brain tumor. When the company finally gained its listing on the New York Stock Exchange, the stock symbol that flashed across the Big Board, and has subsequently graced every newspaper stock page every day of the year, was not "MBNA," as the investment bankers had originally recommended. Rather, it was "KRB," in honor of the heroic contributions of Ken R. Bowman. A perpetual tribute to such heroes and heroines of MBNA is housed in the corporate museum at company headquarters in Wilmington, Delaware.

The telling of stories always creates heroes or heroines—and sometimes, even villains. As described in chapter 5, Northwestern Mutual was involved in the case of a child who died of SIDS before his physician could be bothered to complete the routine medical section of the life insurance application. In that case it was the physician, a professional too important or too busy to tend to the interests of his patients, who was clearly the villain. The agent and underwriter who applied the right principles and paid on the policy were the heroes.

Southwest Airlines, in line with its principle of being picky about hiring employees, selects only applicants who indicate that they will treat others with respect. One story embedded in the company culture features a pilot who applied for a job at a time when the scarcity of qualified candidates was limiting the firm's growth. This pilot had the finest credentials, both in the military and as a civilian pilot; technically, he was outstanding. But during the interview process he offended the employee responsible for scheduling his appointments, making it clear that as a hot-shot pilot he felt entitled to look down his nose at a mere secretary. He was not offered a job. This rude pilot has become an antihero at Southwest Airlines—and the secretary a heroine for having courageously spoken up in the candidate-evaluation process.

MAKE JOURNALISTS YOUR ALLIES

In light of John Chambers's ardent preaching and memorable stories, it's no surprise that all of Cisco's partners are well versed in the core principle of "no technology-religion." But increasingly, people outside the company have come to understand the concept because they have learned about it in the business media. Chambers's lively stories have enticed many a journalist to help him spread the Chambers gospel by retelling them to a broad audience of readers, listeners, and viewers. Realizing that journalists are always looking for good stories, Chambers has additional incentive to develop a collection of compelling ones, stories that manage to entertain and convey Cisco's message at the same time.

Chambers often recounts how his former employer, IBM, began to focus excessively on its bottom line by pushing the technologies it considered to be in the company's competitive best interests and utilizing its market strength to bully customers and employees. He vividly describes how this misguided initiative spiraled into a cycle of events that diminished the loyalty of customers and employees and eventually created serious financial performance problems. The story of Wang's foray into "technology religion" and subsequent demise is another part of Chambers's personal history that is becoming similarly well known outside Cisco. Chambers was personally responsible for many of the massive layoffs at Wang, and he tells the story to make sure people understand the real pain and suffering created by such blunders. The point of Chambers's didactic story was reported to *Time* magazine's vast readership: "Laying off workers in a tough job market was the worst feeling in the world. . . . It made me physically ill."[11]

Another story that has made the rounds of the business press stresses the wisdom of making results for customers the top priority at Cisco:

> Chambers was twenty minutes late for his first board meeting as CEO because he was on the phone with a distraught [customer]. "The board members were not happy campers when I arrived, but when I told them why, they said I could use that excuse any time."[12]

Chambers wants everyone to understand how fanatical devotion to the service of customers reigns supreme as Cisco's most fundamental principle, so he will continue to tell stories like this one—and win over journalists to help him spread the gospel.

Failure to recruit business journalists as your allies can sometimes be more costly than merely missing an opportunity to have talented writers help tell your tale. Unless you work hard to convince journalists of your commitment to high-road principles, they may automatically presume that your firm fits into the more common profits-first paradigm. Then you become far more susceptible to the kind of bad press that can embarrasses your customers, your employees, and your entire community of partners.

Consider, for example, how State Farm Insurance was vilified in most national newspapers for failing to pay for name-brand replacement parts, insisting that customers settle instead for what were described as inferior, generic products. Anyone who really knows State Farm understands that its leaders are committed to high-road principles, and that the leaders considered the lower-cost, generic equivalent parts simply a far better value for State Farm customers. These are the parts they would buy to repair their own personal cars. Although some companies do look for ways to shortchange customers in order to boost short-term profits, State Farm does not. As a mutual, its leaders have nothing to gain by such a move. Any savings from using generic parts are passed directly back to the customers. Nonetheless, a public opinion campaign, orchestrated by trial lawyers and name-brand parts manufacturers, who had much to gain from a class action suit, managed to put State Farm in a very bad light.

If State Farm had done a better job of publicly promoting its core principles and recounting its inspiring stories, far fewer journalists would have been duped by the misinformation they received. And far fewer readers of those misguided news stories would have falsely assumed that one more firm had veered onto the low road. Media scrutiny is an asset if you are committed to the high road, so be accessible to journalists. Be sure they hear the stories that help define your principles and distinguish your company. Otherwise you run the risk of letting your enemies or your detractors create the stories that define you—and undo your sermon.

BEGIN AT THE END

As you near the end of this book, it is time to turn to your own story, your own sermon. If you aspire to preach with great impact, you must realize that the greatest sermons have one thing in common. They remind us that we are going to die. Although most of us try to ignore this fact, confronting the end is the best way to understand the full import of living a life committed to the right principles and to building relationships worthy of loyalty. The greatest preachers help us think more clearly about how we want our stories to end and, therefore, what we must do today and tomorrow to achieve our ultimate goals. Similarly, the job of business leadership is not simply to exhort our partners to tend to the list of actions that must be taken on Monday morning; it is also to help ensure that when there are no more Mondays, those partners will have made the most of their lives. In his leadership videotape, Herb Kelleher puts it this way: "Everyone wants to make a mark, to accomplish something truly meaningful with their life." He urges his colleagues at Southwest to consider their responsibility to help others accomplish something important. Good leaders, he says, must not only make the most of their own gifts, they must give those around them an opportunity to earn an epitaph for their tombstone that will make them proud.

How can this "tombstone leadership" create the basis for success in the digital age? When partners focus on how they want their stories to end, they will naturally concentrate on those priorities that can help them build a life with purpose, a life that will enrich those it touches, a life that will serve something bigger and more timeless than its own immediate gratification. They will realize the importance of building trustworthy, mutually valuable relationships with the kind of people who make them proud. They will recognize the importance of following the high road because it is the only path to lasting success.

With this realization, the apparent paradox of business loyalty described in chapter 1 will be resolved. It will become clear that the essence of loyalty is not self-sacrifice. On the contrary, loyalty is the only way to achieve your long-term interests. A vital step toward building loyalty is to show your partners that loyalty is a logical strategy for the pursuit of self-interest when self-interest is defined in the context of lifelong success, not success just for today, this quarter, or this year.

Maintaining the right time frame resolves one of the basic confusions surrounding loyalty, but raises another. Too many of us think about loyalty as if it had more to do with the past than the future. Classic measures of loyalty, such as defection rates, reinforce the notion that loyalty looks in the rearview mirror. But when you think about crafting your own life's story and your legacy for future generations, then it becomes clear that loyalty—the enlightened notion of loyalty espoused in this book—focuses firmly on the future. It is centered on the principles and on the relationships that bring those principles to life and that enable us to achieve our highest aspirations.

Loyalty to the right relationships and to the principles that underpin them does not impede change. On the contrary, it accelerates progress. Loyalty is the key to managing your way through a changing and unpredictable world. In fact, the more chaotic the environment and the more constant the change, the greater the need for loyalty. Today's evolving Internet economy is a prime case in point. In any environment where frontline troops have to act quickly and make decisions on their own initiative, they must be able to trust one other to behave in the best interests of the team and to remain committed to core principles. Whenever creative responses and rapid adaptation are critical, then loyalty becomes an even more vital asset.

The business leaders included in this book have demonstrated how loyalty provides the key to success in today's world. Their lives have had enormous impact, and they have created great personal fortunes by committing themselves to the success of their partners. Your life has the same potential, but only if your sermon is truly worthy of trust and commitment—and if you make that sermon your life.

Just how do you get started? Your journey cannot succeed if it begins as a quest to make your partners more loyal to you. Your progress will accelerate only as you discover ways to be more loyal to your partners. So muster the courage to take the Loyalty Acid Test Survey, which is detailed in the appendix. Using this simple framework, ask your customers and partners to grade your relationship along the dimensions that drive trust and commitment. Quiz them to see how well they understand your core principles and their consistency with the rules of loyalty. Have them grade your efforts at putting these principles into practice. Finally, ask them what you must do better to be more worthy of their loyalty. When this becomes the process by which you establish your life's priorities, you will be well on your way to building lasting relationships—well along in your journey on the high road to success. To monitor your progress, continue to take the acid test. When your results show that most of your partners agree that you deserve their loyalty and that their loyalty is growing stronger, only then can you be sure that you are on the right path.

ACTION CHECKLIST

- **Take the Loyalty Acid Test Survey**
  Ask customers, employees, and other partners for feedback on how successfully you have preached your sermon. Search out the gaps in their understanding of your principles and any gaps between your principles and the practices they observe. Use the survey forms provided in the appendix to grade your performance and to prioritize action plans for improvement. Pay special attention to the following statements: *The company values people and relationships ahead of today's profits; I trust the company's leaders to behave with fairness and integrity; I understand the values and principles that guide the company's leadership; I believe that the company deserves my loyalty;* and *Over the past year, my loyalty to the company has grown stronger.*
- **Write your retirement speech**
  Fast forward to the day you eventually retire, and write the speech you want

to give. Be specific about the five characteristics you care most that partners will ascribe to their relationship with you and the five accomplishments you care most about including in that speech. Then study that list every week when you make out your schedule, and rebalance priorities. Ask yourself if you're spending time with the right people and doing whatever is needed to build lasting relationships.

- **Craft the sermon that illustrates your fundamental business principles and their relevance in today's business world**
  Write down your core principles, and share them with your closest partners and customers to get their feedback. Begin to expand this dialogue to a wider circle. Ask your partners whether these principles can form the basis for successful, mutually beneficial relationships in the new economy. Reflect and revise until you get it right.

- **Make sure that your actions and your words are in sync**
  In an off-site meeting with your management team, review how well your team is living up to the core principles and whether any of your current systems or procedures are discouraging loyalty. Invite other partners to join the discussion. Ask the group to grade you on how well you are living up to each principle in practice. Coax out the bad news by rank-ordering your performance relative to each principle. To keep striving for even better alignment, establish a round-table forum with like-minded executives for collecting ideas and loyalty leaders' best practices.

- **Build a repertoire of teachable stories**
  Collect and catalogue the best in-house stories that illuminate your loyalty principles. Encourage your partners to recognize teachable moments. Develop a communications strategy for circulating these stories; include journalists when appropriate.

- **Use case studies to show your organization how to put principles into practice**
  Write up a collection of case studies about some of the most difficult decisions your management team has faced, especially decisions involving difficult trade-offs. Teach the case studies to your people, and train others to use them in similar classes.

- **Establish a corporate hall of fame**
  Develop a process for recognizing and rewarding the heroes in your organization, heroes whose actions best embody your core principles. Visit the headquarters of MBNA or Chick-fil-A, and consider whether their museums could serve as models for your organization.

- **Accept your responsibility as a preacher**
  Teach the class on values and culture at new employee orientation, and ask your most senior executives to join you. Make sure that your speeches and reports link key decisions and actions to at least one core principle.

- **Incorporate the role modeling of corporate principles as a formal promotion criterion**
  Use the announcement of job promotions to reinforce values and spotlight role models. Write a brief biographical note detailing how each successful candidate's actions have exemplified the core principles of the firm.
- **Study the experts**
  Read the books written by the loyalty leaders featured in *Loyalty Rules!* Share these books with your partners.
- **Consider writing or commissioning an article or a book about the role of loyalty in your own organization's success**
  Explain your company's principles and how following the high road has been a winning strategy; include the best stories and heroes from your years of experience. Start with a videotaped speech or a pamphlet that clarifies your ideals and goals. Write an article that explains why loyalty principles make practical sense in this day and age. Invite debate on this topic in roundtable discussions to sharpen your own understanding of the most complex issues. Invite one of the prominent loyalty-bashers to debate you on the relevance of loyalty to success in today's world.

Appendix

■

The Loyalty Acid Test

To provide leaders with a reliable tool to monitor and diagnose the health of key relationships, my colleagues at Bain and I have created the Loyalty Acid Test Survey. Sample questionnaires for consumers and employees are illustrated on the following pages. All the surveys—including adaptations for business customers, dealers, suppliers, and investors—are available at www.loyaltyrules.com; you may use them freely with no need for additional approvals from the author or publisher.

In partnership with Walker Research, a leading research organization specializing in stakeholder research, we have administered these surveys to a sample of customers and employees from loyalty leader companies highlighted in this book, including Vanguard, Enterprise Rent-A-Car, Northwestern Mutual, Intuit, Harley-Davidson, SAS, and USAA. Summary results of these surveys are provided on the Web site so that you can compare your results with a sample of best-in-class organizations. As our database of loyalty leader results grows, we will continually update the site.

Companies interested in more than summary benchmarks will have the opportunity to analyze results in greater detail. In return for contributing their survey results to our database, we will provide detailed comparisons with the full range of benchmark results. Individual scores for all companies as well as for individual loyalty leaders will always remain strictly confidential. To learn more about this opportunity, consult our Web site.

At www.loyaltyrules.com, you will find additional advice about survey techniques to help ensure that your results are statistically reliable and comparable to our benchmarks. We will also provide a link to Walker Information's Web site, where you can learn more about their services.

THE LOYALTY ACID TEST
CONSUMER SURVEY

Visit www.loyaltyrules.com for the most recent version and results of this survey.

Please answer each question by checking (✔) or filling in (●) the circle that best describes how you feel. An example is shown below. If you change your mind, cross out or erase your answer.

For most questions, labels for the circles are printed at the top of each section. In this example, the five choices range from "Strongly Agree" to "Strongly Disagree."

Example:

1. I am proud to be associated with [company].

○	○	●	○	○
Strongly Agree	Agree	Neither Agree nor Disagree	Disagree	Strongly Disagree

Section 1:

Your Feelings about [company]

How likely are you to . . .
continue buying [company]'s products and/or services?

○	○	○	○	○
Extremely Likely	Very Likely	Somewhat Likely	Not Very Likely	Not at All Likely

How much do you agree or disagree that . . .
I am very committed to [company]?

○	○	○	○	○
Strongly Agree	Agree	Neither Agree nor Disagree	Disagree	Strongly Disagree

it would matter a lot if I could not continue buying from [company]?

○	○	○	○	○
Strongly Agree	Agree	Neither Agree nor Disagree	Disagree	Strongly Disagree

Overall, how satisfied are you with [company]?

○	○	○	○	○
Very Satisfied	Satisfied	Neither Satisfied nor Dissatisfied	Dissatisfied	Very Dissatisfied

Section 2:

Your Relationship with [company]

①	②	③	④	⑤
Strongly Agree	**Agree**	**Neither Agree nor Disagree**	**Disagree**	**Strongly Disagree**

Use this scale to show how much you agree or disagree that . . .

a. customers can rely on [company] to deliver outstanding quality, service and value.
①   ②   ③   ④   ⑤

b. [company] really cares about building a relationship with me.
①   ②   ③   ④   ⑤

c. [company] attracts and retains outstanding people.
①   ②   ③   ④   ⑤

d. [company] sets the standard for excellence in its industry.
①   ②   ③   ④   ⑤

e. [company] communicates openly and honestly.
①   ②   ③   ④   ⑤

f. [company] values people and relationships ahead of today's profits.
①   ②   ③   ④   ⑤

g. [company] listens well and responds quickly to feedback.
①   ②   ③   ④   ⑤

h. I would like to do more business with [company] in the future.
①   ②   ③   ④   ⑤

i. customer loyalty is appropriately valued and rewarded at [company].
①   ②   ③   ④   ⑤

j. I understand the values and principles that guide [company] employees.
①   ②   ③   ④   ⑤

k. I provide enthusiastic referrals for [company].
①   ②   ③   ④   ⑤

l. I trust [company] personnel to behave with fairness and integrity.
①   ②   ③   ④   ⑤

m. I am proud to be associated with [company].
①   ②   ③   ④   ⑤

n. I believe that [company] deserves my loyalty
①   ②   ③   ④   ⑤

o. over the past year, my loyalty to [company] has grown stronger.
①   ②   ③   ④   ⑤

How would you rate the overall quality of the products and services provided by [company]?

○	○	○	○	○
Excellent	**Very Good**	**Good**	**Fair**	**Poor**

What is the single improvement that [company] could make to increase your loyalty to it?

_____

_____

_____

_____

_____

Section 3:

Descriptive Information

This last question will help us divide the interviews into groups.

How long have you been a customer of [company]?
- ○ Less than one year
- ○ One to less than three years
- ○ Three to less than five years
- ○ Five to less than ten years
- ○ Ten years or more

How many different products/services do you purchase from [company]?
- ○ One
- ○ Two
- ○ Three
- ○ Four or more

Thank you for your time and valuable feedback.

(Insert instructions here for returning the questionnaire by mail or the Internet.)

LOYALTY ACID TEST
EMPLOYEE SURVEY

Visit www.loyaltyrules.com for the most recent version and results of this survey.

Please answer each question by checking (✔) or filling in (●) the circle that best describes how you feel. An example is shown below. If you change your mind, cross out or erase your answer.

For most questions, labels for the circles are printed at the top of each section. In this example, the five choices range from "Strongly Agree" to "Strongly Disagree."

Example:

1. I am proud to be associated with [company].

O	O	●	O	O
Strongly Agree	**Agree**	**Neither Agree nor Disagree**	**Disagree**	**Strongly Disagree**

Section 1:

Your Feelings about [company]

How likely are you to ...
Be working at [company] two years from now?

O	O	O	O	O
Extremely Likely	**Very Likely**	**Somewhat Likely**	**Not Very Likely**	**Not at All Likely**

How much do you agree or disagree that ...

O	O	O	O	O
Strongly Agree	**Agree**	**Neither Agree nor Disagree**	**Disagree**	**Strongly Disagree**

I really feel like part of the family at [company]?

O	O	O	O	O

I am proud to work for [company]?

O	O	O	O	O

I feel a strong personal attachment to [company]?

O	O	O	O	O

when [company] has problems, I think of them as my problems too?

O	O	O	O	O

Section 2:

Your Relationship with [company]

① ② ③ ④ ⑤
Strongly **Agree** **Neither Agree** **Disagree** **Strongly**
Agree **nor Disagree** **Disagree**

Use this scale to show how much you agree or disagree that ...

a. customers can rely on [company] to deliver outstanding quality, service, and value.
① ② ③ ④ ⑤

b. [company] values my relationship, really cares about me, and invests in my success.
① ② ③ ④ ⑤

c. [company] attracts and retains outstanding employees and partners.
① ② ③ ④ ⑤

d. [company] sets the standard for excellence in its industry.
① ② ③ ④ ⑤

e. [company] communicates openly and honestly.
① ② ③ ④ ⑤

f. [company] is committed to win/win solutions and will not profit at the expense of partners or customers.
① ② ③ ④ ⑤

g. [company] listens well and responds quickly to feedback.
① ② ③ ④ ⑤

h. I would like to see my relationship with [company] grow in the foreseeable future.
① ② ③ ④ ⑤

i. I understand the values and principles that guide [company] leadership.
① ② ③ ④ ⑤

j. I provide enthusiastic referrals for [company].
① ② ③ ④ ⑤

k. I trust [company] leaders to behave with fairness and integrity.
① ② ③ ④ ⑤

l. I understand our strategy and the role I must play for our success.
① ② ③ ④ ⑤

m. [company] has a winning strategy (superior economics in serving our customers).
① ② ③ ④ ⑤

n. [company] focuses all of its energy and resources in areas where it can be the best.
① ② ③ ④ ⑤

o. I always know where I stand with [company].
① ② ③ ④ ⑤

p. [company] has sufficient opportunities to grow its business.
① ② ③ ④ ⑤

q. [company] provides me with the information I need to make good decisions.
① ② ③ ④ ⑤

r. [company] involves the right people in decisions and then takes action quickly.

① ② ③ ④ ⑤

s. employee loyalty is appropriately valued and rewarded at [company].

① ② ③ ④ ⑤

t. at [company], we keep organizational structure simple by utilizing small teams.

① ② ③ ④ ⑤

u. people are fairly rewarded for their contributions to [company]'s long-term success.

① ② ③ ④ ⑤

v. leaders respect my time and help me manage my time effectively.

① ② ③ ④ ⑤

w. [company] treats me like a real partner.

① ② ③ ④ ⑤

x. customer loyalty is appropriately valued and rewarded at [company].

① ② ③ ④ ⑤

y. I believe that [company] deserves my loyalty.

① ② ③ ④ ⑤

z. over the past year, my loyalty to [company] has grown stronger.

① ② ③ ④ ⑤

How would you rate the overall quality of the products and services provided by [company]?

O **Excellent**　　O **Very Good**　　O **Good**　　O **Fair**　　O **Poor**

What is the single improvement that [company] could make to increase your loyalty to it?

_____

_____

_____

_____

_____

Section 3:

Descriptive Information

This last question will help us divide the interviews into groups.

How long have you been an employee of [company]?

O Less than one year
O One to under three years
O Three to under five years
O Five to under ten years
O Ten years or more

At which location do you work?

O Corporate/administrative headquarters
O Field

What is your position?

O Executive/upper management
O Middle management
O Supervisor
O Individual contributor

Thank you for your time and valuable feedback.

(Insert instructions here for returning the questionnaire by mail or the Internet.)

Notes

CHAPTER 1: TIMELESS PRINCIPLES

1 This passage and others in the chapter draw on and extend the research presented in Frederick F. Reichheld and Phil Schefter, "E-Loyalty: Your Secret Weapon on the Web," *Harvard Business Review* (July–August 2000), 105–113. Copyright © 2000 by the President and Fellows of Harvard College. All rights reserved. Material used with permission.

2 Walker Information and Hudson Institute, "National Employee Relationship Report," Bain & Company, Boston, 5 May 2000.

3 Ibid.

4 Bain & Company and Mainspring, "Bain/Mainspring Online Retailing Survey" (joint survey of 2,116 online shoppers in the categories of apparel, groceries, and consumer electronics), Bain & Company, Boston, December 1999.

5 Frederick F. Reichheld with Thomas Teal, *The Loyalty Effect* (Boston: Harvard Business School Press, 1996).

6 Meg Whitman, as quoted in Reichheld and Schefter, "Customer Life-Cycle Economics," 107.

CHAPTER 2: LOYALTY LEADERSHIP

1 Andy Taylor, interview by author, Master Class, Wellesley, MA, 6 October 1998.

2 Ibid.

3 Ibid.

4 John Bogle, interview by author, Malvern, PA, 25 September 1996.

5 Jack Brennan, interview by author, Malvern, PA, 26 September 1996.

6 Gus Sauter, interview by author, Malvern, PA, 25 September 1996.

7 John Bogle, interview by author, n.d.

8 Jack Brennan, "Embrace Change," *The Vanguard Leader* (Malvern, PA: The Vanguard Group, 1998), 21.

9 Jack Brennan, telephone conversation with author, 27 September 1999.

10 Thomas Easton, "The Gospel According to Vanguard," *Forbes*, 8 February 1999, 115.

11 Harley-Davidson, Inc., *Annual Report*, 1997, 15.

12 Gary Hamel, "Killer Strategies That Make Shareholders Rich," *Fortune*, 23 June 1997, 70.

13 Dylan Machan, "Is the Hog Going Soft?" *Forbes*, 10 March 1997, 117.

14 Rich Teerlink, interview by author, Master Class, Wellesley, MA, 13 October 1998.

15 Rich Teerlink, in Harley-Davidson, Inc., *1997 Annual Report*, 16–17.

16 Bob Filipczak, "Values Keep Harley-Davidson on the Road to Success," *Training*, February 1996, 38.

17 Michael Dell, *Direct from Dell: Strategies That Revolutionized an Industry* (New York: HarperBusiness, 1999), 32.

18 Ibid.

19 Ibid., 140.

20 Ibid., 173, 176.

21 Ibid., 178.

22 Ibid., 187.

23 Ibid.

24 Eryn Brown, "Is Intuit Headed for a Meltdown?" *Fortune*, 18 August 1997, 200.

25 "Intuit Vision-Missions-Operating Values," revised 30 December 1997.

26 Scott Cook, "Chairman Letter," in Intuit, Inc., *Annual Report*, 1998, iii.

27 Pat Dillon, "Conspiracy of Courage," *Fast Company*, October 1998, 186.

28 *Business 2.0*, October 1999.

CHAPTER 3: PLAY TO WIN/WIN

1 Ed Rust, Jr., interview by author, New York, March 1996.

2 Jack Brennan, telephone conversation with author, 29 July 1999.

3 Jeff Bleustein, interview by author, Milwaukee, WI, 13 March 2000.

4 Ibid.

5 Ibid.

6 Daniel Roth, "Dell's Big New Act," *Fortune*, 6 December 1999, 152.

7 Michael Dell, in Dell Computer Corporation, *1998 Annual Report*, 5.

8 Jeff Bleustein, interview by author, Milwaukee, WI, 13 March 2000.

9 Ibid.

10 Jack Brennan, "The Penalty of Leadership," (partnership speech to all employees, Malvern, PA, 8 June 1999).

11 Andy Taylor, interview by author, Master Class, Wellesley, MA, 6 October 1998.

12 Dell, *Direct from Dell*, 57.

13 Ibid., 77–78.

CHAPTER 4: BE PICKY

1 C. William Pollard, *The Soul of the Firm* (New York: HarperBusiness, 1996), 53.

2 Rich Teerlink, interview by author, Master Class, Wellesley, MA, 6 October 1998.

3 General Chuck Krulak, telephone conversation with author, 31 August 1999.

4 Ibid.

5 Dell, *Direct from Dell*, 110.

6 Ibid., 110–111.

7 Jimmy Collins, telephone conversation with author, 12 July 1999.

8 Ibid.

9 Ibid.

10 Ibid.

11 John Bogle, interview by author, Master Class, Wellesley, MA, 6 October 1998.

12 Ibid.

13 Ibid.

14 John Bogle, "Chairman's Letter," *Vanguard Index Trust* (semiannual report for share-holders), 10 July 1995, 2.

15 Jack Brennan, telephone conversation with author, 28 July 1999.

16 Reichheld with Teal, *The Loyalty Effect*, chapters 2 and 3.

17 Jonathan Clements, "Don't Abandon the Vanguard Ship," *Wall Street Journal*, 17 August 1999.

18 Scott Doney, telephone conversation with author, 1 April 1999.

19 John Nagorniak, telephone conversation with author, 26 January 1999.

20 Reichheld with Teal, *The Loyalty Effect*, chapter 4.

CHAPTER 5: KEEP IT SIMPLE

1 Jim Ericson, interview by author, Master Class, Wellesley, MA, 13 October 1998.

2 Scott Cook, telephone conversation with author, 15 July 1999.

3 Ibid.

4 Jimmy Collins, interview by author, Atlanta, GA, 16 November 1998.

5 Bob Herres, CEO Roundtable at The Vanguard Group, Malvern, PA, 12 October 1999.

6 Andy Taylor, interview by author, Master Class, Wellesley, MA, 6 November 1998.

7 Scott Cook, telephone conversation with author, 15 July 1999.

8 Ibid.

9 Jody Hoffer Gittel, working paper, Harvard Business School.

10 Joan Magretta, "The Power of Virtual Integration: An Interview with Dell Computer's Michael Dell," *Harvard Business Review*, March–April 1998, 73.

11 Andy Taylor, interview by author, Master Class, Wellesley, MA, 6 November 1998.

12 Jack Brennan, telephone conversation with author, 28 July 1999.

13 Ibid.

CHAPTER 6: REWARD THE RIGHT RESULTS

1 Scott Heekin-Canedy, interview by author, Master Class, Wellesley, MA, 5 November 1998.

2 Scott Kirsner, "The Customer Experience," *Net Company* (supplement to *Fast Company*), fall 1999, 23.

3 Jack Brennan, telephone conversation with author, 27 September 1999.

4 Meg Whitman, Bain & Company, Inc., partner meeting, 9 May 2000.

5 Scott Doney, telephone conversation with author, 1 April 1999.

CHAPTER 7: LISTEN HARD, TALK STRAIGHT

1 Scott Thurm, "How to Drive an Express Train," *Wall Street Journal*, 1 June 2000.

2 Alice LaPlante, "The Man Behind Cisco," *Electronic Business*, December 1997.

3 Thurm, "How to Drive an Express Train," 1.

4 Andy Taylor, letter to author, 11 March 1999.

5 Ibid.

6 Scott Doney, telephone conversation with author, 1 April 1999.

7 Dell, *Direct from Dell*, 180–181.

8 Ibid., 130.

9 Ibid., 52.

10 Bob Herres, interview by author, Master Class, Wellesley, MA, 5 November 1998.

11 Ibid.

CHAPTER 8: PREACH WHAT YOU PRACTICE

1 Joseph Nocera, "Living with Layoffs," *Fortune*, 1 April 1996, 69.

2 Kim Clark, "Why It Pays to Quit: Changing Jobs Is the New Way to Get Ahead," *U.S. News and World Report*, 1 November 1999, 74.

3 Jim Taylor and Watts Walker, *The 500-Year Delta: What Happens after What Comes Next* (New York: HarperBusiness, 1997), 208.

4 Jack Brennan, telephone conversation with author, 27 September 1999.

5 Scott Cook, telephone conversation with author, 15 July 1999.

6 See, for example, the following publications by the loyalty leaders featured in this book: John Bogle, *Bogle on Mutual Funds: New Perspectives for the Intelligent Investor* (Burr Ridge, IL: Irwin, 1994); John Bogle, *Common Sense on Mutual Funds: New Imperatives for the Intelligent Investor* (New York: John Wiley, 1999); Jack Brennan, *The Vanguard Leader* (pamphlet) (Malvern, PA: The Vanguard Group, 1998); Stan Burns, *Exceeding Expectations: The Enterprise Rent-A-Car Story* (Lyme, CT: Greenwich Publishing Group, 1997); S. Truett Cathy, *It's Easier to Succeed than to Fail* (Nashville, TN: Thomas Nelson Publishers, 1989); Michael Dell, *Direct from Dell: Strategies That Revolutionized an Industry* (New York: HarperBusiness, 1999); C. William Pollard, *The Soul of the Firm* (New York: HarperBusiness, 1996); Paul T. Ringenbach, *USAA: A Tradition of Service, 1922–1977* (Dallas: Donning Company, 1977); and Rich Teerlink and Lee Ozley, *More than a Motorcycle: The Leadership Journey at Harley-Davidson* (Boston: Harvard Business School Press, 2000).

7 Pollard, *The Soul of the Firm*, 41.

8 "Why John Chambers Is the CEO of the Future," *Chief Executive*, July 2000, 27.

9 Vernon Altman, interview by author, Rancho Mirage, CA, 9 May 2000.

10 Dan Cathy, telephone interview by author, 28 September 2000.

11 Karl Taro Greenfield, "Do You Know Cisco?" *Time*, 17 January 2000, 74.

12 Andy Reinhardt, "Meet Mr. Internet," *Business Week*, 13 September 1999, 136.

Index

■

Suzuki, 66

Taylor, Andy
  in creating branch office teams, 108
  in creating rewards systems, 128, 129,
    135, 137–138, 145
  in dealing with partnerships, 56–57
  leadership role of, 19–20, 33, 44
  in maintaining organizational rules and
    practices, 103
  in practicing loyalty principles, 178, 179,
    183
  in promoting decentralized organization,
    21–22, 114–115
  in promoting e-commerce, 22–23
  in promoting effective communication,
    154–155, 166
  in promoting employee performance,
    23–24, 83, 84
  in recruiting employees, 76–77
  strategic focus of, 20–21, 59
Taylor, Jack, 19, 20, 21, 65
Taylor, Jim, 174
teams
  advantages and flexibility of small,
    110–112, 117, 119, 120
  in boosting employee performance,
    117–118
  simplicity and loyalty of small, 106–110
Teerlink, Rich, 30–32, 54, 74, 115–116, 168,
    178
telecommunications industry, rewarding
    customers in, 142–143
Thomas, Carol, 102–103
Toyota, 126. *See also* Lexus U.S.
trust
  in building online relationships, 8, 149,
    151, 153
  communication in building, 170–171
  Vanguard in building, 28–29

USAA
  communication networks of, 161–163,
    164, 166, 168–169
  customer retention rates at, 14
  ECHO (Every Communication Has
    Opportunity), 164–165, 172

employee rewards systems of, 131–132,
    138
  ODOCE (Online Documentation,
    Employees), 162–163, 164
  small-team structure of, 107–108
  win/win strategy of, 68
U.S. Marine Corps, 15, 75, 82, 83

value creation
  measuring customer loyalty for, 124–127
  measuring profits and, 122–124
  rewarding employees for, 128–130, 147
Vanguard Group
  communication networks of, 163,
    165–166
  customer loyalty to, 13, 28–29
  customer selection and acquisition at,
    85–87, 90
  employee loyalty and performance at,
    26–27, 82
  leadership of, 25–26, 41
    change in, 27–28
  loyalty-based strategy of, 44, 48–49, 58,
    62–63
  nature of, 24–25
  outsourcing of investment management
    at, 93, 113
  putting loyalty principles into practice
    at, 177, 179
  in reducing bureaucracy, 116–117
  rewards systems of, 129–130, 136, 137,
    144–145, 146
  Swiss Army, 166
vendors. *See* partnerships

wages. *See* compensation
Wall Street
  in analyzing scorekeeping systems,
    104–105
  effects of, on business strategy, 66–67
Wall Street Journal, 12
Wal-Mart, 64
Wellington Management, 25
White, Eddie, 181
White, Henry, 181
Whitman, Meg, 1, 12, 58, 140
Williams, Doris, 103

About the Author

■

Fred F. Reichheld is a Director Emeritus of Bain & Company and in January 1999 was elected the firm's first Bain Fellow. He founded Bain's worldwide Loyalty Practice, which remains unique among the major consulting organizations. Reichheld's pioneering work in the area of customer, employee, and investor retention quantified the linkage between loyalty and profits. This work forms the conceptual foundation for the practice, which helps clients achieve superior results through improvements in customer, employee, and partner loyalty.

Reichheld's work has been featured in publications such as the *New York Times*, *Business Week*, and *The Economist*, and his writings, including articles in the *Harvard Business Review* and the *Wall Street Journal*, have been widely published. He is a frequent keynote speaker for major business forums and groups of senior executives.

A graduate of Harvard College and Harvard Business School, Mr. Reichheld lives in the Boston area with his wife, Karen, and their four children, Chris, Jenny, Billy, and Jimmy.

Additional information about Mr. Reichheld and his work can be found at www.loyaltyrules.com.